Negotiated Reform

T0345895

MAX-PLANCK-INSTITUT FÜR GESELLSCHAFTSFORSCHUNG
MAX PLANCK INSTITUTE FOR THE STUDY OF SOCIETIES

Renate Mayntz is Professor and Director emeritus at the Max Planck Institute for the Study of Societies (MPIfG) in Cologne.

Renate Mayntz (ed.)

Negotiated Reform

The Multilevel Governance of Financial Regulation

Campus Verlag
Frankfurt/New York

Publication Series of the Max Planck Institute for the Study of Societies, Cologne, Germany, Volume 85

ISBN 978-3-593-50551-0 Print
ISBN 978-3-593-43300-4 E-Book (PDF)

Copyright © 2015 Campus Verlag GmbH, Frankfurt-on-Main
Cover design: Campus Verlag GmbH, Frankfurt-on-Main
Cover illustration: Building of Max Planck Institute for the Study of Societies, Cologne
Typesetting: Jeanette Störtte, Berlin
Printing office and bookbinder: CPI buchbücher.de, Birkach
Printed on acid free paper.

For further information:
www.campus.de
www.press.uchicago.edu

Contents

1 Introduction: Regulatory Reform in a Multilevel Action System

Renate Mayntz

The reform process

The near-collapse of financial markets in 2008, generally perceived as a global crisis, has widely been attributed to the failure to properly regulate a financial system that had undergone international expansion and become increasingly autonomous. Surprised and shocked by the crisis and its threatening economic impact, politicians focused first on crisis management, but soon there appeared to be agreement that comprehensive regulatory reform was needed. Reform initiatives were launched at all political levels, national, European, and international. Given the nearly global expanse of the financial system, it was obvious that these various initiatives should be coordinated.

At the time of the crisis, there existed no coherent governance structure that would have made possible a coordinated, international response to the regulatory challenge. Regulatory competences were concentrated at the national level. The EU had largely refrained from using its legislative powers for the purpose of market shaping rather than for market making, its dominant goal. At the international level, there existed a number of separate bodies of different types (see Baker 2009), but no treaty-based organization to regulate international finance. This is in stark contrast, for instance, to the international trade regime, where the World Trade Organization (WTO) is a recognized international authority. The International Monetary Fund (IMF) is a classic international organization, but its mandate is to assist countries in danger of default, rather than to regulate financial markets. International financial regulation was instead based on "soft" law standards designed by transnational networks of national regulators (Verdier 2013: 1405–1406). These international standardization bodies – the Basel Committee on Banking Supervision (BCBS), the International Organization of Securities Commissions (IOSCO), the International Association of Insurance

Supervisors (IAIS), and the International Accounting Standards Board (IASB) – depend on voluntary compliance with the rules they develop. In addition, there were international deliberative bodies such as G7, G10 and G20, where mainly the finance ministers and central bank governors of a limited number of countries meet to discuss emerging financial market problems. Finally, there were two platforms with loosely defined functions of coordination: the Joint Forum for the coordination of work by the standard setters and the Financial Stability Forum (FSF) that was to promote collaboration and information exchange among the different bodies dealing with financial regulation and stability. This fragmented international governance structure was the result of developments that took place after the end of the Cold War; they are more closely analyzed in Chapter 2 of this volume.

Given the extreme time pressure, a general overhaul of the regulatory structure prior to starting regulatory reforms was out of the question, so the task was shouldered by already existing authorities and standard-setting institutions. But it was evident that some form of coordination, both internationally and across political levels, was necessary if the crisis was to be overcome and a repeat of it prevented. The reform process that started at the same time at the different political levels had a substantive and an organizational aspect. At the national level, there was a flurry of disparate regulatory interventions in immediate response to the crisis, and there were also changes in the regulatory structure, although their nature and extent varied considerably between countries. In Germany, for instance, a shift of competences from the Federal Financial Supervisory Authority (BaFin) to the German central bank was discussed, but not enacted in the end. In contrast, substantial organizational reforms were initiated and finally realized in the United States and the United Kingdom, the two Anglo-Saxon countries in which deregulation of financial markets has been most pronounced. In both countries, competences were shifted and new agencies were created.[1] Organizational change also took place at the level of the EU, where a new agency, the European Systemic Risk Board, was created, while the three previously existing committees that were supposed to coordinate national supervisors were transformed into European supervisory agencies. These agencies have some decision-making power and the competence to intervene under certain conditions in areas so far under exclusive national jurisdiction (Figure 1-1).

Institutional change at the international level was least evident. No new agencies were established, nor were existing bodies given the competence to make binding decisions for lower level jurisdictions and market actors. There were,

---

1 For details, see the chapters by Handke and Zimmermann, Wooley and Ziegler, and Johal, Moran and Williams, in Mayntz (2012).

Figure 1-1   European governance of financial markets

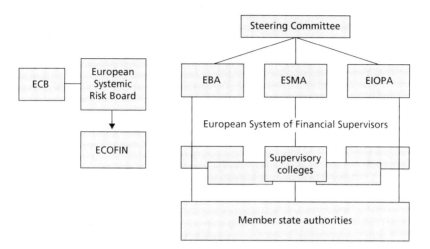

Source: Max Planck Institute for the Study of Societies.

however, changes in the mandate, composition, and weight of some agencies in the overall process of regulation. The G20 had been established in 1999 as a low-key body of central bank governors and finance ministers (who rarely attended in person) to discuss financial matters. In 2008, the G20 heads of government themselves started to meet at highly publicized summits, thus transforming the G20 into the "premier forum of our international economic cooperation" (G20 2009b). The Financial Stability Forum that had mainly served as informa-tion broker also changed substantially. Transformed into the Financial Stability Board (FSB), it has since worked closely with the G20. The IMF was given additional resources. Among the standard setters, the BCBS quickly assumed a focal role in the reform process because stricter capital requirements had quickly become a central reform demand. Figure 1-2 shows the international govern-ance architecture as it had developed by 2010, and as it still looks today.[2]

By the middle of 2011 there had thus been a – limited – upward shift of de facto regulatory power, and an (even more limited) upward shift of formal competences in the multilevel governance of financial markets. Because legis-lative competence is still concentrated at the national level, this upward shift has meant that the downward connection between levels has also become more

2 All figures in this text were prepared by Natalie Mohr.

Figure 1-2   International governance of financial markets

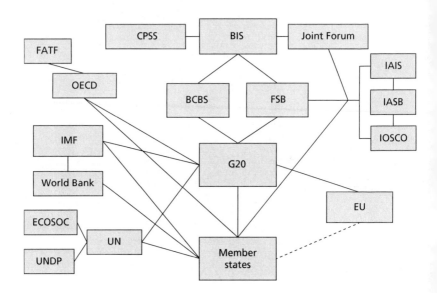

Source: Max Planck Institute for the Study of Societies.

important. The G20 summits have strongly voiced the need for specific reforms and have "tasked" international organizations, as well as national and regional jurisdictions, to become active. The standards formulated by international bodies, notably the BCBS, have served as a template for EU decisions and have also shaped regulatory decisions taken by non-EU countries. EU member states, expecting a new or amended EU directive, often put off introducing new rules by themselves. National decisions were affected by higher level demands and rulings, but national actors were active in formulating these very demands and rulings. By virtue of these upward and downward connections, the policy-making process had become, if not more centralized, more international, and activities at different political levels became more closely linked.

Reform demands voiced after the outbreak of the crisis were radical and comprehensive. At the second G20 summit meeting in London in 2009 the assembled heads of government proclaimed: "We have agreed that all systemically important institutions, markets, and instruments should be subject to an appropriate degree of regulation and oversight" (G20 2009a). Similarly comprehensive reform demands were voiced by the Stiglitz Commission of the UN (United Nations 2009) and the OECD (2009). Banking regulation was to become stricter, rules were to be extended to cover previously unregulated components of the financial system, and regulatory standards were to be harmonized or at least coordinated at the international level in order to make regulatory arbitrage unattractive. Financial market reform quickly became the object of research, by political scientists and political economists alike. The crisis had been a "big bang", and radical regulatory change appeared to loom. At the Max Planck Institute for the Study of Societies (MPIfG) an international group of researchers was formed in 2010 to study the reform initiatives undertaken at the international and the European level, and by selected individual states. This collective research enterprise was concluded in the summer of 2011; the results were published in Mayntz (2012).

By this time it had become obvious that, contrary to early demands for radical reform, regulatory change would be neither comprehensive nor internationally coordinated. As had to be expected, reform plans met with the resistance of the powerful financial industry, but politicians themselves were careful not to strangle a financial system whose functioning was considered essential for the economy. The reforms adopted by the summer of 2011 were admittedly insufficient to discipline risk taking by financial institutions, to deal with the problem of moral hazard presented by banks deemed to be "too big to fail", and to counter the threat of domino effects resulting from the high degree of interconnectedness among market actors. At this stage in the reform process the international financial market crisis was superseded by the European sovereign debt crisis and the related euro crisis. When the attention of political leaders and international organizations turned towards the new issues of sovereign debt, currency problems and economic recession, this had to affect financial reform and in particular banking reform efforts in one way or another. The financial crisis had been a banking crisis; the sovereign debt crisis again involved banks, but now the banks were not the culprits. Banks had been chided for issuing high-risk "subprime" mortgages on a large scale, and for investing heavily in risky securitized mortgages; now they were urged to continue giving credit to the productive economy and to buy government bonds of highly indebted states. The relationship between politics and the finance industry appeared to be reversed: political authorities bent on disciplining financial institutions suddenly found themselves in the position of petitioner. This shift in the balance of power between prospective regulators and the objects of regulation could conceivably have brought the regulatory reform process to a standstill in the fall of 2011. In fact, however, regulatory reform did not come to a standstill. What initially may have appeared to impede a concerted regulatory response – namely the fact that the reform task devolved upon the incoherent set of already existing institutions involved in some way or other in financial market regulation – now worked in favor of a continuing reform process: Once activated by the financial crisis, these institutions simply continued in their job.

Overall, the reform process triggered by the financial crisis has a clear time-profile, moving from the earlier emphasis on bankers' excessive risk-taking and insufficient bank capital to more complex issues, such as the moral hazard posed by increasingly global financial institutions that were deemed "too big to fail" and the threats posed by the unregulated "over-the-counter" trading of complex derivatives. Although the financial crisis had put financial regulation on the political agenda, politicians lacked knowledge of the structure and dynamics of the financial system. Unsurprisingly in this situation, and despite the fact that the crisis was quickly seen as a macro-prudential, systemic problem, the reform approach was micro-prudential at first, targeting individual banks, and the financial incentives that encouraged bankers to engage in increasingly risky trades. Higher capital requirements were another easily understandable measure against risk-taking by banks. Because bank runs threatened, increased deposit insurance was called for and enacted, and consumers – typical small investors – were supposed to receive better information about the risks attendant on specific investments. Measures addressing over-the-counter (OTC) derivatives markets and systemically important financial institutions (SIFIs) started later.

The reform process has also remained selective, if judged against a complete model of the factors contributing to the financial crisis. The agenda for financial market reform was set at the very beginning and has not been significantly revised, let alone extended when attention shifted to different problems. The initial reform discourse has defined the issues to be dealt with by the FSB and international standard-setting organizations, by the European Union, and by individual governments. Potential reform topics that were not on this agenda have not been taken up. One might mention in this regard issues of taxation, the liability of bankers for the consequences of bank activities, and complex forms of securitization, so-called innovative financial instruments (including asset-backed securities [ABS], collateralized debt obligations [CDO], CDO-squared, and credit default swaps [CDS]). The only tax measure discussed – off and on – at various levels, although without a chance of finding international approval, is the so-called "financial transaction tax". Bankers have been held to account for knowingly selling "toxic" securities to unsuspecting customers, but not for the damage caused by risky policy decisions. In addition to the resistance of the financial industry, the complexities of legislation may have inhibited reforms in taxation and liability. The regulation of innovative financial instruments was confronted with the fact that the use of "innovative" forms of securitization was considered to be useful for investors, and not only profitable for banks. The specific selectivity of financial market reform will evidently limit any salutary effects.

The questions

Financial market reform is an ongoing process; it started in another century and will continue, if something similar to our current type of society survives, into the next. The earlier MPIfG project on the reforms triggered by the financial crisis broke off before the process had run its course. By now, however, the reform process has achieved something like an intermediate outcome. In the Communiqué of the Brisbane G20 summit in November 2014, the heads of governments proudly proclaim: "We have delivered key aspects of the core commitments we made in response to the financial crisis. [...] The task now is to finalise remaining elements of our policy framework and fully implement agreed financial regulatory reforms" (G20 2014: 2). It is therefore feasible to treat the reform decisions that took place between 2009 and November 2014 as a "case" to be analyzed.

The reform process that constitutes this case can be analyzed from various theoretical perspectives: by evaluating its outcome and explaining possible shortcomings; by asking about its effects on the international financial system; by focusing on the problem of the democratic legitimacy of a policy process dominated by experts and executives; by comparing reforms in the "varieties-of-capitalism" perspective; or by investigating the interactions between the national, regional, and international institutions involved in the process. At a workshop in December 2013, scholars who had contributed to the volume resulting from the earlier project on financial market reform (Mayntz 2012) met at the MPIfG to discuss the continuation of the reform process. At this workshop, the participants decided to produce a joint volume focusing on the multilevel interactions in the process of regulatory reform. The multilevel perspective on the process of regulatory reform was chosen for a variety of reasons. The effects that reforms will ultimately have on the structure and functioning of the financial system will become visible only when agreed reforms have been implemented, and it will be extremely difficult to attribute observable changes causally to specific reform measures rather than to geopolitical developments and changes in the global economy. To adopt the VoC perspective, as Peter Hall has done in analyzing the euro crisis (Hall 2014), would have required a substantially broader selection of countries than the three figuring in this book. The issue of shortcomings in terms of democratic input legitimacy has frequently been raised in the post-crisis literature on financial market governance, but there is a dearth of studies focusing on the multilevel character of the regulatory reform process. Joined by some new authors, the group presented and discussed the draft chapters of the planned book at the MPIfG in December 2014.

The dominant concern in this book is the way in which the given multilevel structure of financial regulation shapes the process of regulatory reform. Obviously, the vertical and horizontal interactions in this multilevel governance structure affect the outcome of the reform process. But our interest is less in a summary assessment of reform results than in the extent and forms of coordination in a policy process that stretches over several political levels, from the national to the international. Ours, however, is not a typical case of multilevel governance. In typical cases of multilevel governance – that is, in federal systems or the European Union – higher *and* lower level entities have decision-making competences, and interact in a process of joint decision-making (Scharpf 2010: 201–207). This theoretical model does not entirely fit the case of financial regulatory reform, where crucial top-level bodies do not have formal decision-making competences. Thus we set out to study empirically the interactions between the national, regional, and international levels in the process of financial market reform from the perspective of actors at given levels. Have regulatory initiatives conceived at the international level been taken up and translated into binding rules at lower levels? Have the United States, the former regulatory pace-setter, complied with regulatory changes asked for at the international level, or have they tried to imprint US preferences on these templates? How have member state preferences shaped European Union decisions? Has the European Union translated the G20 reform agenda into directives and framework laws, or has the EU developed its own initiatives? Have countries copied reforms from each other or have they formed coalitions to push for or to defeat a given reform? From the chapters in this book, we hope to derive answers to these questions.

In the conceptual framework guiding the joint work on this book, we focused on vertical and horizontal interactions in the policy process spanning multiple levels. Initially we used three core concepts for the interactions we focused on: "downloading", meaning adoption of a higher-level rule by a lower-level jurisdiction; "uploading", meaning shaping a higher-level rule according to lower-level preferences; and "crossloading", meaning horizontal policy transfer. But this conceptual frame soon proved too simple. "Downloading" need not mean compliant implementation, but may mean only formal adoption, and adoption need not be total but may involve – more or less significant – modification. There are likewise different routes and channels of "uploading" political preferences to a higher level body; different countries can form coalitions to push for or to defeat a given higher-level proposal, or they can act alone. "Crossloading", finally, can mean transfer, simple copying, learning from the solution found by another jurisdiction without copying it, or arriving at a mutually agreed solution. The great variety of horizontal and cross-level interactions in the formation of different parts of regulatory reform will be evident in the different chapters, even where no finer terminological distinctions are made.

The global financial crisis may have had a specific trigger in the US subprime mortgage market, but it had many different causes, both proximate and remote. A reform that aimed to prevent a recurrence of the 2007/2008 crisis therefore had to go to its multiple roots. This called for a bundle of measures, addressing different factors that had contributed to the crisis. It would have been impractical, if not impossible for the small group of scholars attending the December 2014 workshop to trace the multilevel interactions involved in all regulatory reforms triggered by the financial crisis. We therefore decided to focus on a limited set of particularly salient, both early and later reforms. This set consists of (i) the Basel III reforms (bank equity, leverage, liquidity), (ii) the provisions for the resolution of systemically important financial institutions without need for taxpayer bailouts, (iii) over-the-counter trading of derivatives in the shadow banking sector, and (iv) structural reforms to separate commercial banking from the risks involved in investment banking and proprietary trading. As is true of any selection, this one can be challenged. Why have structural reforms been included in our selection, although this issue has hardly been addressed at the international level? Our selection of substantive reform issues thus underlines the fact that in the overall process of regulatory reform, not all issues are dealt with equally on all levels.

In Chapter 2 of the present volume the specific character of the multilevel policy-making system that evolved in response to the crisis is set in the wider perspective of change in the form of global governance. In Chapter 3 the role played and the (non-binding) decisions taken by international bodies with regard to the selected substantive issues are analyzed. Chapters 4 to 7 try to show whether the EU or a given country has tried to influence international agreements on these matters, how they responded to higher-level standards and (binding or non-binding) decisions (rejecting, ignoring, or accepting them, with or without modification), and where they developed independent initiatives. The final chapter attempts to identify the modes of cross-level coordination in the process of reforming financial market regulation shown by these empirical findings, and to reflect this multilevel dynamic in the context of a revised theory of multilevel policy-making.

References

Baker, Andrew, 2009: Deliberative Equality and the Transgovernmental Politics of the Global Financial Architecture. In: *Global Governance* 15(2), 195–218.
G20 (Group of Twenty), 2009a: *Final Summit Declaration. London Summit.* London: G20.

G20 (Group of Twenty), 2009b: *Final Summit Declaration. Pittsburgh Summit.* Pittsburgh: G20.

——, 2014: *Final Summit Declaration. Brisbane Summit.* Brisbane: G20.

Hall, Peter, 2014: Varieties of Capitalism and the Euro Crisis. In: *New European Politics* 37(6), 1223–1243.

Mayntz, Renate (ed.), 2012: *Crisis and Control: Institutional Change in Financial Market Regulation.* Frankfurt a.M.: Campus.

OECD (Organisation for Economic Co-operation and Development), 2009: Policy Framework for Effective and Efficient Financial Regulation: General Guidance and High-Level Checklist. In: *OECD Journal: Financial Market Trends* 20(2), 1–56.

Scharpf, Fritz W., 2010: *Community and autonomy: Institutions, policies and legitimacy in multilevel Europe.* Frankfurt a.M.: Campus.

UN (United Nations), 2009: *Report of the Commission of Experts of the President of the United Nations General Assembly on Reform of the International Monetary and Financial System (Stiglitz Commission).* New York: United Nations.

Verdier, Pierre-Hugues, 2013: The Political Economy of International Financial Regulation. In: *Indiana Law Journal* 88, 1405–1474.

2 The Governance Shift: From Multilateral IGOs to Orchestrated Networks

Lora Anne Viola

Introduction

The 2008 global financial crisis not only exposed the need for regulatory reform but also highlighted the decentralized and largely uncoordinated nature of financial governance institutions. Over the past several decades, the global financial regulatory regime has increased in size and sophistication (for an overview of this evolution see Davies/Greene 2008; Helleiner et al. 2010). The regime comprises a large number of diverse actors, including intergovernmental organizations (IGOs), public standard-setting bodies, and private regulatory bodies. In addition to the original Bretton Woods institutions, including the IMF and the World Bank, central actors include the Basel Committee on Banking Regulations and Supervisory Practices, the Financial Stability Forum (now the Financial Stability Board [FSB]), the International Organization of Securities Commissions (IOSCO), and the International Accounting Standards Board (IASB), along with numerous other industry groups, committees, and national bodies. The crisis made clear that the proliferation of fragmented regulatory bodies had introduced inefficiencies, the potential for regulatory arbitrage, as well as unexploited synergies in the regulation of targets.

As a result, many observers have called for institutional reforms aimed at better coordinating regulatory governance efforts. According to Eichengreen (2009: 18), "[e]fforts to share information, apply peer pressure, and correct regulatory problems through the deliberations of the Financial Stability Forum, the Basel Committee on Banking Supervision and colleges of supervisors [...] have been shown by the crisis to not be up to the task." Eichengreen is among a few analysts who have called for a new supranational IGO, something like a World Financial Organization (WFO) analogous to the World Trade Organization, to centralize financial sector governance (Eichengreen 2008, 2009; Claessens 2008;

Eatwell/Taylor 2000). "The WFO would define obligations for its members; the latter would be obliged to meet international standards for supervision and regulation of their financial markets and institutions" (Eichengreen 2009: 19). Other proposals focus on increasing the capacity and competences of existing organizations, primarily the IMF. In addition to general calls for strengthening IMF surveillance activities and its ability to quickly provide large amounts of emergency liquidity, Eichengreen has proposed increasing the political independence of the IMF, removing power from the Executive Board and giving more power to managing directors, making them similar to central bank policy committees (Eichengreen 2009).

As it happens, the crisis did not give rise to anything resembling a WFO and neither was the IMF's independence and oversight capacity enhanced in a way that would make it a *de facto* WFO. Rather, state leaders quickly turned to the G20 format, which had hitherto existed only in the form of a finance ministers' forum, and used it as a focal institution where they could meet to discuss and coordinate national responses to the crisis. Thus it was the informal G20 leaders' summits, supported by the G20 finance minister meetings, that took the pivotal role in coordinating a global response to the crisis and the subsequent reform efforts (see Figure 1-2 of Chapter 1, this volume). Indeed, at the 2009 Pittsburgh Summit, member states declared the G20 to be the "premier forum" for economic coordination.

From a governance perspective, the turn to the G20 rather than to a WFO or enhanced IMF is puzzling. The G20 has no formal mechanisms for aggregating preferences (for example, voting procedures), it has no institutional capacity (for example, a secretariat or bureaucracy), it lacks expertise, its decisions are not legally binding, and it lacks universal membership (which may present problems of both effectiveness and legitimacy). In contrast, the IMF has both a formal mandate and decades of experience with promoting monetary cooperation, facilitating balanced growth, and guiding economic restructuring. In addition, it has a large staff of experts, formidable institutional capacity, and close contact with regulatory targets. Why, then, did the G20 summits become the nodal institution during the crisis rather than the IMF or a WFO? And, considering its weaknesses, what kind of governance could the G20 offer?

The turn to the G20 at the beginning of the crisis, I argue, is symptomatic of a broader move away from governance centralization and towards a more pluralistic and fragmented institutional environment (see also Baker 2009). A number of factors, including the increasing importance of transnational and transgovernmental actors, issue complexity, and actor heterogeneity are moving governance away from traditional, formal, universal intergovernmental organizations (IGOs) towards a proliferation of less formalized, more ad hoc and specialized "clubs" of common interest. Far from being coordinated multilaterally within a centralized IGO, financial market regulation – as the contributions to this volume demonstrate – happens on multiple levels, ranging across sub-national, national, regional, and international jurisdictions, and involves a number of institutions composed of public, private, and hybrid actors. This fragmented institutional field is becoming familiar terrain for a number of issue areas, including environmental and health policies, and reflects – following Slaughter – the development of a form of network governance (Slaughter 2004; Slaughter/ Hale 2010; see also Alter/Meunier 2009; Woods/Martinez-Diaz 2009).[1]

A crucial question, however, is what kinds of governance modes are available in a fragmented institutional environment? Given diverse specialized, exclusive, and sometimes weakly formalized institutions, traditional modes of governance, including hierarchy and delegation, can be difficult to achieve. A network of institutions, I argue, requires a nodal actor (or actors) in order to be effective at governance and regulation. This nodal actor, in turn, exercises "soft" governance through what Abbott et al. (2015) have termed "orchestration". Indeed, at the international level the G20 has taken on the quality of a nodal actor within the fragmented network of global financial institutions and, despite its weak institutionalization, has exercised governance by enlisting and endorsing the work of other bodies within the regulatory regime. As the global financial crisis recedes and the urgency of coordinating reform and responses slackens, the importance of the G20 as a nodal actor has also begun to wane.

The chapter proceeds in three parts. First, I discuss the governance shift with regard to characteristics of the global financial regulatory regime, including its actors, institutional preferences, and available modes of governance. I argue that issue complexity and increasing actor heterogeneity, including the rise of transnational actors and emerging states, have increased state preferences for less formalized, ad hoc, and more exclusive institutions. Such institutions, however, face difficulties engaging in top-down governance or even delegation. As a result, they will tend to engage in orchestration to coordinate and endorse, rather than centrally control, the fragmented institutional environment. Second, I show how the G20 format fits this development and, consequently, made it more acceptable than the IMF or a potential WFO to serve as a pivotal actor during the crisis. Third, I consider some implications of these arguments for the effectiveness of governance and regulatory reform.

---

1 Even the WTO, the exemplar of global supranational regulation, may be undermined by the proliferation of bilateral and plurilateral trade negotiations such as TPP and TTIP.

The governance shift

The pluralization of governance actors

During the period of institutional creation following World War Two, states created IGOs to assist in the coordination and management of distinct policy areas. IGOs were designed with a high degree of functional differentiation from one another and were meant to concentrate competences within their individual bureaucracies. Specific policy areas were thus to be addressed within the dedicated IGO, such as health (World Health Organization), security (United Nations Security Council), nuclear energy (International Atomic Energy Agency), the international monetary and financial system (International Monetary Fund), and development (World Bank). Over the past several decades, and especially since the end of the Cold War, however, there has been a dramatic increase in the number and type of institutions involved in any given governance issue. This has been true in the fields of global health, where the World Health Organization no longer has a monopoly on global health policy but shares the policy stage with the Bill and Melinda Gates Foundation, GAVI, many health-related NGOs, and others (Viola 2013; Hanrieder 2015). It is true of the environment, where failure to come to a global solution on climate change has spurred a number of arrangements located at various other governance levels and including a diversity of actors (Biermann/Battberg/van Asselt 2009). And it has certainly been true of financial governance where regulatory policy is developed not only by states in the traditional Bretton Woods institutions, but also within issue-specific committees, public/private standard-setting bodies, and private (industry) regulatory bodies. Overall, the increasing number and importance of these new actors has changed the international institutional environment by weakening the traditional monopoly of field-specific IGOs and by making the institutional environment more pluralistic. This means a more crowded and fragmented governance environment, including more potential for both complementarity and competition.

In the area of financial governance, functional needs resulting from issue complexity and the policy relevance of non-state actors contribute to this change (Büthe/Mattli 2011). As the financial system has become more complex, regulatory policies have relied on increasingly complex modeling and risk management strategies. Issue complexity means that regulation relies on information and expertise that is highly specialized and distributed among a larger number of actors at multiple levels of governance.[2] It has also meant breaking down regulatory

---

2 Even in those areas in which the issues per se are not changing in complexity, we see the international level becoming more engaged in the governance of complex and technical questions that were once addressed exclusively at the domestic level (Zürn 2008).

goals to specific tasks requiring a high level of knowledge and expertise – some of which may be embedded in the industry to be regulated. In complex policy areas where public regulators have difficulty establishing expertise and information on their own, they tend to be highly dependent on industry actors. This is reflected, for example, in how to measure risk for the purposes of calculating banks' capital requirements. The complexity of these calculations has led to an approach towards banking regulation that allows banks to use their own internal models to calculate regulatory capital requirements based on underlying estimates of variables, such as default probabilities. As a result, regulation depends on specialized agencies, public-private partnerships, and industry self-regulation.

A second factor driving the pluralization of governance actors is a change in the number and type of state actors relevant for financial governance. A central lesson of the Asian financial crisis of 1997–1999 was that existing international financial institutions' focus on a handful of core OECD states made them ill prepared to predict or prevent the Asian crisis. Those states most important for the Asian financial crisis were under-represented in most international financial institutions and not at all represented in the G7. The creation of the G20 in 1999 was in direct response to the need to include more "systemically significant" states in core group discussions in order to improve the effectiveness of global economic governance.

Institutional design in an age of issue complexity and actor heterogeneity

Whereas there are circumstances in which states will delegate a significant degree of sovereignty to international institutions, issue complexity and actor heterogeneity are likely to make states more wary of delegating authority to institutions. The reasons are that complexity increases uncertainty about policy outcomes and actor heterogeneity increases the likelihood of distributional conflicts. These concerns, in turn, induce states to seek institutions over which they maintain significant control and which are only loosely binding.

Complexity increases uncertainty because it makes it more difficult for actors to anticipate the outcomes of policy agreements, and therefore more difficult to choose the "best" policies. States seeking to protect themselves from possible adverse consequences of uncertainty will have incentives to protect their sovereignty while cooperating with other actors (Koremenos et al. 2001; Vabulas/Snidal 2013). These protections include creating institutions that are member-driven rather than staff- or institution-driven, thus preserving autonomy and control. States facing policy uncertainty are also likely to seek flexible arrangements that allow them to adjust to unanticipated outcomes or to default on agreements at little or no cost. Finally, states will prioritize information-sharing, negotiation, and coordination of policy positions over "hard law" instruments (Koremenos et al. 2001: 792–793; Vabulas/Snidal 2013: 209–212). The result is a tendency to prefer institutions that are not tightly binding, with no strong commitments, and with no or weak institutional autonomy.

The FSB exemplifies this type of institutional response. According to the FSB's self-description,

[p]olicies agreed by the FSB are not legally binding, nor are they intended to replace the normal national and regional regulatory process. Instead, the FSB acts as a coordinating body, to drive forward the policy agenda to strengthen financial stability. It operates by moral suasion and peer pressure, to set internationally agreed policies and minimum standards that its members commit to implement at national level.[3]

At the 2011 Cannes summit, the G20 agreed to further strengthen the FSB's capacity, resources, and governance, including its establishment as a permanent and legal organization. Tellingly, however, a working group considered making the FSB a treaty-based organization but then decided it "not to be an appropriate legal form at this juncture", opting instead to establish the FSB as an "association" under Swiss law (International Monetary Fund 2013). The chairman of the FSB, Mark Carney, noted that "[a]s it institutionalises, the FSB intends to maintain its lean structure, its member-driven character, and its tight connection to the G20."[4]

The second motivation to protect sovereignty stems from costs associated with increasing actor heterogeneity. Actor heterogeneity makes interest divergence more likely and, consequently, distributional problems more severe (Kahler 1992). Existing differences in, for example, resources, economic growth, economic-sector strength, population, military power, and regime type are likely to translate into different priorities across issues. When goals and interests are divergent, achieving joint decisions on policies becomes more difficult and more costly. The consequences for governance institutions include a reliance on member-driven institutions and incentives to work within institutions that are more likely to homogenize interests.

While there are strong incentives for states to pursue financial regulation, especially given the large negative externalities resulting from global financial crises, there is also sufficient divergence of interests on the areas, extent, and details of regulation to prevent significant delegation of governance authority to a supranational IGO, such as a WFO. A central reason for this is that financial power is concentrated in the hands of a few states, traditionally the United

---

3 <www.financialstabilityboard.org/what-we-do> (accessed 13 November 2014)
4 Financial Stability Board Press Release, 19 June 2012. Available at <www.financialstabilityboard. org/wp-content/uploads/pr_120619a.pdf?page_moved=1> (accessed 13 November 2014).

States and the United Kingdom, which can exercise unique power through the importance of their financial markets, firms, and currencies. These states can act as "pacesetters" or "uploaders", trying to get their preferred policies transferred to the international level and adopted (or adapted) by other states (see Ryan and Ziegler, Chapter 4, this volume; James, Chapter 6, this volume). In this way, power has been used within institutions and in the standard-setting process to shape the nature of regulation and compliance in areas of preference divergence.

For similar reasons, increasing actor heterogeneity can create powerful incentives for regulatory governance to move to institutions that preserve actor homogeneity while being inclusive enough to remain functional in the policy area. This is because in an environment of actor heterogeneity, so-called "clubs of common interest" facilitate policy coordination and consensus. As a result, we should see governance institutions form around specific issue areas and/or around actor attributes. The G-groupings are a prime example of this dynamic. On one hand, the G7 designed the G20 to be more inclusive and more representative of systemically important actors than previous groupings and even other international financial institutions. The economic significance of the emerging economies made their inclusion functionally necessary to any serious effort at global financial coordination. At the same time, the G20's membership is selective and significantly less diverse than the universal membership of organizations such as the IMF.[5] Indeed, when the G7 created the G20 in 1999 it was concerned that including too many new members would compromise the intimacy and effectiveness of the Group, limiting its ability to reach joint decisions (G20 2007: 12–20).

Ultimately, concerns arising from uncertainty about policy outcomes and distributional conflicts resulting from actor heterogeneity underscore state tendencies to protect their sovereignty by relying on institutions over which they have control, which are not highly institutionalized, and which maintain a degree of exclusivity rather than universality in order to increase the likelihood of interest convergence.

Network modes of governance

The complexity of issues now being addressed at the international level along with a diversification of governance actors is shifting governance away from traditional, universal IGOs to more flexible, less formalized, ad hoc and non-universal institutions. The resulting institutional landscape is more fragmented

---

5 While the G20 argues that its members must be "systemically important", there are no explicit criteria for assessing this status.

and pluralist, with governance taking place in specialized institutions that are connected with one another more or less formally. A number of scholars have referred to this new configuration as "network governance" (Slaughter 2004; Slaughter/Hale 2010; Kirton 2010). Such "transgovernmental networks" "have no formal legal authority, but instead operate through exchanging and distilling information and expertise" (Slaughter/Hale 2010: 54).

A key question that arises in networks, however, is how they can be managed and by what mechanisms such a diffuse form can result in regulatory governance in practice. Traditional IGOs typically govern through hierarchy or, more commonly, delegation. Hierarchy relies on the ability of institutions to coerce governance targets into compliance through, for instance, sanctions or penalties (Abbott et al. 2015). Delegation relies on a principal investing an agent with authority for the purpose of implementing a policy, where the agent has a contractual obligation to the principal and is subject to some control mechanisms (Nielson/Tierney 2003). But if regulatory institutions are highly fragmented, and individual institutions have limited capacity, no universal mandate, and relatively informal structures, hierarchy and delegation become problematic. While hierarchy relies on instruments of coercion, and delegation relies on a certain authority of the principal over its agents, network governance would seem to be open, fluid, and self-organizing.

Drawing on business literature, however, several authors have pointed to the importance of "orchestrating networks" (Slaughter/Hale 2010: 57; Abbott et al. 2015). The idea is that, in order to collaborate and control governance, a network requires a leader or nodal actor who is in a position to support, empower, and coordinate other actors in the network. Nodal or focal institutions are those institutions that are perceived as naturally relevant or salient, usually because they have special authority, legitimacy, or capacity. According to the orchestration model developed by Abbott et al. (2015), focal actors that are unable to engage in hard or direct regulation can work through other public or private actors called "intermediaries". Orchestration is distinct from delegation because the orchestrator cannot invest intermediaries with authority vis-à-vis targets nor does it have the power or resources to sanction or rescind the intermediaries' authority. Intermediaries are other available institutions present in the network that may accept or decline to carry out a request by the orchestrator, as this is a voluntary interaction.

The G20 as a nodal actor

If we consider the global financial regulatory regime to be a network of inter-connected but not hierarchically organized institutions, we can characterize the role of the G20 during the crisis as a focal institution or nodal actor. Before the global financial crisis, the G20 existed as a relatively low-key and technical finance ministers' forum. At the onset of the crisis, heads of state quickly identified the G20 format as a focal point where they could meet to discuss possible reforms to global financial institutions and specific reactions to the crisis. In 2008, President George W. Bush invited leaders from the G20 member states to Washington to create a plan for restoring financial stability and preventing a worsening of the crisis and so transformed the G20 into a leaders' summit. The institutionalization of the Leaders' G20, now held in addition to the Finance G20, shifted decision-making and policy coordination efforts to the highest levels of leadership and lent the forum increased authority and political (rather than simply technocratic) clout (Helleiner/Pagliari 2010; Moschella/Tsingou 2014). The G20 took on a widely recognized but informal leadership or steering committee role during the crisis. This new role and the high expectations accompanying it were articulated by Christine Lagarde, who commented that "[o]nly the G20 can provide the impetus to major economic restructuring, fiscal and financial discipline and sustainable and balanced growth." She called on the G20 "to implement decisions, deepen interaction between countries and institutions to create fairer and more legitimate global governance, and define new areas in which the group can make a difference" (Lagarde 2011).

Why the G20?

The G20 was able to function as a nodal actor first because there were essentially no other immediately available institutions capable of playing this role. The IMF, with its expertise and universal weighted membership, was – in theory – best positioned to become a leader in financial governance. At its creation in 1945, the IMF was formally charged by treaty with promoting monetary co-operation, facilitating balanced growth, providing oversight over international monetary cooperation, as well as technical and financial support for individual states. However, before the crisis the IMF had been experiencing a period of decline, especially since the shock of the Asian crisis, and the failure of the IMF to adequately respond had left it severely weakened, with both its legitimacy and efficacy in doubt. In fact, after the 2008 crisis the IMF was able to retain its central institutional position largely because of the G20's strong endorsement and use of it as intermediary (Cooper/Bradford 2010: 4).

In addition to the absence of rivals, the G20 had specific characteristics that made it suitable to function as a nodal actor. One notable attribute is its membership composition. Unlike the IMF, the G20 is homogenous enough to avoid some of the more severe conflicts of interest that are present in universal membership institutions while still being sufficiently inclusive of significant economies as to remain functionally relevant. Its limited membership facilitates discussion and joint recommendations. Moreover, being comprised of powerful state leaders gives the G20 unprecedented visibility and decision-making power and is the main reason why its weak institutional structure does not unduly hinder its ability to be a governance actor. The leadership composition of the G20 has significantly increased the role of political actors in global financial governance and the group discussions and recommendations succeeded, at least initially, in articulating a common agenda, establishing issue salience, and prioritizing attention to specific regulatory areas.

Another important attribute of the original G20 that the leaders' summit capitalizes on is its close connections to finance ministers and other international financial institutions. The dual nature of the G20 – meeting at both the level of finance ministers and at the level of leaders – allows it to combine detailed policy knowledge with high-level negotiations because minister meetings provide a strong basis for preparing the leaders' agenda (see Mayntz Chapter 3, this volume). Moreover, the G20 is one of only a few institutions that bring together advanced industrial economies, emerging economies, and representatives from the Bretton Woods institutions (it includes the chairs of the IMFC and Development Committee as well as the heads of the IMF and the World Bank as ex officio members).[6] The G20's close working relationship with the international financial institutions, especially the FSF/FSB, the IMF, and the World Bank, also facilitate its role as coordinator and orchestrator, enabling it to both endorse and influence regulatory policies that are developed within other institutions. When the G20 leaders "call upon" other international financial institutions, such as the FSB or the IMF to enact items on its agenda, the G20 performs and confirms its role as the nodal actor, convening and coordinating other institutions within the network (Cooper/Bradford 2010: 4).

Finally, during the crisis leaders turned to the G20 format instead of working within the IMF because of its relatively informal structure, which reduces sov-

---

6 This is generally true of both the finance ministers' meetings and the leaders' summits. The first summit included the 19 G20 states, leaders from the European Union (as the twentieth member), representatives of the IMF, the World Bank, and the FSF, as well as the Netherlands and Spain as guest countries. Subsequent summits have extended guest invitations to various non-member countries and institutions.

ereignty costs for states while conferring a certain flexibility and autonomy. The absence of a secretariat or other bureaucratic apparatus allows members institutional control and flexibility and avoids the costs associated with supranational delegation. The costs associated with delegation to agents, faced within most other institutions, are not relevant. In addition, because decisions are arrived at on a consensus basis and there are no formal control mechanisms or monitoring arrangements, negotiations can happen more quickly as states are unencumbered by procedures and less concerned that their commitment will be strongly binding. States concerned with uncertainty – either regarding policy outcomes, the behavior of others, or even their own preferences – have some flexibility to revisit, adapt, or ignore policy recommendations. The IMF, in contrast, has formalized procedures and is legally binding, and has layers of rules and procedures that make it difficult to adopt substantial departures from past policies. It has a deeply embedded organizational culture and requires the involvement and approval of many mid-level bureaucrats as well as a large and heterogeneous Executive Board, making quick, flexible, and innovative policies difficult to achieve.

By virtue of its informal institutional attributes, the G20 summit is a semi-permanent institution, meeting regularly only for as long as leaders agree. It can be discarded or left to peter out when no longer needed, or it can be transformed to focus on a new set of issues with a new agenda. By the same token, the G20's role as nodal actor depends on the extent to which its members actively use it as a coordinating platform. Whereas during the first few years of the crisis all eyes were on the G20, there is evidence that financial sector reform has slowly taken a back seat at the G20 summits, with the Group claiming to have met its core commitments. In its Brisbane communiqué, the G20 announced that "the task now is to finalise remaining elements of our policy framework and fully implement agreed financial regulatory reforms while remaining alert to new risks" (G20 2014). Indeed, as shown in Chapter 3, recent summits have turned to more generic goals, such as "balanced growth" and "job creation", while at the same time expanding to new issues, such as infrastructure investment and climate change. Overall, a dilution of its focus, together with flagging attention on the part of leaders, may weaken the nodal role of the G20 in global financial governance.

The G20 as a governance actor

Without a bureaucratic apparatus of its own, without formal procedures and legally binding relationships, the G20 cannot directly implement or even authoritatively delegate policy regulations.[7] Indeed, its informal and member-driven

---

7 This section draws on ideas developed in Viola (2015).

nature means that the G20 acts as a collective body and exercises governance functions in a way different to most traditional IGOs. During the financial crisis, the G20 summits did not act as a quasi-supranational authority, a top-down directorate, or even as a collective principal. Rather, the G20 uses soft and indirect government techniques to articulate and endorse a common regulatory agenda, to convene and coordinate pertinent international financial institutions, and to offer political endorsement and material assistance to other institutions during the governance cycle.

The G20 is an aggregate or composite actor because it brings together multiple individual actors to achieve a common purpose. When the G20 summit issues a communiqué, for instance, it is a joint statement and clearly different from a statement issued in the name of an individual state. But what kind of composite actor is it? Using a distinction made by Fritz W. Scharpf (1997: 54–57) we can distinguish between two types of composite actors: collective and corporate. Whereas IGOs are corporate actors, the G20 is best understood as a collective actor. Corporate actors are typically "top-down", hierarchical organizations that "have a high degree of autonomy from the ultimate beneficiaries of their action and whose activities are carried out by staff members" (Scharpf 1997: 54). "Corporate actors may thus achieve identities, purposes, and capabilities that are autonomous from the interests and preferences of the populations they affect and are supposed to serve" (Scharpf 1997: 57). Collective actors, in contrast, "are dependent on and guided by the preferences of their members" (Scharpf 1997: 54). Actors in this arrangement, however, do pursue largely convergent or compatible purposes by using separate resources in coordination. Concerted action is actively sought, even if the utility of strategies or policies is evaluated based on individual interests. Such groups may exist to facilitate agreement on policies that look individually unattractive. Indeed, one of the purposes of the G20 is to help build coalitions and shape preferences.

Collective actors can be more or less "collectivized" in terms of how they manage resources and the extent of responsibility invested in a staff. In Scharpf's terms, the G20 mostly resembles a coalition of actors, where individual actors negotiate, build coalitions, and strive toward joint outcomes without relying on collectivized resources. In the immediate response to the 2008 global financial crisis, the G20 provided a format for leaders of a limited group of "systemically relevant" states to coordinate national responses to the crisis and to build coalitions for regulatory reform. Early on, facilitated by the urgency of the crisis, G20 leaders were able to reach consensus on the importance of avoiding protectionist measures and stimulating their domestic economies. After the crisis lost urgency, the G20 provided a place for leaders to negotiate over policy differences.

A central role of the G20 during the crisis was to articulate and endorse a regulatory agenda. Beginning with the first G20 summit in Washington at the end of 2008, leaders have issued joint communiqués articulating a set of common goals, as well as action plans that outline steps to be taken toward those goals. The regulatory agenda itself is developed as a result of ongoing meetings of national ministers and relevant international financial institutions, especially the FSB, but these points are discussed at summits and informally "ratified" by the explicit endorsement of powerful leaders. Summit documents also serve to signal the policy priorities of leading states. In the first few years of the crisis, the G20 emphasized the need for international prudential regulation and monitoring mechanisms for public and private financial actors. The first G20 summit in Washington in November 2008 articulated a range of immediate, medium, and long-term goals regarding transparency and accountability, coherence in regulatory regimes, financial market oversight, risk management, and reform of the Bretton Woods institutions (G20 2008). These goals both endorsed existing regulatory regimes, such as the IOSCO Code of Conduct Fundamentals for Credit Rating Agencies, and endorsed recommendations to extend regulatory principles to new areas, such as with the Principles for Sound Liquidity Risk Management and Supervision and the Principles for Sound Compensation Practices. Subsequent summits have emphasized the creation of a single standards regime, the extension of regulatory principles to the shadow banking system, and the institutionalized monitoring of systemically important financial institutions (see Mayntz, Chapter 3, this volume). For example, leaders have used the G20 summits to endorse their commitment to the Key Attributes of Effective Resolution Regimes and to Basel III (for example, G20 2013: §67–70). More recent summit documents, however, indicate that the G20's emphasis is moving away from financial market governance and turning to questions of economic growth and employment (G20 2014: §1–8).

Another important way in which the G20 has served as a central governance actor is by providing material assistance to existing international financial institution programs. In 2009, for example, leaders at the second G20 summit in London agreed to substantially increase the resources available to international financial institutions to ensure that they can address the crisis "in a coordinated and comprehensive manner", and they also agreed on a capital increase for the Multilateral Development Banks (G20 2009). G20 support helped the IMF to realize its long-standing plans to create crisis prevention facilities, such as the Flexible Credit Line and then the Precautionary and Liquidity Line (G20 2011: §15). In this context, in 2011 the G20 leaders stated, "[w]e will ensure the IMF continues to have resources to play its systemic role to the benefit of its whole membership, building on the substantial resources we have already mobilized since London in 2009. We stand ready to ensure additional resources," including bilateral contributions and voluntary contributions to a special administered account (G20 2011: § 16). In 2012, G20 leaders committed $450 billion to increase the temporary resources available to the IMF for enhancing global safety nets (G20 2012: § 32).

While it can articulate and endorse a common regulatory agenda, the nature of the G20's institutional structure means that it cannot coerce other actors or legally delegate to potential agents in order to implement its joint policy recommendations. In the absence of these governance mechanisms, a practice of "orchestration" developed within the G20 process whereby the G20 assigns "tasks to the multilateral economic institutions related to specific issues, with instructions to report back to the next meeting of G20 leaders" (Hillman 2010: 13). In its own words, the G20 "calls upon" institutions such as the FSB, the IMF, and the World Bank to carry out specific regulatory tasks. This process began with the Washington Action Plan which, for example, "called on" the IMF, with its emphasis on surveillance, and the FSB, with its emphasis on standard-setting, to strengthen their collaboration; to work together with the BIS to develop recommendations to mitigate procyclicality; for the IMF and FSB to work together to monitor asset prices; and for the IMF and FSB to work together to analyze the causes of the crisis (G20 2008). Subsequent summits have continued to orchestrate other institutions in this way, by calling on them to carry out specific tasks and to then report back to the G20 with progress reports. In 2013 at the St. Petersburg Summit, for example, leaders also called

on the FSB, in consultation with standard setting bodies, to assess and develop proposals by end-2014 on the adequacy of global systemically important financial institutions' loss absorbing capacity when they fail. We recognize that structural banking reforms can facilitate resolvability and call on the FSB, in collaboration with the IMF and the OECD, to assess cross-border consistencies and global financial stability implications, taking into account country-specific circumstances, and report to our next Summit.   (G20 2013: § 68)

In its interactions with the international financial institutions, the G20 does not merely confirm but also initiates programs that are implemented with the assistance of the international financial institutions. The Pittsburgh Framework for Strong, Sustainable and Balanced Growth (FSSBG), for example, was designed by the G20 and announced at the Pittsburgh Summit with the aim of promoting cooperation on policy planning, assessment, and implementation. The FSSBG depends, however, on the IMF for implementation. G20 tasks to the IMF are not authorized under Article IV, and the G20 has no legal standing or authority as a principal over the IMF. Rather, the IMF acts as an advisor to the G20 based on a request for assistance from members (Cooper/Bradford

2010: 6; International Monetary Fund 2009: 6). This is the essence of network governance: relationships are informal, horizontal, and largely voluntary, but still involve governance.

Implications for governance

A loosening of governance from the traditional post-World War Two institutions opens up new flexibilities and possibilities for governance. The proliferation of new actors and new institutions has allowed for the inclusion of some relevant players who have been marginalized by the traditional Bretton Woods institutions. On a functional level, the proliferation of institutions may be a pragmatic approach to managing issue complexity. Cooperation within various selective and specialized institutions, rather than within a large inclusive bureaucracy, may create an effective division of labor. Finally, institutional fragmentation and network governance may inject necessary flexibility and speed into rather lethargic and cumbersome traditional IGOs, such as the IMF. Governance fragmentation, however, also raises a number of potential challenges for governance effectiveness and legitimacy.

First, rather than leading to a smooth division of labor, institutional fragmentation may lead to institutional competition and conflict, exacerbating overlap and coordination problems (Cooley/Ron 2002; Drezner 2009). Thus far, the international financial institutions have been cooperating with the G20. Over time, however, disagreements and turf-battles are bound to appear. The G20's relationship to the UN General Assembly, for example, is already marked by tension directly related to the question of which body has governance authority. The G20 has avoided cooperating with the UN General Assembly and thus has been able to circumvent or only selectively address the concerns of non-G20 states (Heinbecker 2011a: 11, 2011b: 236–246). Moreover, as the urgency of the financial crisis recedes, conflicts of interests within the Group and across institutions, initially suppressed in the face of a greater challenge, may re-emerge.

A related concern here is that the G20 and its orchestration techniques are too weak to effectively coordinate financial governance once the immediate post-crisis goals have been reached. While G20 summits refer to and build on the work of previous meetings, each new summit generates its own set of policy recommendations and new action plans. These plans show a tendency to expand the G20 agenda away from financial regulatory reform. Most recently in Brisbane 2014, the G20 addressed broad economic issues, energy policy, climate change, and food security in addition to financial market governance (G20

2014). Without greater institutionalization and centralization this may lead to a more chaotic and less binding governance regime.

A second problem is that informal and selective institutions such as the G20 have low transparency and few accountability mechanisms (Baker 2009). At the G20, for example, there are no reporting requirements to domestic governments or external monitors, and there is a limited paper trail and little official documentation of meetings. Furthermore, there are no formal mechanisms for the G20 to consult with or report to non-member countries affected by its policies. The G20's selective membership means that a handful of self-appointed states have a disproportionate say in matters of global governance – in this case, financial governance – that can have substantial implications for all actors in the system, including non-members. Among non-member states, such as many Latin American countries, there is concern that the G20 can use its influence within international financial institutions to dictate new rules to outsiders, especially with regard to financial market regulation and international development.

Finally, informality, selectivity, and orchestration may enable powerful states to avoid deeper reforms. While it seems to have been effective at handling the immediate aftermath of the crisis (Cooper 2010; Cooper/Helleiner 2010; Heinbecker 2011; Drezner 2014), the G20 does not have the mandate, enforcement mechanisms, or political independence to impose reforms that prudential regulation might require but that states resist. The regulatory reform agenda of the G20 has been motivated by the need to put out fires and to adapt and respond to crisis, rather than the pursuit of a "grand design" approach to preventing crises. Especially as compared with areas such as trade, in which the World Trade Organization (WTO) has developed significant authority, international financial regulation remains institutionally weak. By showing leadership and results on some issues in moments of crisis, the G20 is able to deflect calls for a more centralized and authorized institution, such as a WFO. However, as crises dissipate, there is no permanent institution charged with maintaining the momentum on global financial governance.

Conclusion

The global financial crisis was an occasion to rethink not only financial regulation, but also the institutional architecture charged with developing, implementing, and monitoring those regulations. Indeed, while there has been much debate about the extent and success of regulatory reform efforts (see, among others, Drezner 2014; Moschella/Tsingou 2013), less attention has been paid to organizational developments. It has long been clear that early calls for a World Financial Organization were never going to be realistic. The prominence of the G20 during the crisis, in contrast, has led to expectations that it would take on a new and important leadership role in financial governance. This chapter has sought to put these developments in the context of larger shifts in global governance. It has argued that the significance of the G20 is symptomatic of a move away from universal multilateral IGOs toward a more pluralistic and fragmented governance landscape. Issue complexity, actor heterogeneity, and resulting state concern over sovereignty costs are factors driving the proliferation of less formal, more specialized, and more selective governance institutions. If the governance environment is no longer organized by a central IGO, as was attempted after World War Two, but resembles more of a network of actors, questions about the effectiveness and quality of governance arise. I have argued that during the global financial crisis, the G20 emerged as a nodal actor to "orchestrate" the diffuse network of financial governance institutions. The G20 has institutional characteristics that make it suited to such a role. On one hand, an orchestrated network imbues governance efforts with speed, flexibility, and a division of labor. On the other hand, however, it also raises several concerns for governance. In the absence of a supranational institution with enforcement mechanisms, a clear mandate, and authority, networked governance may lead to more fragmentation and coordination problems, exacerbate accountability concerns, and may be used by states to avoid deeper and more far-reaching reforms.

References

Abbott, Kenneth, et al., 2015: Orchestration: Global Governance Through Intermediaries. In: Kenneth Abbott et al. (eds.), *International Organizations as Orchestrators*. Cambridge: Cambridge University Press, 1–36.

Alter, Karen J./Sophie Meunier, 2009: The Politics of International Regime Complexity. In: *Perspectives on Politics* 7, 13–24.

Baker, Andrew, 2009: Deliberative Equality and the Transgovernmental Politics of the Global Financial Architecture. In: *Global Governance: A Review of Multilateralism and International Organizations* 15, 195–218.

Biermann, Frank/Philipp Battberg/Harro van Asselt, 2009: The Fragmentation of Global Governance Architectures: A Framework for Analysis. In: *Global Environmental Politics* 9(4), 14–40.

Büthe, Tim/Walter Mattli, 2011: *The New Global Rulers: The Privatization of Regulation in the World Economy*. Princeton: Princeton University Press.

Claessens, Stijn, 2008: The New International Financial Architecture Requires Better Governance. In: Barry Eichengreen/Richard Baldwin (eds.), *What G20 Leaders Must Do to Stabilize our Economy and Fix the Financial System*. London: VoxEU.org Publication, 29–32.

Cooley, Alexander/James Ron, 2002: The NGO Scramble. In: *International Security* 27(1), 5–39.

Cooper, Andrew F., 2010: The G20 as an Improvised Crisis Committee and/or a Contested "Steering Committee" for the World. In: *International Affairs* 86, 741–757.

Cooper, Andrew F./Colin Bradford, 2010: *The G20 and the Post-Crisis Economic Order*. CIGI (Centre for International Governance Innovation) G20 Paper 3. Waterloo, ON: CIGI.

Cooper, Andrew F./Eric Helleiner, 2010: The G-20: A "Global Economic Government" in the Making? In: Christoph Pohlmann/Stephan Reichert/Hubert René Schillinger (eds.), *The G-20: A "Global Economic Government" in the Making?* Berlin: Friedrich-Ebert-Stiftung, Department for International Policy Analysis, 4–11. <http://library.fes.de/pdf-files/id/ipa/07284.pdf>

Davies, Howard/David Green, 2008: *Global Financial Regulation: The Essential Guide*. Cambridge: Polity Press.

Drezner, Daniel, 2009: The Power and Peril of International Regime Complexity. In: *Perspectives on Politics* 7(1), 65–70.

——, 2014: *The System Worked: How the World Stopped Another Great Depression*. Oxford: Oxford University Press.

Eatwell, John/Lance Taylor, 2000: *Global Finance at Risk: The Case for International Regulation*. Cambridge: Polity Press.

Eichengreen, Barry, 2008: Not a New Bretton Woods but a New Bretton Woods Process. In: Barry Eichengreen/Richard Baldwin (eds.), *What G20 Leaders Must Do to Stabilise our Economy and Fix the Financial System*. London: VoxEU.org Publication, 25–28.

——, 2009: *Out of the Box Thoughts about the International Financial Architecture*. IMF Working Paper 09/116. Washington, DC: International Monetary Fund.

G20 (Group of Twenty), 2007: *The Group of Twenty: A History*. Toronto: University of Toronto. <www.g20.utoronto.ca/docs/g20history.pdf>

——, 2008: *Washington Action Plan*. Washington, DC: G20. <www.mof.go.jp/english/international_policy/convention/g20/g20_090905_3.pdf>

——, 2009: *Global Plan for Recovery and Reform*. Toronto: University of Toronto. <www.g20.utoronto.ca/2009/2009communique0402.html>

——, 2011: *Cannes Summit Final Declaration: Building Our Common Future: Renewed Collective Action for the Benefit of All*. Toronto: University of Toronto. <www.g20.utoronto.ca/2011/2011-cannes-declaration-111104-en.html>

——, 2012: *G20 Leaders' Declaration*. Toronto: University of Toronto. <www.g20.utoronto.ca/2012/2012-0619-loscabos.html>

——, 2013: *G20 Leaders' Declaration, Saint Petersburg Summit*. St. Petersburg: g20.org. <https://g20.org/wp-content/uploads/2014/12/Saint_Petersburg_Declaration_ENG_0.pdf>

——, 2014: *G20 Leaders' Communiqué, Brisbane Summit*. Brisbane: g20.org. <https://g20.org/wp-content/uploads/2014/12/brisbane_g20_leaders_summit_communique.pdf>

Hanrieder, Tine, 2015: WHO Orchestrates? Coping with Competitors in Global Health. In: Kenneth Abbott et al. (eds.), *International Organizations as Orchestrators*. Cambridge: Cambridge University Press, 191–213.

Heinbecker, Paul, 2011a: *The Future of the G20 and Its Place in Global Governance*. CIGI (Centre for International Governance Innovation) G20 Paper 5. Waterloo, ON: CIGI.

——, 2011b: The United Nations and the G20: Synergy or Dissonance? In: Colin Bradford/ Wonhyuk Lim (eds.), *Global Leadership in Transition: Making the G20 More Effective and Responsive*. Washington, DC: Brookings Institution Press, 236–246.

Helleiner, Eric/Stefano Pagliari, 2010: Crisis and the Reform of International Financial Regulation. In: Eric Helleiner/Stefano Pagliari/Hubert Zimmermann (eds.), *Global Finance in Crisis: The Politics of International Regulatory Change*. London: Routledge, 1–17.

Hillman, Jennifer, 2010: *Saving Multilateralism: Renovating the House of Global Economic Governance for the 21ˢᵗ Century*. Brussels Forum Paper Series. Washington, DC: The German Marshall Fund of the United States.

IMF (International Monetary Fund), 2009: *The G-20 Mutual Assessment Process and the Role of the Fund*. Washington, DC: International Monetary Fund; Strategy, Policy, and Review Department and the Legal Department. <www.imf.org/external/np/pp/eng/2009/120209a.pdf>

——, 2013: *IMF Membership in the Financial Stability Board*. Washington, DC: International Monetary Fund; Legal and Monetary and Capital Markets Departments. <www.imf.org/external/np/pp/eng/2013/022213.pdf>

Kahler, Miles, 1992: Multilateralism with Small and Large Numbers. In: *International Organization* 46(3), 681–708.

Kirton, John, 2010: The G-20 Finance Ministers: Network Governance. In: Alan Alexandroff/ Andrew Cooper (eds.), *Rising States, Rising Institutions*. Waterloo, ON: The Centre for International Governance Innovation, 196–217.

Koremenos, Barbara/Charles Lipson/Duncan Snidal, 2001: The Rational Design of International Institutions. In: *International Organization* 55, 761–799.

Lagarde, Christine, 2011: How the G20 can prevent another financial crisis. In: *Financial Times*, 24 January 2011. <http://on.ft.com/1Mhianq>

Martinez-Diaz, Leonardo/Ngaire Woods, 2009: Introduction: Developing Countries in a Networked Global Order. In: Leonardo Martinez-Diaz/Ngaire Woods (eds.), *Networks of Influence: Developing Countries in a Networked Global Order*. Oxford: Oxford University Press, 1–18.

Moschella, Manuela/Eleni Tsingou (eds.), 2013: *Great Expectations, Slow Transformations: Incremental Change in Post-Crisis Regulation*. Colchester: ECPR Press.

Nielson, Daniel/Michael Tierney, 2003: Delegation to International Organizations: Agency Theory and World Bank Environmental Reform. In: *International Organization* 57, 241–276.

Scharpf, Fritz W., 1997: *Games Real Actors Play. Actor-centered Institutionalism in Policy Research*. New York: Westview Press.

Slaughter, Anne-Marie/Thomas Hale, 2010: Transgovernmental Networks and Emerging Powers. In: Alan Alexandroff/Andrew Cooper (eds.), *Rising States, Rising Institutions*. Waterloo, ON: The Centre for International Governance Innovation, 48–62.

Vabulas, Felicity/Duncan Snidal, 2013: Organization without delegation: Informal intergovernmental organizations (IIGOs) and the spectrum of intergovernmental arrangements. In: *Review of International Organizations* 8, 193–220.

Viola, Lora Anne, 2013: Institutioneller Wandel durch Wettbewerb: Wie die Zivilgesellschaft die WHO verändert hat. In: Michael Zürn/Matthias Ecker-Ehrhardt (eds.), *Die Politisierung der Weltpolitik – Umkämpfte Internationale Institutionen*. Berlin: Suhrkamp, 287–311.

——, 2014: The G-20 and Global Financial Regulation. In: Manuela Moschella/Catherine Weaver (eds.), *Handbook of Global Economic Governance: Players, Power, and Paradigms*. New York: Routledge, 115–128.

——, 2015: Orchestration by Design: The G20 in international financial regulation. In: Kenneth Abbott et al. (eds.), *International Organizations as Orchestrators*. Cambridge: Cambridge University Press, 88–113.

Woods, Ngaire/Leonardo Martinez-Diaz, 2009: *Networks of Influence: Developing Countries in a Networked Global Order*. Oxford: Oxford University Press.

Zürn, Michael/Gunnar Folke Schuppert (eds.), 2008: *Governance in einer sich wandelnden Welt*. Wiesbaden: Springer VS.

3 International Institutions in the Process of Financial Market Regulatory Reform

Renate Mayntz

Regulatory reform: The international level

The financial crisis that became manifest with the bankruptcy of Lehman Brothers in 2008 triggered immediate policy responses at all political levels involved in financial market regulation: national, European, and international. Demands for regulatory reform were radical and comprehensive. At the second G20 summit meeting in London in 2009 the assembled heads of government proclaimed, "[w]e have agreed that all systemically important institutions, markets, and instruments should be subject to an appropriate degree of regulation and oversight" (G20 2009a). Comprehensive reform demands were also voiced by the UN's Stiglitz Commission (United Nations 2009) and by the OECD (2009). Banking regulation was supposed to become stricter, and rules were to be extended to cover previously unregulated components of the financial system. Most importantly, regulatory standards were to be harmonized or at least coordinated at the international level. Given the international scope and high degree of connectedness of large financial institutions and financial market transactions, international coordination was imperative in order to make regulatory arbitrage unattractive and to preserve a "level playing field". More than in some other policy fields, the international level thus played a crucial role in the process of financial market reform.

As shown by Figure 1-2 in Chapter 1, a large and heterogeneous set of international institutions have been involved in the process of reforming financial market regulation, including the OECD, the UN, the Bank of International Settlements (BIS), the World Bank, and the Financial Action Task Force (FATF). As it turned out, however, only a small set of institutions became core actors in the process of regulatory reform; of these, the G20, the Financial Stability Board (FSB), the International Monetary Fund (IMF), and the international standard-setting organizations the Basel Committee on Banking Supervision (BCBS) and the International Organization of Securities Commissions (IOSCO) have been singled out for closer analysis in this chapter.[1] The activities of these bodies with regard to financial market reform will be traced mainly on the basis of documentary materials concerning the relevant regulatory output up to the fall of 2014. The available literature provides only scant insight into the internal decision-making processes that shaped these outputs. Obviously, however, national preferences, and compromises between diverging national interests, played a major role. It is a special characteristic of the policy field that at the international level representatives of nation-states rather than a big professional bureaucracy are the decisive actors in financial market regulation. The fact that representatives of nation-states negotiate policy decisions at higher levels links the reform activities at these levels: national actors carry whatever they consider problematic and in need of change directly into the reform discourse at the next higher – European or international – level. The subsequent chapters in this book will provide more detailed information on efforts of nation-states and the EU to influence the international regulatory discourse.

The fragmented international governance of financial markets did not undergo radical organizational change in response to the crisis. But the amorphous set of institutions involved in different aspects of financial market regulation crystallized, as it were, around the G20 as a hub. The G20 worked closely together with the Financial Stability Board (FSB), which in turn tightened relations with the IMF and with the international standard-setting organizations. In Chapter 2 of this volume, Lora Viola showed why the G20 became the nodal actor in the reform process that was triggered by the financial crisis, and how this choice corresponds to a more general trend in the development of global governance, away from big treaty-based international organizations towards sectional, club-like, high-level fora of decision-makers sometimes summarily labeled "G-bodies" (see also Cooper/Alexandroff 2010; Cooper/Schrumm 2011). The G20 was established in 1999 as a forum in which the finance ministers and central bank governors of the economically most important countries meet to discuss issues of financial stability; before the recent financial crisis, however, ministers and governors rarely attended these meetings in person. The chair of the G20 rotates between member countries, the country whose turn it is to chair the G20 in a given year being responsible for organizing the meetings. The "acting secretariat" of the G20 thus moves from country to country, just like the household

---

1 Other standard-setting organizations, such as the International Association of Insurance Supervisors (IAIS) and the International Accounting Standards Board (IASB), will not be dealt with in this chapter, because reforms in accounting standards and insurance do not belong to the substantive reform areas singled out for this study.

of medieval monarchs always on the move in their reign. Up until 2007, the G20 had been a body of low political visibility, but it had a sectional mandate that fitted the task at hand when the financial crisis erupted. Besides that, G20 membership is restricted, which meant that consensus-building would be easier than in an international organization such as the IMF, or a United Nations unit with a similar sectional mandate. Together these features predisposed the G20 for its role as nodal actor, which it in fact became when, beginning in 2009, the heads of the G20 governments also started to meet at highly visible summits.

In contrast to the G20, the FSB and the international standard-setting organizations BCBS and IOSCO are formally constituted institutions, but they differ from international organizations such as the IMF. In a typical international organization such as the IMF, the International Labour Organization (ILO), or the OECD, the top decision-making body (or bodies, if there is both an executive council and a plenary) consists of representatives of the member countries, and the organization has a large bureaucratic staff that prepares policy decisions and implements them (Barnett/Finnemore 1999). The top decision-making bodies of the FSB, BCBS and IOSCO similarly consist of national representatives, but they have only a rudimentary administrative staff, so that their task – to formulate recommendations and rules for the behavior of financial market actors – is discharged by the representatives of national authorities at top-level meetings, and by national delegates to numerous working groups. As a member of the FSB secretariat put it, these are "member driven" institutions, in contrast to the "staff driven" organizations the IMF and the OECD.[2] FSB, BCBS and IOSCO are not regulators in the strict sense. They can at best produce what is generally classified as soft law – rules that become legally binding only if ratified at lower political levels. In the following sections of this chapter, the reform activities of, and the interactions among the core actors involved in the multilevel reform process will be looked at in more detail.

G20, FSB and IMF in the reform process

With a recession threatening in the wake of the financial crisis, and with the growing sovereign debt and euro crises, the substantive focus of the international policy discourse changed. But the shift of political attention to government debt and economic recession did not occur uniformly in all institutions that had

---

2 The interviews referred to in this chapter were conducted in 2010 by Till M. Kaesbach with members of the FSB and BCBS secretariats.

become active in the early phase of financial market reform. The shift has been most noticeable in international institutions with a broader mandate, while the specialized international standard-setting organizations continued, small step by small step, with financial market reform in their respective fields, elaborating regulatory frameworks and making extant rules operational. Organizational identity serves as a filter for the impact of challenges arising in their environment on the activity of regulatory institutions.

When, at the height of the financial crisis, the need was felt for concerted international action, the G20 appeared to offer a suitable forum. The decision to assemble the G20 heads of government for regular summit meetings was explicitly intended to establish the G20 as the "premier forum of our international economic cooperation" (G20 2009b). The commitments and tasks proclaimed at summit meetings both legitimize – and have circumscribed – the regulatory activity of European and national bodies. When political attention shifted from financial market regulation to new problems, the G20 continued to serve as "apex policy forum" (Baker 2010), but financial market regulation was no longer the paramount concern at G20 summits (see Figure 3-1). The reform of the financial sector and of international financial institutions dominated the first two summit declarations (Washington 2008 and London 2009), but already the Pittsburgh summit declaration in the fall of 2009 devoted only four out of nine sections to these topics. At Cannes in 2011 the stability and resilience of the international monetary system became a new focus, while the Leaders' Declaration of Los Cabos in 2012 (G20 2012) opens with the statement that "[w]e are united in our resolve to promote growth and jobs", with financial reform moving further down the agenda. Financial sector reform continued to be a topic at G20 summits even after it lost top priority, but has been pushed more and more into the background; at the most recent Brisbane summit, concerns with economic growth, job creation, cross-border tax avoidance, and monetary policy issues dominated the agenda (G20 2014d).

Summit meetings are regularly preceded by the meeting of G20 finance ministers and central bank governors. From the very beginning in 1999, the G20 finance ministers and central bank governors (or their deputies) discussed not only financial matters. As stated at their second meeting in October 2000, they "discussed the state of the world economy, particularly the associated policy challenges and ways of addressing potential vulnerabilities" (G20 2000). The new practice of summits upgraded also the normal G20 meetings; after 2008 they took place several times a year, top-level attendance became routine, and their agenda reflected the concerns voiced at summits. Heads of government necessarily respond to whatever problems appear paramount for the economic well-being of their countries in general, and not only for the stability of their financial

Figure 3-1   G20 reform concerns in summit declarations

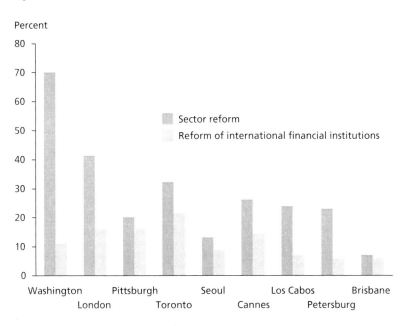

Percent

Legend:
- Sector reform
- Reform of international financial institutions

X-axis labels: Washington, London, Pittsburgh, Toronto, Seoul, Cannes, Los Cabos, Petersburg, Brisbane

Source: Quantitative analysis of G20 final summit declaration documents. Word count by Natalie Mohr and Moritz Höfeld of statements on »financial sector reforms« and »international financial institutions reform« as a percentage of total words per declaration.

systems. While the G20 meetings preceding a summit appear to shape, even dictate summit agendas, their own agenda has clearly been influenced by the acute political concerns of their governments. The shift of concerns observed at summit meetings parallels corresponding shifts at the meetings of G20 finance ministers and central bank governors. In 2014, three meetings of G20 finance ministers and central bank governors – in February in Sydney, in April in Washington, DC, and in September in Cairns – preceded the November Brisbane Summit (G20 2014a, b, c, d). Analysis of the four Communiqués shows that the dominant summit concerns with economic growth and job creation, monetary policy, and cross-border tax avoidance were voiced in very similar ways in the three preceding G20 meetings. The statement in the September Communiqué that signals the end of financial reform as a priority – "[w]e have delivered key aspects of the core commitments we made in the wake of the financial crisis in 2008 to build a stronger and more resilient financial system" – recurs in nearly identical form in the Summit Communiqué (G20 2014c, d). Only for two of the issues addressed at the Brisbane summit – energy provision and climate change – do we find no counterpart in the preceding 2014 G20 communiqués. The two tiers of the G20 have become substantially integrated. But today's G20 differs from the pre-summit G20 not only in structure; the functions attributed to it by Lora A. Viola in Chapter 2 could not have been performed in the same way by the G20 before its transformation in 2009.

Summit agendas are set in negotiations that take place in countless informal exchanges between G20 member governments, the G20 finance ministers and central bank governors, and the FSB, which regularly addresses them before their meetings. In its reports to the G20 finance ministers and central bank governors, the FSB emphasizes the issues to be discussed with priority. This process serves as a filter that does not let all initiatives pass. G20 summits are used by member governments to put their own preferred topic on the agenda. In 2013, for instance, emerging market countries wished to discuss the negative effects that a reduction of "quantitative easing" by the American Federal Reserve would have on their economies, but due to strong US resistance, the topic did not make it to the St. Petersburg agenda. Instead, measures to combat tax evasion by private individuals and corporations – a goal supported by all major countries – became one of the issues dealt with. The political context in which G20 summits take place has changed repeatedly since the financial crisis dominated international concerns; this is reflected in summit agendas, which have extended even beyond cooperation in economic matters. In the St. Petersburg Leaders' Declaration (G20 2013) for instance, the fight against climate change is one of the twelve topics dealt with. The tendency towards overloading the G20 agenda, which is also reflected in the growing number of G20 work groups (40 in 2013), is now being openly criticized even by G20 members such as the Australian treasurer (FAZ, 14 October 2013: 19).

Looking only at those issues dealt with at G20 summits that refer specifically to financial market reform, the reform of the banking sector has been the dominant concern, with the reform of international financial institutions a close second (see Table 3-1). In the category "other regulatory concerns" tax havens and tax information exchange have attracted most, non-bank financial institutions least attention. The relatively high frequency of references in summit declarations to peer reviews and progress reports, as well as frequent references to non-cooperative jurisdictions, reflect the fact that the G20, lacking any decision-making powers as an institution, is restricted to monitoring and coordinating the reform process. True, it is heads of government who meet at G20 summits, but even where they do agree on the desirability of a given measure, their ability to commit their countries is strictly limited. This is also fairly evident in the use of phrases such as "we remain committed", "we reaffirm", "we renew", or "we reiterate our commitment", which abound in the 2013 Summit Declara-

Table 3-1   G20 financial market reform topics

		N Total	Percent
Reform of international financial institutions	Increase in resources generally	14	11.76
	IMF	57	47.90
	World Bank and MDBs	22	18.49
	FSF/FSB	19	15.97
	Cooperation between IFIs	7	5.88
	Sub-total	119	24.14
Banking sector	Capital and liquidity	36	28.13
	Supervision	16	12.50
	G-/SIFIs	33	25.78
	Bank resolution	10	7.81
	Cross-border banking	16	12.50
	Accounting standards	17	13.28
	Sub-total	128	25.96
Other regulatory concerns	Non-bank financial institutions	9	9.09
	Financial instruments	29	29.29
	Tax-havens/tax-information exchange	38	38.38
	Credit rating agencies	23	23.23
	Sub-total	99	20.08
Convergence of regulations and standards	Convergence of regulations	18	21.18
	Cooperation and information sharing	14	16.47
	Peer reviews, progress reports	34	40.00
	Stress testing	2	2.35
	Non-cooperative jurisdictions	17	20.00
	Sub-total	85	17.24
Financial market integrity	Risk management and compensation schemes	26	41.94
	Consumer protection	5	8.06
	Market transparency	6	9.68
	Money laundering and shadow banking	23	37.10
	Financial benchmarking	2	3.23
	Sub-total	62	12.58
Total		493	100 %

Source: Qualitative text analysis of G20 final summit declaration documents. Analysis by Natalie Mohr and Moritz Höfeld: all statements on financial regulation were codified, with codification depending on the addressed area of regulation. The table represents the sum of all G20 commitments and delegations per area of regulation, and for all summit declarations between 2008 and 2013.

tion. The G20 summits have been strong on formulating goals, but the G20 has been criticized for failing to deliver on promises and to see policy choices implemented (for example, Alexandroff/Kriton 2010). After the Cannes summit meeting in 2011, for instance, the Financial Times featured articles entitled "Forum's high ambitions deliver meagre results" and "Summitry once again proves its own irrelevance" (Financial Times, 7 November 2011). Vestergaard (2011) criticizes the G20 both on account of its limited representational legitimacy and for lacking effectiveness, notably with regard to IMF reform. In fact, even at the Brisbane Summit in 2014 the assembled heads of government stated that they were "deeply disappointed with the continued delay in progressing the IMF quota and governance reforms agreed in 2010" (G20 2014d). While admitting that the G20 played an important role in managing the financial market crisis by supporting national stimulus programs, helping to restrain protectionist tendencies, and generally boosting financial market confidence, Helleiner (2012) maintains that the absence of a dollar crisis was more important in preventing a global financial and economic collapse in 2007/2008.

As already alluded to in the Introduction (Chapter 1), the banking sector reforms taken up at the international level and discussed by the G20 have a specific time-profile, moving from simple to complex challenges. When the crisis hit in 2008, politicians still had little exact knowledge of the structure and dynamics of the financial system. Though the crisis was quickly seen as a macro-prudential, systemic problem, for lack of better knowledge the reform approach remained micro-prudential at first, targeting individual banks and the financial incentives inducing bankers to engage in increasingly risky trades. Another easily understandable measure to prevent bank failure was to require banks to hold more capital. The G20 heads of government welcomed – and endorsed – the corresponding initiatives of the Basel Committee. Over time, however, the reform process moved from the earlier emphasis on bankers' excessive risk-taking and insufficient bank capital, to more tricky issues, such as the moral hazard posed by increasingly global financial institutions that were "too big to fail", and the threats posed by the unregulated over-the-counter trading of complex derivatives. Understandably, causal factors that are easy to identify and relatively easy to manipulate are addressed first in a reform process triggered by an acute crisis, before measures to tackle more complex aspects of the problem are considered. It is easier to devise rules controlling the behavior of (certain categories of) actors, individual or corporate, than to address complex structures, intricate interconnections, and kinds of transactions that are difficult to keep track of. The same holds for the regulation of the financial instruments that were suspected of having contributed to the crisis. The various kinds of derivatives are extremely complex regarding their hidden risks. The fact that "innovative" forms of securitization were useful for investors, and not only profitable for banks, militated further against their reform. Below I will come back to some of these issues discussed at the international level in more detail.

The mandate of the IMF – one of the so-called Bretton Woods institutions – included, but was not narrowly focused on issues of financial stability. After the Asian crisis, the IMF had become involved in market supervision. Not only was the IMF authorized to inspect the financial market supervision of IMF members asking for credit; together with the World Bank it developed a new, quite intrusive instrument, the Financial Sector Assessment Program (FSAP). The FSAP exercises evaluate the "extent to which national regulators complied with internationally agreed upon best practices. The results of inspection would then be shared with the country under examination to help that country's policymakers identify the 'strengths, vulnerabilities and risks' of their financial systems" (Brummer 2014: 103). In the course of the reform process that started in 2008, the FSAP developed into a valuable instrument. From the first summit onwards the G20 asked for the collaboration of the IMF. To strengthen the IMF's capacity to play its expected role in the reform process, the G20 devoted much attention to the issue of institutional reform, including changes in the representation of different countries and regions in its decision-making bodies (quota reform). Already in the early phase of financial crisis management, IMF resources were increased, and though the intended quota reform had still not been achieved in 2014, the IMF was drawn into the reform network coordinated by the FSB, and was given specific tasks by the G20. These tasks involve monitoring and information-processing more than the development of specific rules. The financial stability reports published regularly by the IMF reflect a shift of attention parallel to corresponding shifts in G20 attention: until April 2011, issues of financial stability and specific aspects of regulatory reform dominate the IMF's financial stability reports, while the April 2012 report deals extensively with the sovereign debt crisis (IMF 2012). In 2013, policies to revive credit markets are discussed, and the monetary policies of the American Federal Reserve, the Japanese central bank, and the economic policy of the Chinese government are critically reviewed (IMF 2013). The April 2014 Global Financial Stability Report was devoted to growth and emerging markets (IMF 2014a); the last issue here considered was concerned with risk taking, liquidity, and shadow banking (IMF 2014b). The IMF has become an important collaborator of the FSB, particularly in monitoring the implementation of agreed reforms. But with all that, the IMF did not become the focal actor in the process of regulatory reform. With the sovereign debt crisis, the IMF recovered instead some of its previously lost importance as lender, becoming involved in saving especially some European states from bankruptcy.

In contrast to the G20 and the IMF, the attention of the FSB has remained fixed on financial market regulation. The FSB was established by the G20 in

2009 by upgrading the Financial Stability Forum (FSF) that had served to coordinate the work of the international standard setters. The FSB was to

coordinate and direct the future development of financial market regulation at the international level, with a view to ensuring the stability of the financial system. It would be a stronger institution than its predecessor [...] with the capacity not just to compile international standards, but actively to promote higher quality and effectiveness for financial market activity as a whole. (Donnelly 2012: 263)

To this purpose, the charter of the FSB charges it to coordinate the work of national authorities and international institutions "in order to develop, and promote the implementation of effective regulatory, supervisory and other financial sector policies" (FSB 2009a: Article 1). This sounds like a tall order. In fact, the self-description of the FSB is more realistic and more modest; it describes itself as being "responsible for coordinating and promoting the monitoring of the implementation of agreed G20 and FSB financial reforms" (FSB 2011d: 1). In any case, the FSB has become a core actor in matters of financial market regulatory reform. This warrants a closer analysis.

The FSB is located in Basel at the Bank for International Settlements (BIS), which largely covers its budget without being involved in its work. Figure 3-2 shows the focal position the FSB enjoys in the network of financial market governance by virtue of the composition of its membership. The official membership of the FSB includes 25 jurisdictions (including the European Commission), five international institutions (BIS, IMF, OECD, World Bank, and European Central Bank), and six standard-setting organizations. Depending on their internal organization, jurisdictions can be represented by up to three delegates – from their central bank, finance ministry, and supervisory authority; the number of official representatives is therefore larger than the number of official members. The large membership of the FSB contrasts with the miniscule size of its staff. When we conducted interviews in Basel in 2010, the FSB secretariat consisted of 20 people, the majority of them on secondment; currently the FSB secretariat comprises 29 staff members.[3] The Plenary is convened at least twice a year, the official members being represented by high ranking officials, such as organization chairs or deputy finance ministers and deputy central bank governors. The Steering Committee and the three Standing Committees draw their members from this group, with Steering Committee members also serving on Standing Committees. In addition and not shown in Figure 3-2 there are working groups, mostly small and set up to deal, often for a limited time, with a special issue; the members of these groups are experts delegated from FSB member organizations.

---

3 See <www.bis.org/publ/arpdf/ar2014e7.pdf#page=3>.

Figure 3-2   Members and organization of the Financial Stability Board

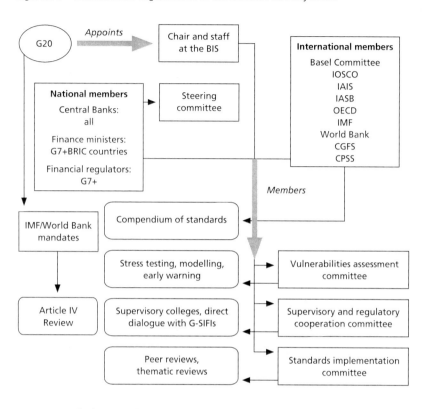

Source: Donelly (2012: 269).

Except for regular meetings, the persons in these committees and groups work from their home base where they use domestic resources, but it is these persons who do the work of the FSB, which means that the FSB members, not the staff, play the focal role in developing policy. As one staff member put it, "the ideas come out of our membership [...] the ownership of the FSB decisions is fully within the membership" (Interview K2). The results of the projects undertaken by working groups and standing committees are submitted to the Plenary, either in the form of reports or as proposals for decision. As Lora Viola points out in Chapter 2 of this volume, the weak autonomy of such a member-driven rather than staff-driven institution fits the preference of nation-states for international institutions that do not produce binding rules. Instead, the FSB plans and organizes the completion of specific envisaged reforms, assigning specific tasks to various international bodies and setting time lines. It is not the size, but the composition of its membership that enables the FSB "to deliver". The FSB membership includes all institutions actually involved in financial market regulation, and the representatives who meet in the permanent committees and the plenary are persons of high rank: they are

people who are pulling the levers of policy themselves, so when they are at a meeting and a new policy topic, a new policy recommendation comes up, they can agree it, and commit their organization to do it, at the meeting. They don't have to say "O goodness that's a new thing, I am going to have to report back and get back to you next week on what our view is." (Interview K1)

This statement, however, must be somewhat qualified where international organizations like the IMF are concerned, because here the FSB interacts with their bureaucracy, not their board or chiefs, as in the case of deputy finance ministers.

The working relationship between the FSB and the G20 is very close, but "[t]he FSB is run by its members and not by the G20. The G20 is a different membership to ours" (Interview K1). Indeed, the fact that the G20 has only national representatives – finance ministers and central bank governors – as official members, while FSB members include important international organizations and standard-setters, establishes the FSB as prime coordinator. The FSB's coordination extends both horizontally and vertically: it links different kinds of international organizations and different political levels in the process of financial market reform. Formally, the FSB has only an observer role at G20 meetings, but the FSB chairman "goes to the G20 leaders and will brief them on what we are doing, and the Secretary General of the FSB will go to the finance ministers to brief them" (Interview K2); "so by the time something gets to the G20, the actual finance ministers and central bank governors, or to the summit, it is not a surprise anymore, they have been fully involved in the policy process of developing it" (Interview K1). There is of course "the possibility that the G20 leaders will identify an issue separately from us and then the FSB has to look into it" (Interview K2), but as pointed out above, the agenda of G20 summits is generally not of its own making. Summit meetings have high symbolic value; they underline the necessity of reforms and legitimize reform initiatives at lower political levels. The critical function of the FSB is as linking pin in consensus building across authorities, levels, and organizations. This function is presumably enhanced by overlaps between different international institutions created by the multiple memberships; representatives of given institutions will meet in different fora, and sometimes it is even the same persons who meet.[4] But the FSB does not serve merely as bro-

---

4 Although this has not been studied empirically for the case of financial regulation, Gehring and Faude (2014) have demonstrated the effect of multiple memberships in a study on the regula-

Figure 3-3   Coordination framework for the monitoring of regulatory implementation

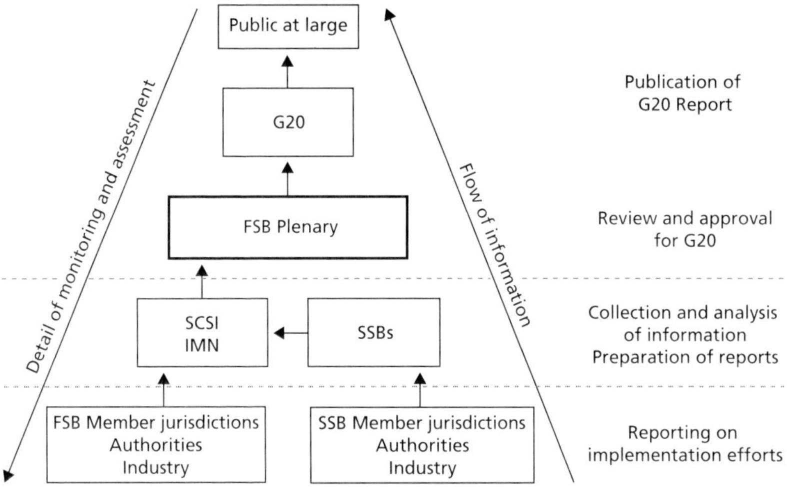

Note: SSB = standard-setting body.
Source: Financial Stability Board (FSB 2011a: 5).

ker; as will become evident in the next section, the FSB has played a focal role in the reform process by making G20 summit commitments operational. Without the FSB, the G20 summit declarations would have remained largely ineffectual.

Over time, the FSB's emphasis has shifted from the formulation to the realization of agreed regulatory reforms (FSB 2011d). Already in 2011, a framework for monitoring the implementation of agreed G20/FSB reforms was formalized (FSB 2011b). The main monitoring mechanisms used by the FSB are progress reports from the standard-setting bodies (SSBs), and thematic and country peer reviews. Figure 3-3 shows the structure of information flows. The FSB Standing Committee on Standards Implementation (SCSI) was created expressly for the peer review program. A peer review is conducted by a small team of experts appointed by the chair of the Standards Implementation Committee, who may be a deputy finance minister or deputy central bank governor. The experts are volunteers from membership organizations. The FSB secretariat assists with writing the review, which is then discussed by the standing committee, submitted to the plenary, and published if endorsed by the latter. The review team collects

tion of genetically modified organisms (GMOs) in agriculture and health-related intellectual property rights.

information from national authorities within the framework of the FSB Implementation Monitoring Network (IMN). Another important information source is the already mentioned Financial Sector Assessment Program (FSAP), run by the IMF and the World Bank.

The FSB's practical influence on reform is, of course, strictly limited. Membership of the FSB implies an obligation to conform to the core international standards that were already operative before 2007, plus any new standard issued by the FSB itself. But this happens rarely: most FSB reform proposals have the character of recommendations, one notable exception being the Principles on Compensation (FSB 2009b) – and these are only principles, not rules. FSB monitoring extends only to the formal adoption of reforms by competent jurisdictions, not to subsequent practice. The FSB has no sanctioning powers of its own to encourage implementation (Helleiner 2010), and its staff members are intensely conscious of this. "Well, there is a commitment, but there is nothing that requires [anyone] to actually do what is agreed" (Interview K1). In 2013, the FSB obtained legal personality (FSB 2013a), but this does not mean that it is now empowered to issue rules that have the force of international law. As before, the binding nature of any rules it develops and that the G20 leaders endorse depends ultimately on the commitment of its member countries. The measures the FSB can take largely boil down to naming and shaming, and reminding G20 leaders of their commitments, trying in this way to put pressure on implementation laggards. If the FSB does not collect information, and reports whether implementation is "on track", an issue may well "fall off the agenda. We are internally putting pressure on through the peer review process and externally through the publication of the peer review" (Interview K1). It is hard to tell whether peer pressure in fact ensues, and whether it works.

Substantive reforms: Bank capital, bank resolution, and derivatives trading

Neither the G20 nor the IMF are standard-setting organizations, and this also holds for the FSB, despite its pro-active stance in the process of regulatory reform. Turning now to the substantive reforms singled out for analysis in this book, the focus shifts to the international standard-setting bodies that have developed operative rules for the behavior of financial market actors. Prominent among these is the Basel Committee on Banking Supervision. The BCBS was in the process of developing new capital rules for banks when the financial crisis erupted, and so was standing ready as first mover in the ensuing reform process.

Established in 1974, the BCBS started by developing rules for banking supervision, but soon turned to the development of rules for bank capital reserves in order to forestall a banking crisis. In 1988 the BCBS adopted the "Basel Accord" on capital requirements for licensed (and hence regulated) banks. This was followed by a revised framework known as Basel II, which was finally published in 2005. However, further revisions continued to be discussed. The ability of the BCBS to pitch in as soon as reforms were called for helped to focus attention on bank equity as reform issue.

The BCBS is hosted by the BIS and located, like the FSB, in Basel. Its members are central banks and supervisory authorities, represented in committee meetings by senior officials. In response to the financial crisis of 2008/2009 the BCBS expanded its membership; at the time of writing it includes 42 organizations from 27 states. The full Committee meets several times a year; these meetings are also attended by observers (among the five regular observers are the IMF and the ECB), and by invited industry representatives. The actual work is done by member state representatives in several subcommittees and in task forces. The standards they devise have to be approved by the Group of Central Bank Governors and Heads of Supervision, the highest decision-making body. Decisions are not made by voting, but based on consensus. The BCBS has a Secretary General, supported by a staff that counted 14 in 2010 when we conducted interviews in Basel; most staff members are seconded by member organizations.

Basel II contains three sections or "pillars", referring respectively to minimal capital requirements for banks, risk management, and information disclosure. The financial crisis of 2008 made evident that this set of rules was insufficient to prevent a banking crisis. As analyzed in detail by Goldbach and Kerwer (2012), the BCBS responded to the financial crisis first by amending Basel II, but simultaneously work started on a new set of capital adequacy standards. Before the crisis, the BCBS had no relations with the G20, but was present together with representatives of the other standard-setting organizations at the meetings of the Joint Forum and of the Financial Stability Forum (FSF), the FSB's predecessor; at these meetings, information was exchanged, but no regulatory decisions were taken. With the transformation of the FSF into today's FSB, the BCBS became a member of the FSB, and was "tasked" by the G20 to develop what has come to be called Basel III. Basel III – officially called "[a] global regulatory framework for more resilient banks and banking systems" – was completed in 2010. Submitted to, and endorsed by the G20 leaders in November 2010, Basel III was published on 16 December 2010 (BCBS 2011a), the first finished piece of regulatory reform.

Basel III rules define stricter minimum capital requirements in relation to banks' risk-weighted assets; in addition, they introduce counter-cyclical and capital conservation buffers that banks are required to hold and demand that banks observe a fixed leverage ratio and a fixed liquidity ratio. Including the capital conservation buffer, banks' minimum capital requirements in relation to risk-weighted assets increased to 10.5 percent; at the same time, the risk weights of several asset categories were raised – with the notable exception of state bonds, which enjoy an official zero-risk to this day. The liquidity coverage ratio is supposed to improve a bank's ability to withstand short-term liquidity shortages, such as occurred in 2009, by requiring them to hold a buffer of highly liquid assets, while the net stable funding ratio is intended to promote stronger resilience over a one-year period. While the minimum capital requirements were to be implemented by the end of 2013, rules on liquidity and leverage are to be phased in over a period up to 2019. The newly introduced provisions of Basel III take up what had already been discussed but not included in Basel II; already in 2000, for instance, the BCBS had published guidelines for countering liquidity risk. But guidelines are not standards: Basel III would not have been possible without the shock of the crisis.

While international banking organizations have criticized the capital requirements of Basel III as too restrictive, experts consider them to be insufficient (Admati/Hellwig 2013). The effective influence of the banking industry on Basel III is assessed differently by Lall (2012) and Young (2012); Goldbach and Kerwer (2012) side with Young, stating that the effective influence of the industry on Basel III has been only modest. As shown in more detail in the following chapters of this book, the representatives of EU member states in the Basel Committee disagreed among themselves on a number of points, and while the United States and the United Kingdom opted for higher capital requirements, continental European countries opposed them. The finally adopted standard is a compromise.

Since the publication of Basel III, the Basel Committee has been concerned with clarification, technical elaboration, and fine-tuning of its rules, providing interpretive guidance on the liquidity coverage ratio and net stable funding ratio. Fine tuning offered new opportunities for national and industry representatives to try to soften unwelcome provisions. Rules that had been considered too restrictive have meanwhile been modified; this is true for the risk-weighting of assets, the originally formulated liquidity ratio, and the leverage ratio. The full text of the revised liquidity coverage ratio was published in January 2013, the final text of the leverage ratio and disclosure requirements in January 2014, while the net stable funding ratio is expected to become a minimum standard only by 1 January 2018 (BCBS 2014: 2). The new capital requirements that were to be adopted by the end of 2013 were largely ratified on time by Basel committee member jurisdictions (BCBS 2014: 4–20); already in March 2013, all of them had at least "initiated significant action" to put the Basel III capital requirements in place (BCBS 2013). Since then also the EU, a laggard with respect to the adoption of Basel III rules, has incorporated them – again in a modified form – in its revised Capital Requirements Directive, CRD IV (see Quaglia, Chapter 4, this volume).

While Basel III was being finalized, other reform needs that had been identified as having contributed to the crisis were taken up. Since the beginning of the financial crisis, experts and potential regulators have been aware that large, "systemically important" financial institutions (SIFIs), over-the-counter (OTC) derivatives trading, and the "shadow banking system" played an important role in its occurrence, but substantive knowledge has been lacking. This is one reason why it took a longer time to start dealing with these aspects of the financial system than it took to define new capital requirements for banks, compensation rules for bankers, and conflict-of-interest avoidance rules for rating agencies. By the end of 2011, the "priority areas" singled out for monitoring by the FSB went beyond the implementation of banker compensation rules and the new Basel capital standards to include global systemically important banks, the resolution of failing banks, the market for OTC derivatives, and the shadow banking system (FSB 2011a).

The regulation of OTC derivatives is clearly the responsibility of IOSCO, but the other issues cut across the policy domains of different international institutions, requiring their cooperation. It was the FSB that played the role of coordinator, becoming what the Financial Times called an "umbrella regulatory body" (Financial Times, 11 November 2014). The efforts to deal with the risk posed by global systemically important banks illustrate this well. By bailing out distressed banks, governments had in fact given credence to the belief that big banks will be saved by the state when in trouble. This widely shared belief was exploited by the big banks, which were rated higher and had to pay lower interest than banks deemed less "safe". The aim of regulatory reform has been to prevent the necessity of future bail-outs of financial institutions considered to be systemically important with, as governments like to put it, "taxpayers' money". But before SIFIs can be regulated, the regulatory target must be defined more clearly, something that posed a problem in view of the large variety of, and the lack of data about, existing financial institutions. Already in October 2009, the FSB, together with the IMF and the BIS, had presented "Initial Considerations" on how to assess the systemic importance of financial institutions and instruments (BIS, FSB and IMF 2009). A year later, the FSB presented recommendations on how to reduce the moral hazard posed by SIFIs generally, and by SIBs (systemically important banks) in particular (FSB 2010). In 2011 the regulation of SIFIs became a focal concern for the FSB, IOSCO, and the Basel Committee

BCBS. At its meeting on 3 October 2011, the FSB mentioned "addressing systemically important financial institutions (SIFIs)" first on its list of key financial regulatory reforms (FSB 2011f). By late 2011, the BCBS had developed indicators for measuring the systemic importance of global, systemically important financial institutions (G-SIFIs). Five properties defining G-SIFIs were identified: the cross-jurisdictional activity of an institution, its size, its interconnectedness, its substitutability, and its complexity. These five categories, measured by 12 indicators, are considered to be of equal importance, and given a weight of 20 percent each (BCBS 2011d). Using these indicators, the FSB identified, and published in 2012, a list of 28 global systemically important banks (G-SIBs; FSB 2012).

The main measures discussed in order to curb the risk SIFIs pose to the stability of the financial system are a cap on their size, higher capital requirements, and the introduction of a resolution procedure in case of failure. A cap on the size of big banks is a particularly contested measure, both on theoretical grounds and because of fierce opposition from the banks that would be affected. The easiest measure appears to be the definition of additional loss absorbency requirements for financial institutions categorized as "systemically important". A first step in this direction was taken by the BCBS in the framework of Basel III (BCBS 2011d), but this did not close the issue. The loss-absorbing capacity of global systemically important banks is particularly relevant in the context of bank resolution, which complicates the matter. Towards the end of 2014, the FSB was still seeking comments on policy proposals to enhance the loss-absorbing capacity of global systemically important banks (FSB 2014e).

Regulatory efforts addressing the risk posed by the failure of systemically important banks have focused on the creation of resolution regimes. In October 2011, the FSB issued a framework to guide the regulatory initiatives of its members, formulating key attributes of effective resolution regimes (FSB 2011e). By this time, Germany, for instance, had already moved ahead on its own (see Goldbach/Zimmermann, Chapter 7, this volume). According to the FSB, resolution strategies and plans should be in place for all global systemically important financial institutions identified in November 2011 by June 2013 (FSB 2013a). The EU likewise envisaged reforms; here the issue of resolution has been dealt with in the context of the Banking Union (see Quaglia, Chapter 5, this volume). Reviewing the transposition of the FSB Key Attributes of Effective Resolution Regimes into law by FSB member jurisdictions, the FSB concludes in its report to the G20 that "reforms are under way in many jurisdictions to align national statutory regimes with the FSB Key Attributes, but significant work remains" (FSB 2013b: 5). At the international level, at least, the problem of "too big to fail" has not yet been resolved.

Any bank resolution regime is dependent on supervision. Effective supervision of financial institutions, and particularly of systemically important financial institutions (SIFI), is the precondition of timely intervention. In 2014, the FSB took up the issue of SIFI supervision, stating that "[b]efore the crisis, insufficient attention was being paid to SIFI supervision [...] Many supervisors of SIFIs had inadequate mandates, resources, independence, and supervisory methods" (FSB 2014b: 1). Insufficient knowledge of the real state of affairs permitted the crisis to build up largely unobserved. There have been improvements in supervisory practices, the FSB notes, but enhanced stress testing, better risk measurement, and improved models are still needed (FSB 2014b: 4). Oversight and stress testing, in turn, require data, data that were often lacking in the build-up to the financial crisis. At the March 2014 plenary meeting, the FSB therefore launched a new phase of the Data Gaps project started in 2009 as part of the wider G20 initiative to improve data to support financial stability. The FSB Data Gaps Initiative is developing a data template for global systemically important financial institutions, a highly ambitious exercise in quantitative measuring (FSB 2014d).

Already in September 2009, the G20 Leaders had agreed in Pittsburgh on a substantial reform of over-the-counter – that is, not supervised by an exchange – dealing in derivatives. All standardized OTC derivative contracts were henceforth to be traded on exchanges or electronic trading platforms, cleared through central counterparties, and reported to trade repositories; higher capital requirements were to be imposed on non-centrally cleared contracts. As noted above, the regulation of OTC derivative trading belongs to IOSCO's domain. Deriving from the Inter-American Association of Securities Commissions, IOSCO was founded in 1983. In Baker's terminology, it is a typical "technical problem-solving network" (Baker 2009). IOSCO sets standards for securities regulation and aims to improve enforcement-related cross-border cooperation. IOSCO's membership is truly international, consisting (in 2011) of 119 securities regulators from 108 jurisdictions as voting members, plus 84 non-voting associate and affiliate bodies. There are numerous committees, both technical and regional, where the actual work is done; the staff is again miniscule – 19 persons working full-time, including seven seconded from member organizations, plus one part-time staff member. Following the G20 mandate, IOSCO proposed principles for mandatory clearing, disclosure, and reporting of OTC derivatives trading (IOSCO 2012). In April 2012, IOSCO published a set of international standards for payment, clearing, and settlement systems that apply to OTC derivatives markets; IOSCO members are committed to adopt these principles (IOSCO/CPSS 2012). The anticipated deadline for the implementation of the G20 commitments with respect to OTC derivative market regulation was the end of 2012. In April 2013 the FSB report stated that the implementation of agreed OTC reforms "is still progressing after the end-2012 deadline"; by this time, final legislation or rules concerning central clearing, reporting, and trading on platforms had been introduced in most jurisdictions, though they were mostly not yet in force (FSB 2013c: 1). By April 2014, rules specifying the legal requirements for central clearing were being developed, or had already been adopted, in several jurisdictions, and were even implemented in some countries. Starting near zero in early 2012, client clearing activity had risen exponentially by 2014 (FSB 2014c: 12, 18).

OTC derivative trading is only a small part of the shadow banking system. The term "shadow banking" is generally used to describe credit intermediation that takes place outside the regulated banking system. Neither the entities – for example, money market funds, private equity funds, hedge funds – nor the transactions in the shadow banking system are illegal per se, but being unregulated, the shadow banking system offers opportunities for illegal transactions. It is, however, the unobserved risk generated by transactions within the shadow banking system that poses the main challenge. Since the shadow banking system provides an important alternative source of credit widely used by the real economy, the task is to regulate, not eliminate the shadow banking sector. Regulation of the shadow banking system is a daunting challenge. The size of the global shadow banking system is estimated to represent 25–30 percent of the total financial system and half the volume of bank assets (European Commission 2012: 4). These estimates have recently been confirmed by an FSB Monitoring Report. Using a refined methodology, non-bank financial intermediation in advanced economies is estimated to account for about 25 percent of total financial assets, roughly half of banking system assets, and 12 percent of GDP (FSB 2014f: 2–3). In contrast to the regulated financial sector, however, no reliable data were available concerning the entities and activities in the shadow banking sector. For example, "[m]ore than 60% of the assets that are considered part of shadow banking activities in the euro area are linked to financial institutions for which high frequency statistical information is not available" (European Central Bank 2012: 6). Meanwhile, data collection has improved and methodology has been refined. The Global Shadow Banking Monitoring Report 2014 includes data from 25 jurisdictions plus the euro area, covers about 90 percent of global financial system assets, and contains fine-grained data on the composition of the shadow banking sector and on growth trends of non-bank financial intermediation (see FSB 2014f).

Information gaps and the ambivalent nature of non-bank financial intermediation as useful but risky have long been an obstacle to regulatory initiatives addressing the shadow banking sector as a whole. Only hedge funds, a small part of the sector, were singled out early. While the MPIfG data bank for publications on financial regulation contains four documents dealing with hedge fund regulation already for 2009, the first documents targeting shadow banking occur in 2011, with quickly increasing numbers in the following years. On 27 October 2011 the FSB published a first set of general principles for the future regulation of this sector that were subsequently endorsed by the G20 (FSB 2011c). The IMF, too, has been concerned with shadow banking (IMF 2011). In 2012 the FSB started five work streams to analyze, in cooperation with IOSCO and BCBS, different segments of shadow banking in more detail; both IOSCO and the FSB have since published a series of proposals for regulating specific segments of the shadow banking system. In August 2013, the FSB published an overview of policy recommendations aiming to strengthen oversight and regulate shadow banking (FSB 2013d). The FSB, IOSCO, and the Basel Committee continue to work on the regulation of specific elements of shadow banking, but it is a moving target. Efforts to tighten regulatory rules unavoidably induce attempts to escape costly compliance and are an incentive to escape from regulated banks to the less regulated sector. Current reforms may increase the transparency of shadow banking, as happens by the use of central counterparties in OTC derivatives markets, but they stop short of interfering with "innovative" forms of securitization.

Of the four areas of financial market regulatory reform chosen for analysis in this book, one – structural banking reforms – has not been an issue at the international level. The issues discussed at G20 meetings and summits did not cover the full range of potential reforms. Issues that clearly fall in the domain of national and European jurisdictions with the legal power to organize the governmental apparatus, such as the establishment of new regulatory agencies and reforms of the supervisory structure, were intensely discussed at the national and European, but not the international level. Nor have structural banking reforms been an issue at the international level. The main issue of structural banking reforms has been whether or not, and if so how, to separate core banking activities (commercial banking) from capital market activities of banks (investment banking). While in countries like France and Germany universal banks traditionally dominate, the US had separated commercial from investment banking in the Glass-Steagall Act, which, however, was later repealed. Since the trading activities of banks, and particularly proprietary trading, were generally seen to have contributed to the financial crisis, structural banking reform became a reform issue – but only at the national and the European level. In this case, however, it was not so much the question of regulatory competence, but rather the great diversity between national banking systems that pre-empted the search for a one-size-fits-all international solution. The diverse lower level activities with respect to structural banking reforms did, however, not go unobserved at the international level. Responding to a call from the G20, the FSB together with the IMF and the OECD prepared a report for the November 2014 summit of G20 leaders, informing them briefly about the structural banking reforms under way in some countries and the European Union (FSB 2014g). The report abstains from critical evaluation and makes no recommendations, but raises the question of the cross-border consistency of the different reported reforms. This is in line with the dominant concern of the international reform discourse: the strongly felt need that regulatory reforms be coordinated and avoid growing regulatory divergence.

Conclusion

In the early 2014 report to the G20 finance ministers and central bank governors the FSB states optimistically that "if we remain focused and ambitious, we can complete the remaining core elements of the reforms during the Australian G20 Presidency" (FSB 2014a: 1). In fact, however, important issues – too-big-to-fail, shadow banking, and derivatives markets – were still not resolved when the G20 leaders met at Brisbane. Financial market regulation no longer enjoys political top priority, but it is clear that the FSB and international standard-setters will continue their work into the future.

This chapter has shown in detail what has already been stated at its beginning: that the relations between the fragmented set of international bodies concerned with the stability of the financial system and with developing rules for its regulation have been tightened. With the transformed G20 and the FSB as linking pin, a certain amount of vertical order has also been introduced. This kind of structural change in a formerly loose network is a process taking place over time, as interactions between different institutions become more frequent, and cooperation becomes focused on specific issues. With this there has been, at the international level, a shift away from mutual information and possible one-sided adjustment, to closer cooperation and even instances of joint decision-making.

Looking at the output of international organizations that purport to formulate rules, one notes increasing concern with the technical details of intended reforms, as initial reform demands become operationalized. Policy development is generally characterized by increasing specialization as comprehensive reform demands are broken down and translated into specific measures. To make rules operational raises issues of classification. The BCBS, for instance, took pains to define precisely the criteria for what assets count as common equity tier 1 capital, and how to apply §75 of Basel III rules to derivatives (BCBS 2011b, 2011c, 2011e). The tendency to formulate ever more detailed rules is a reaction to the often explicitly recognized propensity of profit-seeking financial institutions to evade compliance by making use of regulatory gaps and of terms open to interpretation. The formulation of so-called "technical standards" aims to assist in the enactment of rules and to make certain that the rule-makers' intentions are realized. Where regulatory institutions, in recognition that a proposed regulation will be applied under widely different conditions, formulate general principles rather than detailed rules, they either expect lower level legislators to translate the principles into appropriate rules, or they do so in the – often vain – hope that supervisory institutions will insist on compliance not with the letter, but the spirit of a given principle (Mayntz 2012). At this point it is fair to recall that rules proposed by one of the international institutions, even if they have been formulated by delegates and experts with a national passport, have no immediate binding power for lower level jurisdictions, let alone financial market actors directly. In the following chapters it will be seen to what extent lower level reforms have followed international templates, and how lower level actors have tried to shape international policy. Of course both the preferences that national actors pursue in higher level negotiations, and the extent to which they are ready to adopt the resulting recommendations, are shaped by domestic forces. But at the same time, political decisions at all levels are intertwined with cross-level interactions and subject to their influence. The outcome of regulatory reform will be the result of these closely connected processes.

Already in 2010, the Transatlantic Council, a non-partisan network of US American and European leaders, warned of "the danger of divergence" in financial reform (Transatlantic Council 2010). With the feeling that the worst of the financial crisis *strictu sensu* has passed, an increasing penchant for protectionism has become visible in G20 negotiations (Bremmer/Roubini 2011). The renewed expansion of the G20 agenda after it had concentrated on financial market regulation seems to have strengthened the divisive force of diverging national interests. Helleiner and Pagliari (2011) in fact suggest that instead of strengthening, official international standards of financial regulation may weaken in the post-crisis world, because the broadening representational basis of the most important international regulatory bodies makes consensus harder to reach and favors a soft approach. Indeed, it is plausible that the greater economic and political diversity among states participating in international negotiations will lead to an increasing heterogeneity of policy preferences. But this does not mean that regulation will generally become more permissive. Regulation at the national level will be stricter than it was before the crisis, but national interest and regulatory arbitrage on the part of financial institutions will operate against the emergence of big differences in the strictness of regulation. The failure to achieve international regulatory harmonization, combined with the tendency toward stricter national or regional (EU) regulation, may reflect a shift from the self-perception of national power in terms of influence to the perception of "power as autonomy" (Cohen 2006, quoted in Helleiner/Pagliari 2011), the insistence on policy independence; this insistence may be a direct reaction to the increasing drive for financial regulation that is both strict and international.

The politicization of financial regulation following the financial crisis of 2007/2008 has increased rather than decreased the tendency towards protectionism and beggar-thy-neighbor strategies in international negotiations. Political leaders are expected, more so than technical experts, to act in what they define as the interest of their country. Given the importance of banks both for the national economy and for the debt financing of national budgets, it is not surprising that politicians "align themselves with bankers because they want to promote their countries' banks' interests in international competition. In international negotiations they fight for their countries' banks, even if the rules they fight for might endanger financial stability" (Admati/Hellwig 2013: 193). As long as political leaders identify with the interests of their country, and as long as national interests are diverse and often conflict, parametric adjustment rather than positive coordination and collective problem-solving will be the dominant mode of decision-making. This touches on a far-reaching and often discussed theoretical question, namely whether it is the capitalist mode of economic organization, or the political organization into separate states that feeds international competition. Kenneth Waltz ([1954]2001), for one, doubts that in a world of socialist states there would be no violent conflicts, since the reasons for such conflict lie in the nature of states, and are independent of their political economy. If this is so, the hope of arriving at an internationally regulated financial system is vain.

References

Admati, Anat/Martin Hellwig, 2013: *The Bankers' New Clothes.* Princeton: Princeton University Press.

Alexandroff, Alan S./John Kirton, 2010: The "Great Recession" and the Emergence of the G20 Leaders' Summits. In: Alan S. Alexandroff/Andrew F. Cooper (eds.), *Rising States, Rising Institutions. Challenges for Global Governance.* Washington, DC: Brookings Institution Press, 177–195.

Baker, Andrew, 2009: Deliberative Equality and the Transgovernmental Politics of the Global Financial Architecture. In: *Global Governance* 15, 195–218.

——, 2010: Deliberative international financial governance and apex policy forums: Where we are and where we should be headed. In: Geoffrey R. D. Underhill et al. (eds.), *Global Financial Integration Thirty Years On.* Cambridge: Cambridge University Press, 58–73.

Barnett, Michael N./Martha Finnemore, 1999: The Power, Politics and Pathologies of International Organizations. In: *International Organization* 53(4), 699–737.

BCBS (Basel Committee on Banking Supervision), 2011a: *Basel III framework for liquidity – Frequently asked questions*. Basel: BIS.

——, 2011b: *Basel III definition of capital – Frequently asked questions*. Basel: BIS.

——, 2011c: *Basel III definition of capital – Frequently asked questions* (update of FAQs published in July 2011). Basel: BIS.

——, 2011d: *Global systemically important banks: Assessment methodology and the additional loss absorbency requirement*. Basel: BIS.

——, 2011e: *Basel III definition of capital – Frequently asked questions* (update of FAQs published in October 2011). Basel: BIS.

——, 2013: *Report to G20 Finance Ministers and Central Bank Governors on monitoring the implementation of Basel III regulatory reforms*. Basel: BIS.

——, 2014: *Progress report on the implementation of the Basel regulatory framework*. Basel: BIS.

BIS (Bank for International Settlements)/FSB (Financial Stability Board)/IMF (International Monetary Fund), 2009: *Report to G20 Finance Ministers and Governors – Guidance to Assess the Systemic Importance of Financial Institutions, Markets and Instruments: Initial Considerations*. Basel: BIS.

Bremmer, Ian/Nouriel Roubini, 2011: A G-Zero World. In: *Foreign Affairs* 90(2), 2–6.

Brummer, Chris, 2014: *Minilateralism. How Trade Alliances, Soft Law, and Financial Engineering are Redefining Economic Statecraft*. Cambridge: Cambridge University Press.

Cohen, Benjamin J., 2006: The Macrofoundations of Monetary Power. In: David M. Andrews (ed.), *International Monetary Power*. New York: Cornell University Press, 31–50.

Cooper, Andrew F./Alan S. Alexandroff (eds.), 2010: *Rising States, Rising Institutions. Challenges for Global Governance*. Washington, DC: Brookings Institution Press.

Cooper, Andrew F./Andrew Schrumm, 2011: Reconciling the Gs: The G8, the G5, and the G20 in a World of Crisis. In: Paolo Savona/John J. Kriton/Chiara Oldani (eds.), *Global Financial Crisis. Global Impact and Solutions*. Farnham: Ashgate Publishing, 229–244.

Donelly, Shawn, 2012: Institutional Change at the Top. In: Renate Mayntz (ed.), *Crisis and Control: Institutional Change in Financial Market Regulation*. Frankfurt a.M.: Campus, 263–278.

European Commission, 2012: *Green Paper Shadow Banking*, 19 March 2012. Brussels: EC.

European Central Bank, 2012: *Shadow Banking in the Euro Area – An Overview*. Occasional Paper Series 133. Frankfurt a.M.: ECB.

FSB (Financial Stability Board), 2009a: *Financial Stability Board Charta*. Basel: FSB.

——, 2009b: *FSB Principles for Sound Compensation Practices*. Basel: FSB.

——, 2010: *Reducing the moral hazard posed by systemically important financial institutions – FSB Recommendations and Time Lines*. Basel: FSB.

——, 2011a: *A Coordination Framework for Monitoring the Implementation of Agreed G20/FSB Financial Reforms*. Basel: FSB.

——, 2011b: *Intensity and Effectiveness of SIFI Supervision – Progress report on implementing the recommendations on enhanced supervision*. Basel: FSB.

——, 2011c: *Shadow Banking: Strengthening Oversight and Regulation. Recommendations of the Financial Stability Board*. Basel: FSB.

——, 2011d: *Overview of Progress in the Implementation of the G20 Recommendations for Strengthening Financial Stability. Report to G20 Leaders*. Basel: FSB.

——, 2011e: *Key Attributes of Effective Resolution Regimes for Financial Institutions*. Basel: FSB.

FSB (Financial Stability Board), 2011f: *Meeting of Financial Stability Board.* Press Release, 3 October 2011. Basel: FSB.

——, 2012: *Update of group of global systemically important banks (G-SIBs).* Basel: FSB.

——, 2013a: *Report to G20 Ministers and Central Bank Governors: Progress of Financial Regulatory Reforms.* Basel: FSB.

——, 2013b: *Implementing the FSB Key Attributes of Effective Resolution Regimes – how far have we come?* Basel: FSB.

——, 2013c: *OTC Derivatives Market Reforms – Fifth Progress Report on Implementation.* Basel: FSB.

——, 2013d: *Strengthening Oversight and Regulation of Shadow Banking – An Overview of Policy Recommendations,* 29 August 2013. Basel: FSB.

——, 2014a: *To G20 Finance Ministers and Central Bank Governors. Financial Reforms – Progress and Challenges.* Basel: FSB.

——, 2014b: *Supervisory Intensity and Effectiveness. Progress Report on Enhanced Supervision.* Basel: FSB.

——, 2014c: *OTC Derivatives Market Reforms. Seventh Progress Report on Implementation.* Basel: FSB.

——, 2014d: *FSB Data Gaps Initiative – A Common Template for Global Systemically Important Banks.* Basel: FSB.

——, 2014e: *Adequacy of loss-absorbing capacity of global systemically important banks in resolution.* Basel. Basel: FSB.

——, 2014f: *Global Shadow Banking Monitoring Report 2014.* Basel: FSB.

——, 2014g: *Structural Banking Reforms. Cross-border consistencies and global financial stability implications. Report to G20 Leaders for the November 2014 Summit.* Basel: FSB.

G20 (Group of Twenty), 2000: *Press Release – Meeting of the G-20 Finance Ministers and Central Bank Governors, 2000.* Washington, DC: G20.

——, 2008: *Final Summit Declaration.* Washington Summit, 2008. Washington, DC: G20.

——, 2009a: *Final Summit Declaration.* London Summit, 2009. London: G20.

——, 2009b: *Final Summit Declaration.* Pittsburgh Summit, 2009. Pittsburgh: G20.

——, 2010a: *Final Summit Declaration.* Toronto Summit, 2010. Toronto: G20.

——, 2010b: *Final Summit Declaration.* Seoul Summit, 2010. Seoul: G20.

——, 2011: *Final Summit Declaration.* Cannes Summit, 2011. Cannes: G20.

——, 2012: *Final Summit Declaration.* Los Cabos Summit, 2012. Los Cabos: G20.

——, 2013: *Final Summit Declaration.* Saint Petersburg Summit, 2013. St Petersburg: G20.

——, 2014a: *Communiqué Meeting of G20 Finance Ministers and Central Bank Governors.* Sydney Summit, 2014. Sydney: G20.

——, 2014b: *Communiqué Meeting of G20 Finance Ministers and Central Bank Governors.* Washington Summit, 2014. Washington, DC: G20.

——, 2014c: *Communiqué Meeting of G20 Finance Ministers and Central Bank Governors.* Cairns Summit, 2014. Cairns: G20.

——, 2014d: *G20 Leaders' Communiqué.*Brisbane Summit, 2014. Brisbane: G20.

Gehring, Thomas/Benjamin Faude, 2014: A theory of emerging order within institutional complexes: How competition among regulatory international institutions leads to institutional adaptation and division of labor. In: *The Review of International Organizations* 9(4), 471–498.

Goldbach, Roman/Dieter Kerwer, 2012: New Capital Rules? Reforming Basel Banking Standards after the Financial Crisis. In: Renate Mayntz (ed.), *Crisis and Control: Institutional Change in Financial Market Regulation.* Frankfurt a.M.: Campus, 247–262.

Helleiner, Eric, 2010: *The Financial Stability Board and International Standards.* CIGI (Centre for International Governance Innovation) G20 Papers No. 1. Waterloo, ON: CIGI.

——, 2012: Multilateralism reborn? In: Nancy Bermeo/Jonas Pontusson (eds.), *Coping with Crisis: Government Reactions to the Great Recession.* New York: Russell Sage, 35–90.

Helleiner, Eric/Stefano Pagliari, 2011: The End of an Era in International Financial Regulation? A Postcrisis Research Agenda. In: *International Organization* 65, 169–200.

IMF (International Monetary Fund), 2011: *The Nonbank–Bank Nexus and the Shadow Banking System.* Working Paper 11/289, 2011. Washington, DC: IMF.

——, 2012: *Market Developments and Issues. Global Financial Stability Report 2012.* Washington, DC: IMF.

——, 2013: *Transition Challenges to Stability. Global Financial Stability Report 2013.* Washington, DC: IMF.

——, 2014a: *Moving from Liquidity- to Growth-Driven Markets. Global Financial Stability Report 2014.* Washington, DC: IMF.

——, 2014b: *Risk Taking, Liquidity, and Shadow Banking: Curbing Excesses While Promoting Growth. Global Financial Stability Report 2014.* Washington, DC: IMF.

IOSCO (International Organization of Securities Commissions), 2012: *Requirements for Mandatory Clearing.* Madrid: IOSCO.

IOSCO (International Organization of Securities Commissions)/CPSS (Committee on Payments and Settlement Systems), 2012: *Principles for financial markets infrastructures (PFMIs): Disclosure framework and assessment methodology.* Madrid: IOSCO.

Lall, Ranjit, 2012: From failure to failure: The politics of international banking regulation. In: *Review of International Political Economy* 19(4), 609–638.

Mayntz, Renate, 2012: Die Regelung von Finanzmärkten durch internationale Organisationen. In: Stephan Duschek et al. (eds.), *Organisationen regeln: Die Wirkmacht korporativer Akteure.* Wiesbaden: Springer VS, 263–275.

OECD (Organisation for Economic Co-operation and Development), 2009: Policy Framework for Effective and Efficient Financial Regulation: General Guidance and High-Level Checklist. In: *OECD Journal: Financial Market Trends* 2009(2), 1–56.

Transatlantic Council, 2010: *The Danger of Divergence. Transatlantic Cooperation in Financial Reform,* October 2010. Washington, DC: Transatlantic Council.

UN (United Nations), 2009: *Report of the Commission of Experts of the President of the United Nations General Assembly on Reform of the International Monetary and Financial System (Stiglitz Commission).* New York: United Nations.

Vestergaard, Jakob, 2011: *The G20 and Beyond. Towards Effective Global Economic Governance.* DIIS Report 2011:04. Copenhagen: Danish Institute for International Study.

Waltz, Kenneth, [1954]2001: *Man, the State, and War. A theoretical analysis.* New York: Columbia University Press.

Young, Kevin L., 2012: Transnational capture? An empirical examination of the transnational lobbying of the Basel Committee on Banking Supervisions. In: *Review of International Political Economy* 19(4), 663–688.

4 Patchwork Pacesetter: The United States in the Multilevel Process of Financial Market Regulation

Peter J. Ryan and J. Nicholas Ziegler

Introduction

The financial crisis of 2007–2008 put the United States in an unfamiliar position within the international economic order. For six decades, the country had played a clear leadership role in designing and maintaining, and later in adapting, the institutions of the world economy. With the bankruptcy of Lehman Brothers in September 2008, US policy-makers were faced with the need for immediate rescue of financial markets, followed by thorough overhaul of the country's regulatory institutions. While these tasks were first and foremost matters of domestic politics, it was immediately clear that the financial crisis was global in nature. Key US policy-makers recognized that short-term rescue operations, as well as longer-term regulatory reform hinged on cross-border cooperation. Such cooperation was not, however, always aligned with domestic political and institutional constraints.

This chapter examines the role of the United States in the multilevel processes of defining and consolidating a new framework for financial market regulation in the wake of the 2007–2008 crisis. The central position of the United States in the design of international institutions and in the origins of the crisis meant it was destined to play a pacesetting role in efforts to strengthen the

The perspectives expressed in this chapter are solely those of the authors and do not necessarily represent the views of their employers or affiliated organizations.

Peter Ryan is Vice President, Federal Regulatory Affairs for Credit Suisse – Public Policy Americas. During the writing of this chapter he served as Senior Policy Analyst for the Financial Regulatory Reform Initiative of the Bipartisan Policy Center (BPC). The perspectives expressed in this chapter are solely those of the author and do not necessarily represent the views of Credit Suisse or the BPC. *J. Nicholas Ziegler* is Associate Professor in the Travers Department of Political Science, University of California, Berkeley. He thanks Luke Elder, Levon Minassian, Konrad Posch, and Matthew Stenberg for research assistance.

governance of international financial markets. However, the United States was an inconsistent pacesetter in the international regulatory reform process. Sometimes it succeeded – or largely succeeded – in uploading its preferred policies through deliberate consultation that recognized the need for cooperation among multiple jurisdictions from the outset. At other times, US policy-makers set out on their own preferred pathway and exercised a pacesetting role less by way of consultation and more by way of example that was supported by some jurisdictions and resisted by others. Finally, there were instances in which US regulators failed to upload key elements of their preferred policies, leading to the imposition of domestic standards that were distinct and often more stringent than those approved in other jurisdictions.

Clear traces of the hegemonic role played by the United States in earlier decades were apparent in the varying approaches adopted by US regulators in these negotiations. While it remains the world's leading economy and capital-market center, the United States can no longer set the international rules for economic exchange unilaterally. This changed status is visible in those instances in which US regulators tried – but ultimately failed – to upload key policy preferences, leading US regulators to go it alone with more stringent domestic standards, a phenomenon often characterized as "goldplating". By varying its approach across policy domains and sometimes over time, the United States therefore performed a role in international regulatory reform that can best be described as that of a patchwork pacesetter.

If the overall pattern of US engagement in international negotiations reflected its position as hegemon in decline, the specific variation of its approaches to different sub-domains of financial reform can be attributed to the fragmented nature of the US regulatory apparatus. Given the country's longstanding skepticism toward concentrated economic power, most of the key agencies were created only in response to emergencies. For example, the Office of the Comptroller of the Currency (OCC) was established in 1863 during the Civil War to enable the formation of a new system of nation-wide banks. In 1913 the Federal Reserve System was founded as a delayed but clear response to the Panic of 1907. The Great Depression of the 1930s prompted creation of the Federal Deposit Insurance Corporation (FDIC), whose primary mission was to insure deposits, resolve failing depository institutions, and act as a prudential regulator (largely of smaller banks). It also led to the establishment of the Securities and Exchange Commission (SEC) in 1934, with a mandate to protect investors. Authority for regulating derivatives remained within the US Department of Agriculture for decades and was only assigned to an independent Commodity Futures Trading Commission (CFTC) in 1974 (US Treasury 2008; Ryan 2014c; Woolley/Ziegler 2012).

These historical origins endowed the agencies with distinct missions, internal structures and budgetary resources, as well as different professional cultures and levels of prestige. Accordingly, the agencies enjoy varying degrees of autonomy from the legislative branch that delineates their formal powers. While all federal agencies are subject to congressional oversight to varying degrees, they receive different levels of deference from Members of Congress. And based largely on their ability to attract high-caliber employees, the agencies maintain varying reputations for expertise and professionalism among the industry groups whose activities they regulate and the broader policy community (Ryan 2013: 85–94).

Stemming from these historical factors, the five agencies discussed here also possess quite different degrees of experience in international negotiations. There is no single agency or body of analytic thought dedicated to the elaboration of a foreign financial policy in the United States in the same way that foreign trade is assigned to the US Trade Representative or foreign security policy to the National Security Council. Among the key agencies involved in financial services regulation, the Federal Reserve possesses the best-established organizational routines and common language for discussing monetary policy with other central banks. The Board of Governors (hereafter the Federal Reserve Board) is the principal representative of the US delegation within the Basel Committee on Banking Supervision (BCBS), and Federal Reserve officials play a leading role within the Financial Stability Board (FSB). The FDIC and the OCC also serve as part of the US delegation to the BCBS, and the FDIC, although not a formal member of the FSB, has been influential in shaping its work on cross-border resolution issues. By contrast, as business-conduct capital market regulators, the SEC and the CFTC have relatively few resources for international consultation (Ryan 2014a), although the SEC has a solid record of cooperation with European stock-market regulators (Posner 2009).

The ability of US regulators to set rules internationally was also shaped by the presence – or absence – of existing institutional patterns of cooperation. In those areas in which the prudential banking agencies took a lead role, such as capital standards and resolution, well established procedures for international consultation and/or the agency's established expertise helped them to upload important components of their preferred policies internationally or "crossload" them to other jurisdictions. In those fields in which the capital-market regulators were building outreach capabilities for the first time – such as structural change and derivatives regulation – the absence of established routines of international consultation and a lack of resources posed important challenges.

Global capital standards: Pacesetting through leadership and example

Since the passage of the first Basel Accord in 1988, minimum regulatory capital requirements have become the primary form of prudential bank regulation internationally. The Federal Reserve, often acting in concert with the Bank of England, was the primary actor in driving international cooperation (Ryan 2013: Chapter 3). Through the auspices of the Basel Committee on Banking Supervision (BCBS), the Federal Reserve succeeded in institutionalizing global minimum capital requirements for banks based upon a risk-weighted asset metric it had used in the United States since the early 1980s. In the Basel II accord, initially agreed in 2004, it was responsible for the adoption of a new capital regime based on bank-generated internal ratings approaches, which it had begun to incorporate into its supervisory approach in the mid-1990s. In short, from the 1980s to the 2000s, the Federal Reserve demonstrated itself to be a global pacesetter on the issue of capital standards and successfully used the BCBS as a vehicle to "upload" its preferred policies globally.

The Federal Reserve's capacity to "upload" its preferred policies had been diminished by the time a third major round of negotiations over minimum international capital rules began in 2009. One reason was simply that the BCBS membership had grown, encompassing 44 organizations from 27 member countries, with the new members largely coming from major developing economies (G20 members). More importantly, the Federal Reserve had come under attack from US lawmakers on the political right for its relaxed monetary stance, from lawmakers on the populist left for its perceived support for less stringent oversight of the industry, and from lawmakers of both parties for its emergency actions during the crisis. Therefore its room for maneuver was more limited. Finally, the Collins Amendment to the Dodd-Frank Act made permanent the heightened domestic capital requirements imposed in the wake of the financial crisis. This statutory floor further limited the room for negotiation (Davis Polk 2011).

The Federal Reserve Board's priorities had also shifted, both for strategic reasons and owing to a change in key personnel. In particular, the appointment by President Obama of Daniel (Dan) Tarullo as a Federal Reserve Governor proved critical; Tarullo was widely regarded as a "hawk" on regulatory matters, particularly on the need for greater capital requirements (Cook 2013). Then Federal Reserve Chairman Ben Bernanke, who was preoccupied with the ongoing macroeconomic crisis, largely delegated regulatory and supervisory responsibility to Tarullo, including the negotiations surrounding a third Basel Accord. Tarullo had an ally with strong domestic clout in the form of the FDIC and its Chairwoman, Sheila Bair. Bair, who had been lauded domestically for warning about the impending crisis, was also an advocate of higher capital requirements, essentially writing the aforementioned Collins Amendment (Ryan 2013: 198–205).

The US delegation entered the third major round of Basel negotiations in 2009 with agreement on the need to increase the quantity and quality of minimum capital requirements, capital that could be used to absorb a firm's losses and keep it operational. Early in the process, the Federal Reserve Board and the FDIC both produced reports showing that the common equity ratio – that is, the ratio of common equity[1] of the bank relative to risk-adjusted assets – needed to be in the 8–10 percent range. This level was consistent with a report issued by the BCBS staff, which suggested a 7–11 percent range (Bair 2012). The Federal Reserve Board subsequently proposed an 8 percent level plus a surcharge on systemically important financial institutions (SIFIs), which would bring the overall common equity level for such institutions closer to 10 percent. This satisfied the FDIC, which was traditionally more conservative on capital matters and was particularly so under Bair's leadership.

The Federal Reserve Board and the FDIC pursued their goals on common equity ratios by working closely with the UK, Swiss, and Dutch delegations to overcome opposition from other continental European countries (Bair 2012: Chapter 22). France and Germany in particular wanted recognition of silent participations in their firms' capital structure, for example, state guarantees for the German *Landesbanken*, certain kinds of in-house pension funds and other long-term capital claims (see Quaglia 2014: 45–46; Zimmermann 2010; Goldbach/Zimmermann, Chapter 7, this volume), categories of capital that have no clear correlate in Anglo-American banks. The final Basel III Accord put in place a revised common equity requirement – known as "common equity tier 1" (CET1), equivalent to 7 percent of risk-weighted assets.[2] That was nearly three times the amount of common equity previously required for institutions to be considered well capitalized. The Accord also increased the risk-weightings of assets such as mortgage-servicing rights, which comprised a relatively greater share of US bank portfolios, as well as derivatives positions not cleared through a central counterparty. In doing so, it dramatically restructured the investment incentives for banks with the goal of reducing exposure to higher risk activities. Although the Basel III capital standards represented a step in the right direc-

---

1 Common equity shareholders are the last group to be paid out in the event of a firm's liquidation, after all other creditors, bondholders, and preferred shareholders. It is thus considered to be the "purest" form of bank capital.

2 Comprising a minimum requirement of 4.5 percent plus a "conservation buffer" of 2.5 percent.

tion for both the Federal Reserve Board, represented by Tarullo, and the FDIC under Bair, it did not go far enough in the view of either (Bair 2012: 268). The joint statement released by the Federal Reserve, FDIC, and OCC on September 12, 2010, welcomed the agreement, but also made clear that two additional measures were needed to "augment" Basel III. These included "the establishment of more stringent prudential standards, including higher capital and liquidity requirements for large, interconnected financial institutions" and "the development of measures to improve the loss absorbing capacity" for SIFIs (FRB 2010).

Indeed, over the next four years, both agencies would push for international agreements on a SIFI surcharge and minimum standards on loss-absorbing capacity. At the same time, they also proved willing to increase the stringency of US standards – also known as "goldplating" – above the globally agreed Basel III minimums where they felt agreement would be difficult, including on the issue of the leverage requirement and long-term debt. They furthermore imposed an entirely new set of forward-planning capital requirements under the Comprehensive Capital Analysis and Review (CCAR) process that in many ways began to supersede Basel III as the binding constraint on US banks.

G-SIB surcharge

The first issue was the global systemically important bank (G-SIB) surcharge, which the US agencies argued they were required to impose on US institutions as a result of Section 165 of the Dodd-Frank Act. The Federal Reserve Board and the FDIC had proposed that the surcharge be included in Basel III, but the BCBS decided to leave the issue to the FSB to determine. At the FSB, both agencies advocated a surcharge of 3 percent of risk-weighted assets, made up of CET1 (Tarullo 2011; Bair 2012: 268–270).

However, the US delegation at the FSB was split: the Treasury Department and the OCC favored a lower surcharge of 1–1.5 percent. In fact, the head of the OCC, John Walsh, went public with his opposition to the higher figure (Borak 2011). In addition, major US banks such as Citigroup and JP Morgan Chase made clear their opposition to the imposition of the surcharge at all (Bair 2012: 270–271). The reluctance of the Treasury and the OCC to embrace a higher level, coupled with the opposition of the industry to a surcharge, made reaching agreement at the FSB more difficult.

Ultimately, the BCBS retook control of the process in mid-2011 and agreed to a surcharge (or "buffer") that would consist of CET 1 and range from 1 percent to an initial maximum of 2.5 percent (which could later increase to 3.5 percent) of risk-weighted assets for institutions designated by the FSB as G-SIBs, with the actual number for each institution based on its size and interconnectedness. While the Federal Reserve Board and the FDIC had been partially success-ful in uploading rules to the global level, the episode also highlighted how the fragmented nature of the US regulatory system could, at times, frustrate the process of cooperation at the international level. As in other areas of partial up-loading, the US moved quickly toward goldplating these standards domestically, with the Federal Reserve Board proposing a maximum surcharge ceiling of 4.5 percent (FRB 2014f).

Supplementary leverage ratio

One of the most important points of division in the Basel III negotiations was the subject of a minimum international leverage ratio. The leverage ratio refers to capital requirements that are not based on risk-weightings of assets owned by the bank; these risk-weightings have been criticized by some for their complexity, opacity, and tendency to incentivize risk-taking in asset classes with low risk-weightings. The issue had arrayed the US, UK, Swiss, and Dutch regulators, who favored inclusion of a tough leverage ratio, against the other major countries, which opposed its inclusion. US regulators favored a leverage standard because US banks had long been subject to such a requirement (Onaran 2013) and they thought a leverage ratio would discourage banks from manipulating risk weights to reduce their capital funding costs. By contrast, the opposition of most Eu-ropean Union (EU) member states was likely based on their heavy investments in sovereign debt and corporate bonds, against which they would now have to raise significantly more capital (Bair 2012: 265; also Goldbach/Zimmermann, Chapter 7, this volume).

When the Basel III negotiations settled on a compromise leverage ratio of 3 percent, consisting of Tier 1 capital, US regulators saw the figure as insufficient. In 2013, Governor Tarullo publicly acknowledged this inadequacy, stating that "the new Basel III leverage ratio […] may have been set too low" and noted that the Federal Reserve Board could "set a higher leverage ratio for the largest firms" (Stephenson/Miedema 2013). Domestic political pressure was building to in-crease the leverage ratio in 2013 as high-profile proposals by the Vice-Chairman of the FDIC, Thomas Hoenig, former FDIC Chairwoman Bair, and Senators Sherrod Brown (D-OH) and David Vitter (R-LA) all aimed at significantly rais-ing leverage requirements for the largest banks (Stephenson/Miedema 2013; US Senate 2013).

In July 2013, the US regulators proposed a new minimum leverage ratio of 5 percent for bank holding companies with more than $700 billion in assets. This figure was significantly higher than the Basel III minimum. Institutions that failed to maintain this level would be subject to tighter limits on their ability to make capital distributions or make bonus payments (Davis Polk 2013). This new supplementary leverage ratio rule was finalized in September 2014, to become effective on January 1, 2018 (FRB/FDIC/OCC 2014).

While US regulators were successful in their efforts to include a leverage ratio in Basel III, this was again only a partial victory. After the Accord was agreed, the United States set its own pace by enhancing or "goldplating" the Basel requirements. This approach implied recognition that efforts to upload tighter rules would be futile. In part this view was borne out of the difficulty of the Basel III negotiations during 2009 and 2010. It also probably reflected the fact that the EU had not by the end of 2014 finalized a binding version of the leverage ratio for European banks, underscoring the absence of a willing international negotiating partner (Onaran 2013).

Comprehensive capital analysis and review (CCAR)

CCAR is a case in which the United States – and specifically the Federal Reserve Board – set its own pace on capital standards without engaging international partners. In November 2011, the Federal Reserve Board adopted a rule that required bank holding companies with assets greater than $50 billion to submit annual capital plans to the Board for review (Federal Register 2011). CCAR differs from the other capital requirements discussed thus far because it relies on an evolving and complex set of quantitative and qualitative "stress tests" that are designed to evaluate an institution's ability to absorb losses under different scenarios (Tarullo 2014).

Through the CCAR process, the Federal Reserve injected additional stringency into US capital adequacy requirements. In the 2012 CCAR, for example, participating institutions were required to show they could "achieve readily and without difficulty" the ratios required by Basel III under economic and market conditions that were four and a half times worse than those experienced during the financial crisis that began in 2007 (FRB 2014c). The qualitative supervisory component of CCAR adds unpredictability to the process, with some institutions arguing that this has forced them to take a more conservative approach to capital.

Although none of the participating financial institutions were formally required to issue new capital as a result of the CCAR exercises, the Federal Reserve blocked some banks from making capital distributions because they evaluated their capital levels to be inadequate under one or more scenarios (FRB 2014d). In short, CCAR significantly augmented the Basel III minimums, promising to become the "binding" constraint on US banks. Through late 2014, the Federal Reserve Board seemed content to forge its own path on CCAR, without the constraints that would come with additional coordination.

Failure resolution: Pacesetting through bilateral engagement

The United States has been a global pacesetter in the area of failure resolution. This role has involved the "uploading" or "crossloading" of US-style legal frameworks or policies preferred by the two major agencies with responsibility in this area: the FDIC and the Federal Reserve Board. It has also involved obtaining legal recognition of US rules governing the resolution process.

The FDIC and the Federal Reserve Board have worked together across the specific issues that contribute to a general framework for resolving large financial institutions in distress. Most important, the FDIC has taken the lead in outlining a "single point of entry" (SPOE) approach through bilateral agreements that paved the way toward further discussions at the multilateral level. Under the SPOE approach, the FDIC takes over a financial firm's holding company and transfers its assets to a temporary bridge firm, wiping out the firm's equity holders in the process. The new bridge firm is recapitalized by converting unsecured debt into equity. Because the holding company's equity and debt holders absorb the losses, this approach avoids destabilizing insolvency proceedings at the subsidiary level, allowing the firm's critical subsidiaries (both domestic and foreign) to remain open and operating.

Proponents of the SPOE approach believe it would be more straightforward than letting regulators in two or more jurisdictions resolve multiple parts of the failed firm – a challenging task given the complex financial and operational links among cross-national subsidiaries and the extraordinary degree of real-time coordination between the regulators that would be involved (Gordon/Ringe 2014). The FDIC also preferred the SPOE approach because it fitted well with the holding-company organization that almost all large US banks had adopted (Omarova/Tahyar 2011).

With the SPOE approach as a foundation, the FDIC and the Federal Reserve Board have pursued additional initiatives in outlining the terms of an international resolution framework. The Federal Reserve has been a leader in multilateral discussions at the FSB to establish a common standard for total loss-absorbing capacity or TLAC (since these discussions were still ongoing in late 2014, they are not detailed here). In addition, the FDIC and the Federal Reserve have used the powers granted them under US legislation to rewrite the protocols for resolving derivatives contracts, a development summarized later in this chapter.

A common resolution framework

As enacted in July, 2010, Title II of the Dodd-Frank Act established an Orderly Liquidation Authority process that allows regulators to put a major bank through insolvency proceedings without destabilizing the economy or forcing taxpayers to provide emergency financial assistance to the institution. Under this mechanism, losses suffered by a financial institution are borne by its shareholders and creditors, not taxpayers. If resources within the firm are insufficient to avoid systemic consequences, then any gap is to be closed through assessments of other financial firms. These provisions are often referred to as a "bail-in" approach, in contrast to a "bail-out" by the government.

While establishing this joint approach with the Federal Reserve Board at home, the FDIC pursued its vision of a common resolution framework at both the bilateral and multilateral levels. Both initiatives were essential because the FDIC's preferences would be workable only for a large international bank – or G-SIB – if other jurisdictions endorsed a bail-in approach and, ideally, the SPOE resolution model.

The FDIC's first focus replicated a familiar dynamic in international financial negotiations, when the FDIC opened discussions with authorities in the United Kingdom (see, for example, Wood 2005). These discussions had, in fact, begun before the financial crisis, with the FDIC and the UK Financial Services Authority (FSA) signing a memorandum of understanding (MOU) on the exchange of information and cooperation in 2008 (FDIC/FSA 2008). After the crisis (and particularly after the passage of Dodd-Frank), the FDIC continued working with the Bank of England on a common approach to the resolution of G-SIBs. This cooperation became conspicuous in December 2012, when the FDIC and the Bank of England published a joint paper that endorsed the SPOE approach favored by the FDIC – a close relationship that has by all accounts continued since then (FDIC/BoE 2008; Gruenberg 2013).

The common cross-border approach between the two regulators made sense for the FDIC. Over 80 percent of the international assets and derivatives contracts of US G-SIFIs are held in the United Kingdom (FDIC 2012), meaning that an agreed resolution framework between the two countries would be important in the event a US G-SIB failed. It also made sense for the UK authorities, given the depth of British bank holdings in the United States and the fact that many UK banks were, like their US competitors, also organized in a holding company structure (Financial Times, 26 December 2013: Fleming).

Another key relationship arose between the FDIC and the Swiss authorities. The FDIC took the lead in establishing trilateral negotiations between the Bank of England and FINMA, the Swiss Financial Market Supervisory Authority (Gruenberg 2013). These discussions probably contributed to an endorsement of the SPOE approach in a position paper in August 2013 (FINMA 2013). They also informed a change in Swiss regulatory capital policy that encouraged the country's two global banks – Credit Suisse and UBS – to shift their organizational structure towards one that more closely resembled the holding company structure prevalent in the United States (Financial Times, 21 November 2013: Shotter). In addition to its work with the British and Swiss authorities, the FDIC also struck a bilateral agreement with Canada that endorsed SPOE, and engaged in discussions with German and Japanese authorities (Gruenberg 2013). These bilateral relationships appear to have produced a degree of "crossloading" of US rules and policies into these key jurisdictions.

These bilateral relationships also helped to shape multilateral negotiations taking place through the FSB, thereby facilitating a broad consensus on failure resolution among the most important banking jurisdictions. Germany's experience with public bank bailouts in early 2008 and 2009 prompted it to enact legislation in 2010 that included a bank levy and resolution procedures for failed banks (see Goldbach/Zimmermann, Chapter 7, this volume). US regulators also worked with British and Swiss officials who, along with German representatives, took key international positions that allowed them to shape the evolving agenda. For example, representatives of FDIC and FINMA co-chaired the Cross-Border Bank Resolution Group of the BCBS for most of this period, producing a key report in 2009 detailing lessons from the financial crisis and recommendations that laid some of the groundwork for future agreements (BCBS 2010). The Federal Reserve Bank of New York chaired the FSB's Crisis Management Group. And the FSB's Resolution Steering Group was, for most of this period, headed by former Deputy Chair of the Bank of England, Paul Tucker (Financial Times, 10 December 2010: Gruenberg/Tucker).

The FSB's Resolution Steering Group developed the first set of international standards for cross-border resolution, entitled the *Key Attributes of Effective Resolution Regimes*, which was approved by the G20 leaders at the Cannes Summit in 2011 (FSB 2013; G20 2010). The *Key Attributes* recommendations mirror many of the core elements of Dodd-Frank's Title II and the 2010 German law, particularly by endorsing the bail-in approach to resolution (Tarullo 2013). Subsequent to the publication of the *Key Attributes,* there was an assumption that the SPOE strategy would be used in the Consultative Document released by the FSB in 2012 to operationalize the *Key Attributes* document. As Federal Reserve Board Governor Dan Tarullo observed in 2013, "the FDIC's work on the single-point-of-entry approach continues to help frame the terms of international discussions at the FSB" (Tarullo 2013). In short, the FDIC, along with the Bank of England, the Swiss FINMA, and the German BaFin, succeeded in setting the agenda, ensuring the uploading of a "bail-in" plan and, to a large degree, a SPOE resolution strategy to the international level.

These bilateral and multilateral efforts also further influenced the work of the joint Working Group between the FDIC and the European Commission. As James Wigand, then the FDIC's lead international representative, noted in testimony before the US Senate, these meetings were important in informing the European Commission's emerging Recovery and Resolution Directive or BRRD (Wigand 2013). Perhaps unsurprisingly, the final BRRD, published in late 2013, largely mirrored the resolution powers granted to the FDIC under Title II of the Dodd-Frank Act. The BRRD was also clearly designed to accommodate the SPOE strategy (for details, see IIF 2014). In this sense, the BRRD effectively accommodated the preferred strategy of US regulators by "crossloading" much of the US legal framework into their jurisdictions.

Despite the increasing adoption of US-style legal resolution frameworks and a clear preference among many regulators in other countries for the SPOE approach, both the FDIC and the Federal Reserve Board have signaled that they may be unwilling to defer to foreign authorities in the resolution of an institution with significant US operations. For example, the FDIC's Notice did not provide formal recognition to foreign resolution regimes equivalent to the BRRD's Article 85, despite calls from major industry trade associations to do so (Clearing House et al. 2014). Moreover, the Federal Reserve Board's rule implementing Section 165 of the Dodd-Frank Act for foreign banking organizations obliged foreign banks to establish intermediate bank holding companies in the United States that must meet standalone capital and liquidity requirements (FRB 2014b). This rule, together with comments made by Governor Tarullo, was viewed as a signal that US regulators could ring-fence the US operations of a foreign G-SIB in the event of failure rather than permit resolution by the institution's home authority (Davis Polk 2012).

This reluctance to recognize foreign resolution regimes meant that US authorities effectively engaged in a pattern of asymmetric cooperation for several years following the passing of the Dodd-Frank Act. There was a successful uploading of domestic rules and policies through the FSB; crossloading through bilateral MOUs and working groups; and legal recognition of US resolution proceedings. Yet US authorities did not reciprocate by formally recognizing foreign resolution regimes. It may be that US authorities did not currently view foreign resolution regimes as credible, either because of ongoing legal uncertainty, because they had not explicitly adopted their preferred SPOE strategy, or because of doubts regarding the capacity of foreign regulators. Although such an approach is unlikely to be sustainable in the long run, the US authorities were able for several years to shape the global agenda on resolution without conceding their authority to resolve foreign banks with operations in the United States.

Regulation of bank structure: Going it alone

It was in the area of structural change that the domestic determinants of US policy-making left their clearest stamp on the US approach to questions of international harmonization. The fragmentation of regulatory authority, the role of individual policy entrepreneurs, and the periodic eruption of bottom-up pressure for stricter control of the country's largest banks all shaped the way the relevant US agencies approached the task of implementing changes in bank organization.

The idea of requiring changes in bank structure took the form of the so-called Volcker Rule, which soon became one of the best-known parts of Dodd-Frank. Named after Paul Volcker, former Chairman of the Federal Reserve, the Volcker Rule aimed at preventing depository institutions – which enjoy government guarantees through deposit insurance and access to lender-of-last-resort facilities – from engaging in certain high-risk investments. Specifically, the rule bans proprietary trading and limits ownership of hedge funds. To some degree, Volcker's idea hearkened back to the formal separation of commercial from investment banking enacted by the Glass-Steagall Act of 1933, which was incrementally weakened in the 1980s and 1990s until it was formally repealed under the Gramm-Leach-Bliley Act of 1999.

The Obama administration embraced the Volcker Rule in early 2010, when public anger rose against the Wall Street firms that were still paying out handsome bonuses after accepting multi-billion dollar government bailouts (Woolley/Ziegler 2012; Scheiber 2011). As enacted in Section 619 of the Dodd-Frank Act, the Volcker Rule did two things. It prohibited banks that enjoyed government guarantees from engaging in proprietary trading – trading using the bank's funds (rather than its customers') to make a profit. Second, it said that banks could no longer take unlimited ownership stakes in alternative investment vehicles – including hedge funds, private equity funds, and certain other covered funds – that had become highly profitable in the years prior to the crisis (Ryan 2014b).

It was far from self-evident how a clear boundary could be drawn between proprietary trading and several other bank activities, particularly market-making and general risk hedging. Banks often act as intermediaries by buying and inventorying financial instruments in anticipation of client demand. Banks also use derivatives and other instruments for hedging – that is, risk mitigating – purposes. In translating the statutory language into rules that market participants could follow, regulators therefore needed to specify many definitional boundaries and stipulate which transactions would be exempted from the Volcker Rule provisions. Because the rule touched upon so many different activities, the legislation required five different agencies to agree upon the implementing language.

These included the three main prudential bank regulators: the Federal Reserve, the FDIC, and the OCC. In addition, both conduct-of-business regulators, the SEC and the CFTC, had to agree.

All five agencies were responding to vigorous domestic debate in the way they proposed their respective versions of the provision. Progressive groups seized upon the Volcker Rule as a key reform that needed to be implemented fully and stringently. For example, the financial offshoot of the Occupy movement, known as Occupy the SEC, submitted a 325-page letter in early 2012 (Occupy the SEC 2012), that called for limiting the exemptions from the Volcker Rule and for monitoring banks closely to ensure they could not circumvent the ban on proprietary trading. The financial services industry also communicated extensively with regulators on the Volcker Rule, through detailed comment letters and requests for exemptive action. Both individually and through their trade associations, the major banks argued that they should be permitted to continue broadly defined activities in market-making and investment hedging without cumbersome new compliance requirements (for example, ABA/FSR/TCH/SIFMA 2012).

From the viewpoint of European regulators and banks, the tougher drafts of the Volcker Rule carried the threat of imposing US restrictions on non-US market participants. As elaborated by US agencies, the Volcker Rule had an exclusion for transactions conducted "solely outside the United States" (SOTUS). European regulators considered the SOTUS exclusion inadequate. It left non-US banks subject to the ban on proprietary trading if they did business with any US-based market participants, irrespective of the transaction's geographic location. This threatened a significant extension of US rules internationally – something regulators in France, Germany, and the United Kingdom all considered a degree of extra-territoriality that encroached directly on their own jurisdictions (see, for example, Deutsche Bundesbank/Bafin 2012; see also Financial Times, 13 February 2012: Hasiripour/Alloway; and Quaglia 2014: 33–34). The same regulators, as well as Michel Barnier, EU Commissioner for the Internal Market, also objected that the draft rule exempted US government securities from the ban on proprietary trading, but allowed no other sovereign debt instruments under the same exemption. This omission would limit the market for European sovereign issuers – an urgent concern given the sovereign debt difficulties of multiple EU member countries in 2012 (Barnier 2012). European banks, meanwhile, argued that the Volcker Rule should apply only to activities undertaken by their US-based affiliates. They protested over two particular types of transactions left within the rule's draft language: transactions concluded outside the United States but with US counterparties and transactions between non-US parties but executed through a US trading platform or exchange (IIB/EBF 2012).

Even as US regulators debated exactly how the curbs on proprietary trading should work, major US banks started preparing for compliance by eliminating their proprietary trading desks or reassigning traders to asset management divisions where the bank acted as agent for institutional clients rather than as principal on its own account (Woolley/Ziegler 2012; see also Wall Street Journal, 6 July 2010; Reuters, 3 April 2012). While taking such actions in anticipation of the finalized regulations, banks continued to press for less stringent treatment of market-making and hedging activities. It seemed as if a measure of forbearance was possible – especially because the US bank regulators had never thought the Volcker Rule would work as well as capital adequacy standards. The case for more stringent implementation of the Volcker Rule received powerful reinforcement, however, when JP Morgan announced that its London trading desks had incurred multi-billion dollar losses in the early months of 2012. These losses, which became known as the "London Whale", were variously estimated at anywhere from $2 billion to $9 billion. Since they recapitulated the disaster that befell the insurance giant American International Group through its London derivatives desk in 2008, this news served as a reminder that the financial system was still fragile.

The Volcker Rule proved important for international negotiations because it both preceded and was more proscriptive than similar regulation in other jurisdictions. The "Vickers Rule" in the United Kingdom required an arms-length functional separation, or "ring-fencing", of deposit-taking activities from investment activities undertaken by banks as principals (see James, Chapter 6, this volume). This provision, included in the Financial Services (Banking Reform) Act of late 2013, applied to a broader range of activities than the Volcker Rule, but required only that banks establish separate trading divisions for proprietary trading rather than full divestment. French and German regulators also adopted changes designed to segregate different types of risk without, however, abandoning the concept of universal banking. Accordingly, they also followed a ring-fencing approach, but also without forcing a change in the ownership of the trading subsidiaries. These provisions were enacted, respectively, through the French law 2013-672 of 26 July 2013 and the German *Trennbankengesetz* (German Bank Separation Law), announced on 7 August 2013 (see Goldbach/ Zimmermann, Chapter 7, this volume). The relevant guidelines by which these laws would be translated into practice remained to be determined (Woll 2014: 174; Mayer Brown 2014).

As the five US agencies moved towards agreement on final language for the Volcker regulations in late 2013, both the CFTC and the SEC asserted their influence as the primary conduct-of-business regulators who would have to enforce the rule. The details of the hedging exemption emerged as one of the pivotal issues in the final negotiations. The more the final rule limited the scope of hedging activities that US banks could engage in, the more it risked damaging the international competitiveness of those institutions. CFTC chairman Gary Gensler was particularly concerned about the need to prevent unlimited hedging. But in light of the London Whale incident, Gensler also wanted the final rule to make sure large foreign banks were not able to set up deals in the United States and then evade the Volcker restrictions by booking those deals overseas (Schmidt/Brush 2013; Hopkins/Hamilton 2013).

In response to comments from European regulators, the final rule adopted by the five US agencies on December 9, 2013 exempted sovereign debt issued by European and other governments from the ban on proprietary trading. The rule included a relatively narrow exemption for hedging activities, in which banks were required to show that transactions on their own account were linked to specific, identifiable risks that were to be recalibrated continuously rather than only periodically in time intervals that would allow ongoing proprietary trading between risk assessments (Financial Times, 10 December 2013: Chon). Non-US banks were required to satisfy the final regulations for any trades that were arranged or executed by traders in the United States.

In the case of the Volcker Rule, the US agencies were concerned primarily with reaching agreement among themselves instead of undertaking regular consultations with other jurisdictions. To some degree, the go-it-alone approach was also followed by default. There were no corresponding rules in other jurisdictions that could serve as examples for the implementation of the Volcker Rule in the United States. The Volcker Rule also served as a partial template for the European Union's proposal in early 2014. The EU proposal banned proprietary trading for Europe's thirty largest banks and included a series of ring-fencing requirements to be triggered on the basis of case-by-case assessments carried out by national regulators (The Economist, 1 February 2014; Mayer Brown 2014).

As a way of producing international standards, these distinct pathways left the FSB in the predicament of tracking roughly parallel developments rather than issuing specific recommendations or setting guidelines. In October 2014, the FSB noted that concerns among surveyed regulators about national efforts to segregate depository and investment activities were "expressed in fairly high-level terms" with effects still uncertain because "in most cases final rules have not [yet] gone into effect" (FSB 2014: 16). The best fallback in the event of "overlapping requirements with potential inconsistencies" (FSB 2014: 17) would be for jurisdictions to agree to criteria for mutual recognition of one another's requirements. Relative to other domains considered in this volume, however, such efforts at mutual recognition have not been evident in the area of structural banking changes.

Regulation of OTC derivatives trading: Pacesetting through example or a race into the unknown?

Even more than other aspects of financial regulation, the task of regulating derivatives presented regulators with novel challenges. While derivatives were among the main issues that motivated the Volcker Rule's ban on proprietary trading, the creation of an overall framework for supervising the derivatives trade involved a far broader range of non-depository financial firms, asset managers, derivatives end-users, and other market participants. Prior to the crisis of 2008, over-the-counter (OTC) derivatives were traded as bilateral contracts or swaps contracted directly between market participants and regulated only by the master agreements of the industry's trade association, the International Swaps and Derivatives Association (ISDA). In the United States, exchange-traded derivatives, such as futures and certain types of options, had been regulated by the CFTC since the 1970s. But when the CFTC tried to extend its jurisdiction to OTC derivatives in the late 1990s, the Commodity Futures Modernization Act of 2000 explicitly barred it from doing so. Title VII of the Dodd-Frank Act effectively repealed this law and charged the CFTC to work with the SEC to develop a framework for clearing financial derivatives through central counterparty clearing houses (also known as central counterparties or CCPs). These CCPs would then record trades, subject them to competitive bidding, and guarantee the credit risk involved.

These changes presaged a major redesign of regulatory competence as well as market structure (Ziegler/Woolley 2014). The derivatives business was centered overwhelmingly in London and New York, where the largest five to ten banks acted as primary dealers and held large inventories of specific classes of derivatives in which they specialized. In the United States, for example, five banks accounted for 97 percent of the $180 trillion (notional value) of outstanding derivatives contracts in early 2008 (OCC 2008, Graphs 4 and 5A).[3] The task of subjecting this highly concentrated business to regulatory oversight fell primarily to the CFTC, with the SEC responsible for a relatively small segment of equity-based futures. The challenges that confronted the CFTC's new chairman, Gary Gensler, himself a former partner at Goldman Sachs, were immense. His agency was responsible for overseeing an entirely new trading infrastructure, including both CCPs and platforms known as swap execution facilities (SEFs) that were to provide participants with the ability to trade swaps based on competitive bids and offers made by multiple other participants.

---

3 The top five banks in 2008 included JP Morgan, Bank of America, Citibank, Wachovia, and HSBC.

The construction of the new regulatory regime entailed three major steps. First, the CFTC required that swap dealers and participants register with the CFTC and begin to document all swap contracts with trade repositories that would make their information available to regulators. Second, after a phase-in period, all swaps would have to be cleared through a licensed CCP. This step was crucial because the CCPs had to provide necessary margin and capital to guarantee the swap contracts. Finally, after a further phase-in period, the contracts would themselves have to be executed through SEFs or organized exchanges in which some degree of price discovery and competition would be possible.

Because each of these steps required major changes in the information systems and business relationships that swap dealers and clients used, regulators recognized that they would need to undertake similar steps in all jurisdictions. The G20 agreed in September 2009 to improve transparency in OTC derivatives markets and the FSB subsequently recommended that the International Organization of Securities Commissions (IOSCO) should develop a harmonized approach to central clearing in order to minimize regulatory arbitrage across jurisdictions (see also Mayntz, this volume).

While regulators embraced harmonization in principle, it was far harder in practice to agree on the scope and timing of each step. The banks that functioned as major swap dealers were active on both sides of the Atlantic, and very substantial revenue streams could be easily shifted between London and New York. Within the United States, the CFTC faced ongoing opposition from financial industry groups (Ziegler/Woolley 2014; see also Pagliari/Young 2014). Gary Gensler saw cross-border transactions as a potential backdoor escape for banks that wanted to circumvent the changes the CFTC was putting into place. The CFTC's guidance on cross-border transactions, officially proposed in July 2012, interpreted all swap transactions as subject to CFTC rules if they involved a US person, irrespective of the geographic location of the transaction. An exemption for "substituted compliance" under another jurisdiction would apply if that jurisdiction's rules included similar scope, objectives, compliance procedures, and enforcement capabilities. The basic transparency requirements for clearing, trade execution, and real-time reporting requirements would, however, apply to all swaps with US persons, irrespective of location, without any provision for substituted compliance (CFTC 2012).

The proposed guidance would not become effective for a full year, but many firms in Europe as well as the United States started preparing to clear and execute trades in anticipation. It seemed evident that the CFTC's guidance was driving changes in financial industry practices. The US allowance for substituted compliance promised to be more demanding than the EU's provision on third-country clearing (see Quaglia, Chapter 5, this volume). According to one international law firm, the CFTC had gained a "substantial headstart" in implementing its rules, meaning that "a significant part of the US regime could be in force in advance of the corresponding EU rules" (Clifford Chance 2012).

As the one-year delay came to an end, an interesting compromise emerged within the CFTC. Chairman Gensler saw an expansive definition of transactions involving US persons as a precondition for preventing banks from booking trades in other jurisdictions and evading the CFTC's rules by doing so. Gensler's preferred approach would drive the pace and the timing of compliance faster than other US agencies or European jurisdictions wanted. The CFTC's cross-border guidance gained in salience when the New York Times explicitly spoke out in favor of Gensler's approach:

The United States should lead in reform, as the CFTC is trying to do. It should neither wait for the SEC nor outsource the job to regulators in other countries, where derivative rules are weak or nonexistent.   (New York Times 2013)

To gain support from at least two other commissioners, Gensler confirmed the CFTC's expansive guidance but also agreed to a further five-month extension in order to work with the European Commission on a joint document enabling firms to petition for substituted compliance in either jurisdiction.

While differences remained between agency heads regarding the criteria for substituted or mutually recognized compliance, the working groups attached to the FSB were moving forward to define the necessary technical standards. Two of the key steps in lowering the risks of the old system of bilateral trading in derivatives were establishing requirements for clearing houses (CCPs) and setting margin requirements for the customized swaps that would be reported but not cleared through the CCPs. The CFTC proposed its risk minimization rules for clearing houses in 2011. Over the next two years, CFTC officials joined their counterparts from the Federal Reserve and the SEC to shape international deliberations toward a common set of guidelines. Working within an IOSCO group known as the Over-the-Counter Derivatives Regulators Group and jointly with the BIS committee known as the Committee on Payment and Settlement Systems (CPSS), the CFTC helped develop an international standard known as the Principles for Financial Market Infrastructures (PFMI) that established minimum capital and reporting requirements for clearing houses. Given the CFTC's substantial head-start in developing its own rules for clearing houses, these deliberations appear to be a case in which US standards were being uploaded to international norm-setting bodies. When the CFTC confirmed its final rule for clearing houses, consistency with the uploaded principles was a prominent part of the rule's justification (CFTC 2013; for the Final Rule, Federal Register 2013). In this way, the CFTC officials shaped the internationally agreed upon standards and then substantially downloaded these standards as final rules for enforcement within the United States.

A similar pattern emerged from negotiations regarding swap contracts that would not be transacted through a central platform. The mandatory clearing requirements applied to the majority of standardized derivatives, typically for interest rate swaps. Certain customized swaps were exempted from mandatory clearing, but they were still to come under tightened rules for margin and collateral. The CFTC first proposed margin rules for un-cleared swaps in April, 2011. It then advanced its approach as a template for consultations within a working group that drew on representation from both the BCBS and IOSCO. This working group, known as the Working Group on Margining Requirements, published its recommendations in 2013 (BIS 2013), and a year later the CFTC re-proposed its margining rules for un-cleared swaps with extensive justification from the international working group's conclusions (Federal Register 2014). Once again the CFTC played a key role in shaping IOSCO's rules for an important category of derivative transaction and then downloaded much the same rules that it would very likely have to defend against financial industry pressures within the US jurisdiction.

This progress on the technical standards did not translate into broader transatlantic agreement on initial compliance dates and substituted compliance. Toward the end of his term as chairman of the CFTC, Gary Gensler confirmed the agency's expansive cross-border guidance. This decision heightened tension with Michel Barnier's Directorate in the European Commission and unleashed a storm of protest from large banks on both sides of the Atlantic (Bloomberg, 18 November 2013: Schmidt/Brush; New York Times, 21 November 2013: Norris; Financial Times, 24 November 2013: Fleming). The major dealers considered the new guidance so detrimental to their revenues that they decided to contest the CFTC's policies. On December 4, 2013, one of the major banks' trade associations, SIFMA, joined with the industry's self-regulatory body, ISDA, as well as the Institute of International Bankers (IIB), and sued the CFTC in the US District Court. With the CFTC's guidelines on cross-border monitoring in question, there was less reason for Michel Barnier to adopt the CFTC standards quickly. Even when Gary Gensler stepped down as chairman in December 2013, there was little progress on the criteria for mutual deferral or substituted compliance. When Commissioner Barnier announced in June 2014 that the EU had made equivalence assessments allowing Japan, Singapore, Australia, Hong Kong and India to clear swaps written by European banks, the United States was conspicuously absent from the recognized jurisdictions. Barnier released a statement saying,

Our technical talks with the CFTC are progressing well and I am confident that we can agree on outcomes-based assessments of our rules and on aligning key aspects of margin requirements to avoid arbitrage opportunities. If the CFTC also gives effective equivalence to third country CCPs, deferring to strong and rigorous rules in jurisdictions such as the EU, we will be able to adopt equivalence decisions very soon.   (Barnier 2014)

As talks picked up in September 2014, the US courts upheld the CFTC's prerogative in issuing its cross-border guidance (New York Times, 16 September 2014). In practical terms, much as the major banks had started reorganizing their activities in anticipation of the Volcker Rule, most major swap dealers had been moving their swaps contracts to clearinghouses in conformance with the CFTC's anticipated rules. The CFTC efforts on the rules for derivatives appeared to be a case in which it drove the trajectory of international negotiations as much by uploading the rules it wanted to use at home as by securing full agreement from other regulators on the timing and specific guidelines for introducing the new rules worldwide.

Beyond the regulatory challenges they posed for routine transactions, derivatives also raised a set of difficult questions that dramatically complicated the design of any resolution framework that would work in internationalized markets. Derivatives contracts occupied a privileged place because they were to be "netted", or insofar as possible settled, immediately if one party entered bankruptcy proceedings. This approach, written into the ISDA's templates meant that swaps contracts gave their transactors priority in taking assets from a bankrupt institution well before other creditors had a chance to advance their claims (Roe 2011). During the Lehman bankruptcy in 2008, these netting rules produced a powerful ripple effect that delayed other claims by years and deepened the paralysis of credit markets around the world.

The Dodd-Frank Act addressed this problem for US transactions with a provision in Title II that mandated a one-day stay and transfer of derivatives contracts, to a bridge company, in the event of insolvency. Since Lehman and other US banks typically booked as many as half of their swaps contracts in London (Eavis 2014), however, the potential for disorderly termination of these contracts for any internationally active bank remained high.

The FDIC and the Federal Reserve Board both identified the derivatives netting protocol as a major impediment to any emerging international resolution framework. In October 2013, Fed Governor Tarullo compared two potential solutions (Tarullo 2013). First, he observed that cross-border legal recognition of stays imposed in different jurisdictions was unlikely to be achieved. Second, he argued that "modifications to standard contractual cross-default, netting, and related practices" appeared to "be the most promising for tackling this vexing problem." Following Tarullo's second suggestion, the FDIC wrote jointly to the

International Swaps and Derivatives Association (ISDA) with three other regulators – the Bank of England, Germany's BaFin, and the Swiss FINMA. Together the four jurisdictions asked ISDA to amend its standard template contract to provide for a short-term suspension of early termination rights in the resolution of a G-SIB and calling for further dialogue on the issue (BoE/BaFin/FDIC/FINMA 2013).

While forming a united front with other regulators, the Federal Reserve Board and FDIC also relied upon another powerful lever for negotiating directly with the banks that functioned as major swaps dealers. The Dodd-Frank Act (Title I) required that large, complex financial institutions file annual "living wills", or plans that would detail how they would be liquidated if they had to enter bankruptcy proceedings. In August 2014, the FDIC and the Federal Reserve Board jolted many large banks by demanding substantial changes in their living wills. Specifically addressing the derivatives issue, the two agencies asked the institutions involved to amend "on an industry-wide and firm-specific basis, financial contracts to provide for a stay of certain early termination rights of external counterparties triggered by insolvency proceedings."

In October 2014, the Federal Reserve convened senior executives from eighteen of the largest dealers in OTC derivatives and outlined the new proposal for a stay on netting. The eighteen executives in attendance represented the largest banks in Europe and Japan, as well as in the United States.[4] Since the requirement for living wills applied to non-US banks with over $50 billion in global assets as well as US banks, all significant participants in US markets were effectively subject to the Federal Reserve Board's requirements. Despite their earlier misgivings, the banks agreed to sign ISDA's new Resolution Stay Protocol, requiring them to wait up to 48 hours before seeking to terminate derivatives contracts or collect the resulting payments from a failing financial company, effective January 2015 (Eavis 2014). By adhering to the new protocol, the banks expanded the stay's coverage to 90 percent of their derivatives contacts (notional value) and also acknowledged that it would apply to firms entering into proceedings under the US Bankruptcy Code (ISDA 2014).

The two regulatory initiatives examined here both pertained to derivatives, but they clearly differed in scope and difficulty. In constructing a new regulatory infrastructure for trading in derivatives, the CFTC faced an immense task in which its international counterparts had no more experience than it did. In

---

4 These banks were: Bank of America Merrill Lynch, Bank of Tokyo-Mitsubishi UFJ, Barclays, BNP Paribas, Citigroup, Crédit Agricole, Credit Suisse, Deutsche Bank, Goldman Sachs, HSBC, JP Morgan Chase, Mizuho Financial Group, Morgan Stanley, Nomura, Royal Bank of Scotland, Société Générale, Sumitomo Mitsui Financial Group and UBS.

the important areas of clearing and margining, CFTC officials were able to upload parts of their proposed rules to the general frameworks promoted by the FSB. Without a long track record of cooperation with other jurisdictions, however, the CFTC found it difficult to develop agreements that linked the general goals and specific timetables in order to prevent market actors from engaging in regulatory arbitrage across jurisdictions. As of late 2014, therefore, full-blown mutuality between US and European rules on derivatives remained to be achieved.

In developing new protocols for the treatment of derivatives in cases of financial failure, the Federal Reserve Board and the FDIC faced a tough but far better delimited task. The US agencies were able to develop bilateral links with national regulators in the United Kingdom, Germany, and Switzerland before approaching the industry's self-regulatory trade association, ISDA, to propose a change in industry practices. As these preparatory steps were being taken, the Federal Reserve Board played no less aggressive a role than the CFTC had frequently adopted. By convening banks from all major jurisdictions, the Federal Reserve in effect used its position as gatekeeper to the US market to impose the changes it wanted directly on industry practices. In these efforts, the Fed was undoubtedly helped by its partnership with the FDIC, its established channels with other national regulators, and its ability to command attention from all market participants who wanted to remain active in the United States.

Conclusion

The four areas of financial regulatory reform examined in this chapter illustrate the range of approaches taken by different US agencies as they tried to extend their regulatory goals to other jurisdictions. Since the different agencies had different capabilities and resources at their disposal, the approaches they followed were the result of constraint as often as choice. In the field of capital adequacy, the Federal Reserve built on well-established channels of cross-border consultation to deploy its resources in pushing but also persuading other jurisdictions to move toward its standards. It enabled the United States to play the role of pacesetter by leading the Basel negotiations while working steadily to achieve a measure of international agreement. In seeking an international approach to orderly resolution, the FDIC had a lower global profile but more direct experience. Accordingly, the FDIC relied on bilateral understandings, particularly with the British authorities, to help set the agenda for subsequent consultations at the multilateral level.

The course of US policy was less predictable in the domain of structural change. The prominence of the Volcker Rule stemmed in large part from domestic political imperatives and historically rooted suspicions of large, concentrated banks. It was not surprising therefore that US regulators focused first on their own lengthy inter-agency negotiations before they were ready to consider the approaches being defined by their counterparts in other countries. In the field of OTC derivatives, the CFTC played a forceful role in designing a regulatory architecture largely from scratch. However, because the task was so large and the CFTC's resources so constrained, the agency had very limited capacity or experience to engage in international cooperative efforts. As a result, it took on the role of a pacesetter by example, waiting to see if other jurisdictions would follow its lead. Only where the derivatives markets intersected with discussion of a common resolution framework could the Federal Reserve Board and the FDIC apply their resources and experience toward more broad-based international cooperation.

Among the many factors that contribute to these varied patterns of cross-border engagement, two variables stand out. The presence or absence of prior conventions for international cooperation had a clear bearing on the speed with which US agencies could engage their counterparts overseas. The two regulatory domains in which the United States displayed steady international engagement were those in which processes of international consultation were securely established before 2008. In the case of capital standards, these processes were based on the Basel discussions, themselves anchored in a common language that grew up among central bankers in the second half of the twentieth century. To a lesser degree in the area of resolution, the habits of international consultation stemmed from informal but steady bilateral discussions between the FDIC and its counterparts in the United Kingdom. The two domains in which the US regulators led more by example than by engaged interaction – structural change and OTC derivatives – were those in which the Dodd-Frank Act explicitly reversed prior deregulatory legislation. As a result, US agencies in these domains were first confronted with the need for international consultation in response to the crisis of 2008.

The second, related factor that helped produce these different trajectories stemmed from the fragmented nature of the regulatory agencies themselves. For capital standards and the problem of resolving G-SIBs, the US agencies that played the lead role were the Federal Reserve Board and the FDIC, respectively. The Federal Reserve was widely viewed as the most professional of the bank regulators with the deepest staff resources. While the FDIC was not as well staffed as the Federal Reserve, it had a deep reservoir of experience in resolving failed banks. The Volcker Rule, by contrast, required the active agreement of the three prudential regulators as well as the two conduct-of-business agencies. The different missions and expertise of these US agencies created dissension over the rule, exacerbating the difficulties of developing a coordinated international approach. Finally, as the youngest and smallest of the five agencies, the CFTC was given primary responsibility for the vast project of building a regulatory regime for OTC derivatives. This meant the agency had little choice but to climb a steep organizational learning curve as it confronted the innumerable practical tasks involved in bringing such a complex set of markets into the realm of regulatory oversight.

A final, more contingent element was the source of policy initiative. Each of these regulatory domains had its particular champions or policy entrepreneurs. In the area of capital standards, former FDIC chair Shelia Bair and Federal Reserve Board governor Dan Tarullo have worked to keep a regulatory agenda on track at the international level. In developing an international approach to global banks in financial distress, Martin Gruenberg, with support from key British figures such as Paul Tucker, have helped to shape a global consensus in favor of both a bail-in approach and an SPOE strategy for resolution. The goal of restructuring banks to separate their publicly guaranteed activities from proprietary trading took shape without any single advocate inside the regulatory apparatus. Instead, an eminent former official, Paul Volcker, pressed from outside the government for stringent implementation, without regard to how the proposal would be received internationally. And finally in the field of OTC derivatives, Gary Gensler at the CFTC played a pivotal role in pushing other regulators toward more stringent regulations. While the impetus came from different sources, a willingness by these key actors to break out of inherited ways of doing business was part of the process by which organizational missions were expanded and the foundations for international regulatory agreements constructed.

References

ABA/FSR/TCH/SIFMA (American Bankers Association/Financial Services Roundtable/The Clearing House/Securities Industry and Financial Markets Association), 2012: *Letter Regarding Notice or Proposed Rulemaking Implementing the Volcker Rule – Proprietary Trading.* Comment Letter to Multiple Regulators, February 13, 2012. New York: SIFMA. <www.sifma.org/issues/item.aspx?id=8589937353>

Bair, Sheila, 2012: *Bull by the Horns: Fighting to Save Main Street From Wall Street and Wall Street From Itself.* New York: Free Press.

Barnier, Michel, 2012: *Letter from Commissioner Barnier to Mary Schapiro,* 8 February 2012. Washington, DC: Securities and Exchange Commission. <www.sec.gov/comments/s7-41-11/s74111.shtml>

Barnier, Michel, 2014: *Statement by Commissioner Barnier on Global Derivatives Regulation,* 27 June 2014. Brussels: European Commission.
<http://europa.eu/rapid/press-release_STATEMENT-14-211_en.htm>

BCBS (Basel Committee on Banking Supervision), 2010: *Report and Recommendations of the Cross-Border Bank Resolution Group,* March 2010. Basel: Bank of International Settlements. <www.bis.org/publ/bcbs169.pdf>

BIS (Bank of International Settlements), 2013: *Margin requirements for non-centrally cleared derivatives by the Basel Committee on Banking Suvervision,* September 2013. Basel: BIS. <www.bis.org/publ/bcbs261.htm>

BoE/BaFin/FDIC/FINMA (Bank of England/Bundesanstalt für Finanzdienstleistungsaufsicht/ Federal Deposit Insurance Corporation/Swiss Financial Market Supervisory Authority), 2013: *Joint Letter to the International Swaps and Derivatives Association,* 5 November 2013. Washington, DC: FDIC. <www.fdic.gov/news/news/press/2013/pr13099.html>

Borak, Donna, 2011: OCC's Walsh Signals Discord Among US Regulators on Capital Surcharge. In: *American Banker,* 20 June 2011. <www.americanbanker.com/issues/176_118/occ-john-walsh-signals-discord-regulators-1039160-1.html>

CFTC (Commodity Futures Trading Commission), 2012: *CFTC Approves Proposed Interpretive Guidance on Cross-Border Application of the Swaps Provisions of the Dodd-Frank Act.* Press Release, 29 June 2012. Washington, DC: CFTC. <www.cftc.gov/PressRoom/Press Releases/pr6293-12>

——, 2013: *Derivatives Clearing Organizations to Align with International Standards.* Statement of Gary Gensler, 15 November 2013. Washington, DC: CFTC. <www.cftc.gov/Press Room/SpeechesTestimony/genslerstatement111513>

Clearing House/SIFMA/American Bankers Association/Financial Services Roundtable/Global Financial Markets Association, 2014: *Letter regarding the FDIC's Notice and Request for Comments on the Resolution of Systemically Important Financial Institutions: The Single Point of Entry Strategy.* Comment Letter, FR Docket No. 2013-30057, February 18, 2014. Washington, DC: ABA. <www.aba.com/Advocacy/commentletters/Documents/ Joint%20Trades%20Single%20Point%20of%20Entry%20Comment%20Letter%20 %28Feb%2018,%202014%29.pdf>

Clifford Chance, 2012: *Regulation of OTC derivatives markets: A comparison of EU and US initiatives. Client Briefing,* September 2012. Washington, DC: Clifford Chance.
<www.cliffordchance.com/briefings/2012/09/regulation_of_otcderivativesmarkets-.html>

Cook, Nancy, 2013: The Fed's Last Troublemaker. In: *National Journal,* 13 October 2013. <www.nationaljournal.com/magazine/the-fed-s-last-troublemaker-20131031>

Davis Polk, 2011: *Federal Banking Agencies Implement Collins Amendment by Establishing Risk-Based Floor.* Client Memorandum, 23 June 2011. New York: Davis Polk.

——, 2012: *Governor Tarullo Foreshadows Proposal to Ring-Fence Large US Operations of Foreign Banks.* Client Memorandum, December 2012. New York: Davis Polk.

——, 2013: *Basel III Leverage Ratio: US Proposes American Add-on; Basel Committee Proposes Important Denominator Changes.* Client Memorandum, 19 July 2013. New York: Davis Polk.

Deutsche Bundesbank/BaFin (Bundesanstalt für Finanzdienstleistungsaufsicht), 2012: *Letter Regarding Restrictions on Proprietary Trading and Certain Interests in, and Relationsships with Hedge Funds and Private Equity Funds ("Volcker Rule").* Comment Letter to Multiple

Regulators, 10 February 2012. Washington, DC: Securities and Exchange Commission. <www.sec.gov/comments/s7-41-11/s74111-222.pdf>

Eavis, Peter, 2014: Fight Brews On Changes That Affect Derivatives. In: *The New York Times*, 14 August 2014. <http://dealbook.nytimes.com/2014/08/14/fight-brews-on-changes-that-affect-derivatives/?_r=0>

Elliott, Douglas J./Christian Rauch, 2014: *Lessons from the Implementation of the Volcker Rule for Banking Structural Reform in the European Union.* White Paper No. 13. Frankfurt a.M.: SAFE Sustainable Architecture for Finance in Europe. <http://safe-frankfurt.de/uploads/media/Elliott_Rauch_Volcker_Rule_Lessons.pdf>

FDIC (Federal Deposit Insurance Corporation), 2012: *International Resolution Coordination Overview.* Presentation to the FDIC Advisory Committee on Systemic Resolution, 25 January 2012. Washington, DC: FDIC. <www.fdic.gov/about/srac/2012/2012-01-25_inter national-resolution-coordination.pdf>

FDIC/BoE (Federal Deposit Insurance Corporation/Bank of England), 2013: *Resolving Globally Active, Systemically Important Financial Institutions.* Joint Paper, 10 December 2013. Washington, DC: FDIC. <www.fdic.gov/about/srac/2012/gsifi.pdf>

FDIC/FSA (Federal Deposit Insurance Corporation/Financial Services Authority), 2008: *Memorandum of Understanding Concerning Consultation, Cooperation and the Exchange of Information Related to the Resolution of Insured Depository Institutions with Cross-Border Operations in the United States and the United Kingdom,* 25 June 2008. London: Bank of England. <www.bankofengland.co.uk/about/Documents/mous/fsa_fdic.pdf>

Federal Register, 2011: *Capital Plans; Final Rule.* 12 CFR Part 225. Washington, DC: Federal Register, 76/231, Thursday, 1 December 2011. <www.gpo.gov/fdsys/pkg/FR-2011-12-01/pdf/2011-30665.pdf>

——, 2013: *Derivatives Clearing Organizations and International Standards; Final Rule.* 17 CFR Parts 39, 140, and 190. Washington, DC: Federal Register, 78/231, 2 December 2013. <www.lexissecuritiesmosaic.com/gateway/cftc/general-press-releases/file_2013-27849a.pdf>

——, 2014: *Margin Requirements for Uncleared Swaps for Swap Dealers and Major Swap Participants; Proposed Rule.* 17 CFR Parts 23 and 140. Washington, DC: Federal Register, 79/192, Friday, 3 October 2014. <www.cftc.gov/ucm/groups/public/@lrfederalregister/documents/file/2014-22962a.pdf>

FINMA (Swiss Financial Market Supervisory Authority), 2013: *Resolution of Global Systemically Important Banks,* 7 August 2013. Bern: FINMA. <www.finma.ch/e/finma/publika tionen/Documents/pos-sanierung-abwicklung-20130807-e.pdf>

FRB (Board of Governors of the Federal Reserve System), 2010: *US Banking Agencies Express Support for Basel Agreement.* Press Release, 12 September 2010. Washington, DC: FRB. <www.federalreserve.gov/newsevents/press/bcreg/20100912a.htm>

——, 2014a: *Comprehensive Capital Analysis and Review 2014: Assessment Framework and Results,* March 2014. Washington, DC: FRB. <www.federalreserve.gov/newsevents/press/bcreg/ccar_20140326.pdf>

——, 2014b: *Enhanced Prudential Standards for Bank Holding Companies and Foreign Banking Organizations,* 79 Federal Register 13498, 11 March 2014. Washington, DC: FRB.

FRB (Board of Governors of the Federal Reserve System), 2014c: *Dodd-Frank Act Stress Test 2014: Supervisory Stress Test Methodology and Results.* 24 March 2014. Washington, DC: FRB. <www.federalreserve.gov/bankinforeg/stress-tests/2014-supervisory-scenarios.htm>

——, 2014d: *Comprehensive Capital Analysis and Review 2014: Assessment Framework and Results.* March 2014. Washington, DC: FRB. <www.federalreserve.gov/newsevents/press/bcreg/ccar_20140326.pdf>

——, 2014e: Overview of CCAR Process. In: *Comprehensive Capital Analysis and Review 2015: Summary Instructions and Guidance,* October 2014. Washington, DC: FRB, 2–3. <www.federalreserve.gov/newsevents/press/bcreg/bcreg20141017a1.pdf>

——, 2014f: *Risk Based Capital Guidelines: Implementation of Capital Requirements for Global Systemically Important Bank Holding Companies,* 12 CFR Part 217, 10 December 2014. Washington, DC: U.S. Government Publishing Office. <www.gpo.gov/fdsys/pkg/FR-2014-12-18/pdf/2014-29330.pdf>

FRB/FDIC (Board of Governors of the Federal Reserve System/Federal Deposit Insurance Corporation), 2014: *Agencies Provide Feedback on Second Round Resolution Plans of "First Wave" Filers.* Joint Press Release, 5 August 2014. Washington, DC: FDIC. <www.fdic.gov/news/news/press/2014/pr14067.html>

FRB/FDIC/OCC (Board of Governors of the Federal Reserve System/Federal Deposit Insurance Corporation/Office of the Comptroller of the Currency), 2014: *Agencies Adopt Supplementary Leverage Ratio Final Rule.* Joint Press Release, 3 September 2014. Washington, DC: FRB. <www.federalreserve.gov/newsevents/press/bcreg/20140903b.htm>

FSB (Financial Stability Board), 2013: *Implementing the FSB Key Attributes of Effective Resolution Regimes – How far have we come?* Report to the G20 Finance Ministers and Central Bank Governors. 15 April 2013. Basel: FSB. <www.financialstabilityboard.org/wp-content/uploads/r_130419b.pdf?page_moved=1>

——, 2014: *Structural Banking Reforms: Cross border consistencies and global financial stability implications.* Report to G20 Leaders for the November Summit, 27 October 2014. Basel: FSB.

Fleming, Michael/Asani Sarkar, 2014: The Failure Resolution of Lehman Brothers. In: *Federal Reserve Bank of New York, Economic Policy Review* 20(2), 175–206.

G20, 2011: *Final Summit Declaration.* Cannes Summit, 4 November 2011. Cannes: G20.

Gordon, Jeffrey N./Wolf-Georg Ringe, 2014: *Bank Resolution in the European Banking Union: A Transatlantic Perspective on What it Would Take.* University of Oxford Legal Research Paper Series 18/2014. Oxford: Oxford University.

Gruenberg, Martin J., 2013: *Remarks to the Volcker Alliance Program,* 13 October 2013. Washington, DC: FDIC. <www.fdic.gov/news/news/speeches/archives/2013/spoct1313.html>

Hopkins, Cheyenne/Jesse Hamilton, 2013: Lew Said to Warn Banks of Tough Volcker Rule in Meetings. In: *Bloomberg,* 7 November 2013. <www.bloomberg.com/news/articles/2013-11-07/lew-said-to-warn-banks-of-tough-volcker-rule-in-meetings>

IIB/EBF (Institute of International Bankers/European Banking Federation), 2012: *Letter Regarding Joint Notice of Proposed Rulemaking Implementing the Volcker Rule.* Comment Letter, FR Docket No. R-1432 and RIN 7100 AD 82; OCC Docket ID OCC-2011-14; FDIC RIN 3064-AD85; SEC File No. S7-41-11; CFTC RIN 3038-AC, 13 February 2012. Washington, DC: FRB. <www.federalreserve.gov/SECRS/2012/March/20120329/R-1432/R-1432_021312_105308_362705737715_1.pdf>

IIF (Institute of International Finance), 2013: *Letter Regarding the FDIC's Notice and Request for Comments on the Resolution of Systemically Important Financial Institutions: The Single Point of Entry Strategy.* Comment Letter, FR Docket No. 2013-30057, 18 February 2014. Washington, DC: FDIC. <www.fdic.gov/regulations/laws/federal/2013/2013-single-point-entry-c_14.pdf>

ISDA (International Swaps and Derivatives Association), 2014: *Major Banks Agree to Sign ISDA Resolution Stay Protocol.* Press Release, 11 October 2014. New York: ISDA. <www2.isda.org/news/major-banks-agree-to-sign-isda-resolution-stay-protocol>

Mayer Brown, 2014: *Does Volcker + Vickers = Liikanen? EU proposal for a regulation on structural measures improving the resilience of EU credit institutions.* Legal Update, February 2014. Chicago: Mayer Brown.

New York Times, 2013: The Latest Assault on Bank Reform. Editorial. In: *New York Times*, 4 July 2013.

Occupy the SEC, 2012: *Letter Regarding Prohibitions and Restrictions on Proprietary Trading and Certain Interests in Relationships With, Hedge Funds and Private Equity Funds.* Comment Letter to Multiple Regulators, 13 January 2012. Washington, DC: SEC. <www.sec.gov/comments/s7-41-11/s74111-230.pdf>

OCC (Office of the Comptroller of the Currency), 2008: *OCC's Quarterly Report on Bank Trading and Derivatives Activities for 2008, first quarter.* Washington, DC: OCC.

Omarova, Saule T./Margaret Tahyar, 2011: That Which We Call a Bank: Revisiting the History of Bank Holding Company Regulation in the United States. In: *Review of Banking and Finance Law* 31, 111–203.

Onaran, Yalman, 2013: US Weights Doubling Leverage Standard for Biggest Banks. In: *Bloomberg,* 21 June 2013. <www.bloomberg.com/news/2013-06-21/u-s-weighs-doubling-leverage-standard-for-biggest-banks.html>

Pagliari, Stefano/Kevin Young, 2014: Leveraged Interests: Financial Industry Power and the Role of Private Sector Coalitions. In: *Review of International Political Economy* 21(3), 575–610.

Posner, Elliot, 2009: Making Rules for Global Finance: Transatlantic Regulatory Cooperation at the Turn of the Millennium. In: *International Organization* 63, 665–699.

PricewaterhouseCoopers, 2012: *More Intense SIFI Supervision Called for in FSB's G-SIB Update.* FS Regulatory Brief, November 2012. New York: PwC. <www.pwc.com/us/en/financial-services/regulatory-services/publications/assets/pwc-fs-brief-fsb-sib-framework.pdf>

Quaglia, Lucia, 2014: *The European Union and Global Financial Regulation.* Oxford: Oxford University Press.

Roe, Mark J., 2011: The Derivatives Market's Payment Priorities as Financial Crisis Accelerator. In: *Stanford Law Review* 63(3), 539–590.

Ryan, Peter, 2013: *Charting a Course to Autonomy: Bureaucratic Politics and the Transformation of Wall Street.* Ph.D. thesis. Berkeley: University of California.

——, 2014a: *The Omnibus Spending Bill Highlights Contrasts in the Autonomy of Financial Regulators,* 22 January 2014. Washington, DC: Bipartisan Policy Center.

<http://bipartisanpolicy.org/blog/omnibus-spending-bill-highlights-contrasts-autonomy-financial-regulators>

Ryan, Peter, 2014b: *Is Wall Street Really Winning the Financial Reform War? Assessing the Influence of Large US Banks.* Working Paper for the BPC, May 2014. Washington, DC: Bipartisan Policy Center.

——, 2014c: *How the Federal Reserve Became the De Facto Federal Insurance Regulator,* 30 July 2014. Washington, DC: Bipartisan Policy Center. <http://bipartisanpolicy.org/blog/how-federal-reserve-became-de-facto-federal-insurance-regulator>

Scheiber, Noam, 2011: *The Escape Artists: How Obama's Team Fumbled the Recovery.* New York: Simon and Schuster.

Schmidt, Robert/Silla Brush, 2013: Gensler Said to Win Volcker-Rule Limits for Foreign Banks. In: *Bloomberg,* 6 December 2013. <www.bloomberg.com/news/articles/2013-12-06/gensler-said-to-win-volcker-rule-limits-for-foreign-banks>

Stephenson, Emily/Douwe Miedema, 2013: Fed's Tarullo Wants Big Banks to Hold More Capital. In: *Reuters,* 3 May 2013.
<www.reuters.com/article/2013/05/03/us-financialregulation-capital-idUSBRE9420YG20130503>

Sullivan and Cromwell, 2012: *Bank Capital Plans and Stress Tests,* 11 November, 3. New York: Sullivan and Cromwell. <www.sullcrom.com/siteFiles/Publications/SC_Publication_Bank_Capital_Plans_and_Stress_Tests_E739.pdf>

Tarullo, Daniel K., 2011: *Capital and Liquidity Standards.* Testimony by Daniel K. Tarullo before the Financial Services Committee, 16 June 2011. Washington, DC: US House of Representatives. <www.federalreserve.gov/newsevents/testimony/tarullo20110616a.htm>

——, 2013: *Planning for the Orderly Resolution of a Global Systemically Important Bank.* Conference Remarks, 18 October 2013, Federal Reserve Board and Federal Reserve Bank of Richmond. Washington, DC: FRB. <www.federalreserve.gov/newsevents/speech/tarullo20131018a.htm>

——, 2014: *Stress Testing After Five Years.* Speech. Federal Reserve Third Annual Stress Test Modeling Symposium, Boston, MA, 25 June 2014. Washington, DC: FRB.
<www.federalreserve.gov/newsevents/speech/tarullo20140625a.htm>

US Senate, 2013: *Terminating Bailouts for Taxpayer Fairness (TBTF) Act.* Senate 798, introduced 24 April 2013. Washington, DC: US Congress.

US Treasury Department, 2008: *Blueprint for a Modernized Financial Regulatory Structure.* Washington, DC: US Treasury Department. <www.treasury.gov/press-center/press-releases/Documents/Blueprint.pdf>

White and Case, 2014: *Enhanced Prudential Standards For Foreign Banking Organizations: The US Approach to Ring-Fencing.* Banking Advisory, March 2014. New York: White and Case.

Wigand, James R., 2012: *Resolution Strategy Overview.* Presentation by the Director, Office of Complex Financial Institutions, to Systemic Resolution Advisory Committee, FDIC, 25 January 2012. Washington, DC: FDIC. <www.fdic.gov/about/srac/2012/2012-01-25_resolution-strategy.pdf>

——, 2013: *Improving Cross Border Resolution to Better Protect Taxpayers and the Economy.* Testimony before the Subcommittee on National Security and International Trade and Finance, US Senate, 15 May 2013. Washington, DC: FDIC. <www.fdic.gov/news/news/speeches/spmay1513_2.html>

Woll, Cornelia, 2014: *The Power of Inaction: Bank Bailouts in Comparison.* Ithaca: Cornell University Press.

Wood, Duncan, 2005: *Governing Global Banking: The Basel Committee and the Politics of Financial Globalization.* Burlington: Ashgate.

Woolley, John T./J. Nicholas Ziegler, 2012: The Two-Tiered Politics of Financial Reform in the United States. In: Renate Mayntz (ed.), *Crisis and Control: Institutional Change in Financial Market Regulation.* Frankfurt a.M.: Campus, 29–65.

Ziegler, J. Nicholas/John T. Woolley, 2014: *After Dodd-Frank: The Post-Enactment Politics of Financial Reform in the United States.* IRLE Working Paper 110-114. Berkeley: University of California, Institute for Research on Labor and Employment. <http://irle.berkeley.edu/workingpapers/110-14.pdf>

Zimmermann, Hubert, 2010: Varieties of Global Financial Governance? British and German Approaches to Financial Market Regulation. In: Eric Helleiner/Stefano Pagliari/Hubert Zimmermann (eds.), *Global Finance in Crisis: The Politics of International Regulatory Change.* Abingdon: Routledge, 121–136.

5 The European Union and the Post-Crisis Multilevel Reform of Financial Regulation

Lucia Quaglia

Introduction

The global financial crisis that began in the United States in 2007 and subsequently spread worldwide brought into the spotlight the political salience of financial governance. The crisis underscored the need for "fit for purpose" financial regulation and supervision. It also highlighted how financial instability can spread quickly across national borders due to the internationalization or globalization of finance.[1] The regulation of financial services has become increasingly complex due to the large number of cross-border financial institutions that exploit regulatory gaps to engage in risky activities. Moreover, a variety of international, regional, transnational, and national bodies are involved in rule-making and monitoring (Porter 2005). The multilevel governance of financial services is characterized by two main interrelated regulatory phenomena: the interaction between rule-making processes in multiple arenas; and the "accommodation" or "coexistence" of their rule-making outputs.

The multilevel governance of financial services is complicated further in regional jurisdictions, such as the European Union (EU), where an extra (supranational) level of regulation exists, alongside that taking place in national, international, and transnational arenas. Among regional regulatory regimes, the EU is by far the most advanced because its legislation is legally binding on the member states and to a large extent it provides the framework for national financial

The author wishes to acknowledge financial support from the British Academy (SG 120191) and the Fonds Nationale de la Recherche (FNR) in Luxembourg. This chapter was written while the author was visiting fellow at the University of Luxembourg.

1 The academic literature on the global financial crisis is vast. See, for example, Helleiner, Pagliari, and Zimmerman (2009), Mayntz (2012), Hardie and Howarth (2013), Moschella and Tsingou (2013).

services regulation (Quaglia 2010). Moreover, the European Commission is in charge of monitoring the implementation of EU rules in the member states and the European Court of Justice has jurisdiction over compliance with those rules.

Nowadays, the EU is one of the largest financial jurisdictions worldwide. Drezner (2007) considers it one of the "great powers", together with the United States, and Damro (2012) characterizes the EU as a "market power". Over the 2000s, the EU devoted considerable efforts to the completion of the single financial market in Europe (for comprehensive accounts see Donnelly 2010; Mügge 2010; Macartney 2010; Posner 2009a; Quaglia 2010), promoting regulatory harmonization within its borders and strengthening the institutional framework for financial regulation and supervision. In so doing, the EU increased what Bach and Newman (2007) define as "regulatory capacity", that is, the ability to issue, enforce and monitor market rules in a given sector, in this instance, finance. Moreover, the EU has become increasingly active in international financial fora and is one of the main interlocutors of the United States in the policy debate on this subject (Posner 2009b, 2010; Quaglia 2014b). For all these reasons, the EU is an important player in global financial governance.

In this chapter we investigate the role of the EU in the upward and downward dynamics of post-crisis regulatory reforms in finance and the extent to which the EU complies or does not comply with international standards, or whether it chooses its own rules. In line with the rest of the volume, the chapter's empirical coverage includes prudential regulation for banks – that is, capital and liquidity requirements – rules on bank resolution, structural measures in the banking sector and the regulation of over-the-counter derivatives. It also discusses the setting up of a banking union, which was the main response to the sovereign debt crisis in the euro area. Indeed, an important qualification to be made with reference to the post–global financial crisis reform of financial legislation in the EU is that, as of mid-2010 onwards, the attention of EU policymakers was diverted by the need to tackle the sovereign debt crisis and this might have thwarted a more comprehensive reform of financial regulation in the EU.

The EU and reform of prudential banking regulation

The global financial crisis brought into sharp relief the inadequacy of existing capital requirements for banks and therefore the need to revise them. Capital requirements have traditionally been regarded as the main instruments to ensure the stability of the banking sector and hence financial stability *tout court*. Capital requirements are basically regulations limiting the amount of leverage that financial firms can take on. At the peak of the crisis the interbank markets froze, highlighting the importance of banks' holding of liquid assets[2] in order to meet short-term obligations. Hence, besides capital requirements, liquidity rules also came to the fore as a new zeitgeist came to characterize banking regulation.

Traditionally, the EU has downloaded (see Mayntz, Chapter 1, this volume) international capital requirements into EU legislation. The first international accord for capital requirements, the so-called Basel I, was issued in 1988 by the Basel Committee on Banking Supervision (BCBS; Kapstein 1989, 1992; Singer 2007; Simmons 2001). In the EU, the main elements of the Basel I accord had been incorporated into the Capital Requirements Directive (CRD) in 1993 (Underhill 1997), subsequently revised by the CRD II, after a partial modification of the Basel I accord in the late 1990s. The Basel I accord was replaced by the Basel II Accord in 2004 (Tsingou 2008; Underhill/Zhang 2008; Wood 2005). In the EU, the main elements of the Basel II Accord were incorporated into the CRD III in 2006 (Christopoulos/Quaglia 2009). Over time, these "soft" (not legally binding) international rules were incorporated into legally binding national legislation in more than 100 countries. In the EU this was done through the capital requirements directives.[3]

Shortly after the peak of the global financial crisis, the BCBS began working on a major revision of the Basel II Accord, which became the Basel III Accord (see Mayntz, Chapter 3, this volume). The Basel III Accord was eventually issued in September 2010.

In the negotiations on Basel III, various jurisdictions, including the United States and the main EU countries in the BCBS, tried to upload (see Mayntz, Chapter 1, this volume) their domestic regulatory preferences (see also Kudrna 2014). These preferences were rooted mainly in the configuration of national banking systems and existing regulatory frameworks in these jurisdictions (Howarth/Quaglia 2015). Indeed, national banking regulators gathered in the BCBS wanted to make sure that the new Basel III rules would be suitable for their national banking systems without creating a competitive disadvantage for the banks they supervised.

A discussion of national preferences on the main components of Basel III is important because when it was time to download this accord into EU law, these issues and the disagreements that had emerged in the BCBS resurfaced again in EU negotiations, affecting the final outcome, namely EU prudential rules on banks. During the Basel III negotiations, the United States (see Ryan/Ziegler,

---

2 Liquid assets are cash or any other negotiable assets that can be quickly converted into cash.

3 When the financial crisis broke out the United States had not yet implemented Basel II in national legislation.

Chapter 4, this volume) and the United Kingdom (see James, Chapter 6, this volume), which had been heavily hit by the financial crisis, wanted a stricter definition of capital, to be limited to ordinary shares, higher capital requirements (including capital buffers), a leverage ratio, liquidity rules, and a short transition period. Continental countries – in particular, France and Germany – wanted a broader definition of capital, including hybrids and silent participations (which were part of the definition of capital included in their domestic regulatory template) and lower capital requirements. They opposed the leverage ratio, asked for a modification of certain aspects of the liquidity rules and wanted a longer transition period (Howarth/Quaglia 2015; see Goldbach/Zimmermann, Chapter 7, this volume).

Despite attempts by the European Commission to forge a common position, the EU presented a disjointed stance during the Basel III negotiations. As in Basel I, the EU was unable to project a common set of preferences on Basel III. Unlike Basel I, in which the influence of the United States and the United Kingdom was dominant, Basel III was a compromise between the positions of the two coalitions (Quaglia 2014c). In particular, continental Europeans were able to secure longer transition periods and lower capital requirements, as evidenced by the comparison of the initial document issued by the BCBS in December 2009 and the (less ambitious) document eventually agreed in December 2010. Extensive lobbying from the financial industry also accounts for this watering down of the rules (see Young 2012).

Following the agreement on Basel III and during the intra-EU negotiations on the Capital Requirements Directive IV (CRD IV) "package", some of the compromises reached in the BCBS unravelled. Several EU member states, the European Parliament (Greenwood/Roederer-Rynning 2014) and even the Commission itself called for "European specificities" to be taken into account when incorporating the Basel III rules into the CRD IV, reopening some of the issues that had caused friction within the BCBS. This was because Basel III applied to internationally active banks, whereas EU legislation was to apply to all banks and investment firms, making some Basel III provisions – notably the calculation of Tier 1 capital – impossible to apply in EU member states without a massive shift in the structure of a large range of banks and banking systems.

The Commission justified its decision to apply Basel III rules, as with Basel I and Basel II, to all EU banks and investment firms on stability grounds and for reasons linked to the application of EU Competition Policy. Both the Commission and the European Parliament also emphasized competition concerns and the need to ensure an "international level playing field". Of particular concern was the fact that in the United States, the Basel III Accord would be applied only to financial institutions with over 50 billion US dollars in assets, whereas the new rules would apply to all banks in the EU, as in the case of Basel I and Basel II (European Parliament 2010).

In July 2011, after extensive consultations conducted in parallel with the work of the BCBS, the European Commission adopted the CRD IV legislative package designed to replace the "old" CRD III with a directive that governs access to deposit-taking activities (European Commission 2011a) and a regulation that establishes prudential requirements for credit institutions (European Commission 2011b). After its approval, the directive (European Commission 2011a) will have to be transposed by the member states in a way suitable to their own national environment. It contained rules concerning the taking up and pursuit of the business of banks, the conditions for freedom of establishment and freedom to provide services, the supervisory review process and the definition of competent authorities. The directive also incorporated two elements of the Basel III Accord, namely the introduction of two capital buffers in addition to the minimum capital requirements: the capital conservation buffer identical for all banks in the EU and the countercyclical capital buffer to be determined at national level.

The EU regulation (European Commission 2011b) contained prudential requirements for credit institutions and investment firms. It covered the definition of capital, increasing the amount of own funds that banks need to hold, as well as the quality of those funds; it introduced the Liquidity Coverage Ratio – the exact composition and calibration of which will be determined after an observation and review period in 2015 – and the need to consider a leverage ratio, subject to supervisory review. The use of a regulation, which once approved is directly applicable without the need for national transposition, was designed to facilitate the creation of a single rule book in the EU. The regulation was intended to eliminate a key source of national divergence; it was an approach based on so-called "maximum harmonization". In the CRD III, more than one hundred national discretions (differences in national legislation transposing the EU directive) remained. This was because the directive was based on minimum (not maximum) harmonization and unlike a regulation it had to be transposed into national legislation. During the transposition process, the member states deliberately made use of the discretion allowed by the directive to adapt EU rules to their domestic contexts, especially the distinctive features of national banking systems.

The Commission's CRD IV draft was criticized by some regulators (for example, the British authorities, see James, Chapter 6, this volume) and by the International Monetary Fund (IMF) for significantly watering down key Basel III elements (IMF 2011). Speaking at a meeting of the economic and finance ministers held to discuss CRD IV, the British Treasury minister complained that "[w]e are not implementing the Basel agreement, as anyone who will look at this text will be able to tell you" (Financial Times, 2 May 2012). The Commission "softened" its definition of Core Tier I capital relative to the Basel III recommendations in some areas (Howarth/Quaglia 2013a). Notably, the Commission draft allowed "silent participations"; that is, state loans that make up a significant part of the capital of many EU banks, including the publicly owned German *Landesbanken*. The Commission's draft also limited the role of the leverage ratio designed to limit risk-taking at banks. The almost unique reliance on the risk-weighted Core Tier 1 ratio in the Commission's draft CRD IV, which was in line with that agreed in Basel III, was criticized for inadequately representing the health of the European banking sector (Howarth/Quaglia 2013a).

On liquidity, the Commission adopted the less prescriptive definition of liquid assets: the liquidity coverage ratio should include "transferable assets that are of extremely high liquidity and credit quality" and "transferable assets that are of high liquidity and credit quality." The Commission's draft lacked a firm commitment to implement the net stable funding ratio by 2018 called for in Basel III. Most of these modifications to Basel III in CRD IV were owing to the demands of the French and German governments (Howarth/Quaglia 2013a; see Goldbach/Zimmermann, Chapter 7, this volume).

Unlike previous capital requirements directives and the spirit of the Basel accords that set minimum capital requirements, the initial proposal drafted by the European Commission set maximum capital requirements for banks. That meant that national regulators would not be able to impose higher capital requirements on domestic banks should they deem it necessary to do so. The proposed maximum capital ratio was opposed by the British authorities and those who argued in favor of EU standards that exceed the Basel minimum because of prevailing balance sheet uncertainties in the EU, the lack of EU-wide resolution arrangements, and a fully unified fiscal backstop. In the final version of the CRD IV package, national regulators were given the option of imposing higher capital requirements without requesting permission from the EU. It was a victory for the United Kingdom (James, Chapter 6, this volume).

By contrast, an issue on which the British authorities lost their battle in Brussels and that differentiate the CRD IV package from the Basel accords was the legally binding cap imposed on bankers' bonuses. This was an amendment introduced and strongly advocated by the European Parliament with some support from continental countries (Greenwood/Roederer-Rynning 2014) and unsuccessfully resisted by the British authorities (James, Chapter 6, this volume).

The EU and the new rules on bank recovery and resolution

The massive amounts of public funds spent on bailing out banks in several countries at the peak of the global financial crisis highlighted the need for new rules on resolution, whereby banks should be resolved in an orderly manner without the need to prop them up using "taxpayers' money". As explained in Chapter 3, work on bank resolution was undertaken by the IMF, the BCBS and especially the Financial Stability Board (FSB). The principles and guidelines issued by these international bodies were subsequently downloaded and developed further by new EU legislation, the Bank Recovery and Resolution Directive (BRRD). The unfolding of the sovereign debt crisis in the euro area and the launch of banking union brought the issue of bank resolution back onto the EU (to be precise, euro-area) agenda with reference to the Single Resolution Mechanism (SRM), discussed in the following section.

In November 2011, the FSB issued a document entitled "Key Attributes of Effective Resolution Regimes for Financial Institutions" (FSB 2011), which focused mainly on global systemically important cross-border financial institutions (Mayntz, Chapter 3, this volume). In this, the FSB drew upon the work carried out by the BCBS. In March 2010, the BCBS published a report and a set of ten recommendations prepared by its Cross-border Bank Resolution Group (BCBS 2010d). At the June 2010 Toronto Summit, the G20 leaders endorsed the BCBS recommendations and expressed their commitment to implementing them.

The FSB and BCBS standards or recommendations were subsequently downloaded and elaborated further in EU legislation. Indeed, after prolonged consultations, the European Commission put forward a formal legislative proposal for a Bank Recovery and Resolution Directive in June 2012 (European Commission 2012). The proposed directive had been in the making since the peak of the international financial crisis. However, the legislative proposal by the Commission had been delayed for two main reasons. To begin with, international regulatory fora were discussing this issue and the Commission wanted to put forward EU legislation in line with what had been agreed internationally, as the EU subsequently did.

The second reason why the Commission's proposal was delayed until June 2012 is that the issue of bank resolution was controversial in the EU and thus it was subject to extensive consultation. Indeed, the first consultation document was issued by the Commission in October 2009: "Public Consultation regarding

an EU framework for Cross-Border Crisis Management in the Banking Sector."[4]
This was followed by a Commission Communication on Bank Resolution Funds
in May 2010 and a Communication on a New EU Framework for Crisis Management in the Financial Sector in October 2010. In January 2011, there was
a consultation on technical details of a possible European crisis management
framework. Once the Bank Recovery and Resolution Directive was officially
proposed, there was a Commission consultation on a possible framework for the
recovery and resolution of financial institutions other than banks. Reportedly, in
the drafting of the proposal, the Commission was inspired by certain elements
of the new resolution regime put in place in the United States (Ryan/Ziegler,
Chapter 4, this volume).

The Bank Recovery and Resolution Directive had the same scope of application as CRD IV (hence, it applied to credit institutions and certain investment
firms). It distinguished between powers of "prevention", "early intervention" and
"resolution". In the case of prevention, banks were required to draw up recovery
plans and resolution authorities were required to prepare resolution plans both
at group level and for the individual institutions within the group. Authorities
could require a bank to change its legal or operational structures to ensure that
it could be resolved with the available tools. Financial groups could enter into
intra-group support agreements in the form of loans, or the provision of guarantees (European Commission 2012). The harmonized resolution tools and powers outlined in the directive were designed to ensure that national authorities in
all member states had a common toolkit and roadmap to manage the failure of
banks. Resolution colleges were to be established under the leadership of the
group resolution authority and with the participation of the European Banking
Authority (EBA), which was to act as binding mediator if necessary (European
Commission 2012).

There were two main controversial issues in the negotiations on this directive
(see Howarth/Quaglia 2013b). The first to emerge was the proposal to establish
national resolution funds, which would raise contributions from banks propor-
tionate to their liabilities and risk profiles and would not be used to bail out
non-national banks. There was a link between this piece of legislation and the
Deposit Guarantee Schemes (DGS) Directive, which was designed to provide
funding for the protection of retail depositors. Member states were allowed to
merge these two funds, provided that the scheme remained in position to repay
depositors in case of failure (European Commission 2012).

---

4 <http://ec.europa.eu/internal_market/consultations/2009/banking_crisis_management_
en.htm>

When the directive was proposed in June 2012, the Commission noted that ideally, a single pan-European fund should be established with a pan-European resolution authority to manage its disbursal, but at the time of the proposal, the absence of a single European banking supervisor and insolvency regime would make this unworkable.[5] In case of both the pooling of resolution funds and the setting up of a common DGS, the obstacles to far-reaching changes were ultimately political, the main line of division running between potential net contributors to and net beneficiaries from these schemes.

The second controversial issue that emerged later on in the negotiations concerned the bail-in tool, whereby banks would be recapitalized by wiping out shareholders' stakes, and creditors would have their claims reduced or converted into shares. At stake in the negotiations was how much flexibility governments should be granted in making decisions on winding down banks, as well as the hierarchy in the bailing-in of creditors. The Commission's proposal envisaged that only "deposits that are guaranteed in accordance with Directive 94/19/EC" and certain kinds of liabilities – for example, "secured liabilities" – would be excluded from the bail-in (European Commission 2012). However, finance ministers in several countries favored some sort of depositor preference. A coalition led by France and the United Kingdom wanted national authorities to have flexibility when using a bail-in (when, and on whom, losses were to be forced). Germany, Denmark, the Netherlands, and Finland favored harmonized rules with no special treatment for uninsured deposits in order to reduce legal uncertainty for investors. They insisted that the bail-in rules be of limited flexibility, giving national authorities little choice concerning when to force losses on equity and bond holders after a bank collapse, as well as limited room to choose which kinds of liabilities could be exempted from such bail-ins. Spain, which was experiencing a severe banking crisis, wanted deposits of all sizes to be excluded.

In the end, it was agreed that small depositors with less than 100,000 euros would be guaranteed in the event of a bank bailout. Individuals with more than 100,000 euros in deposits and small and medium enterprises with more than 100,000 euros in deposits were given greater protection than large companies and institutional investors with more than 100,000 euros in deposits. National resolution authorities were given some flexibility, hence the power to exclude liabilities on a discretionary basis.[6]

---

5 <http://europa.eu/rapid/pressReleasesAction.do?reference=MEMO/12/416&format=HTML &aged=0&language=EN&guiLanguage=en> (accessed 1 December 2012)
6 <www.consilium.europa.eu/uedocs/cms_data/docs/pressdata/en/ecofin/137627.pdf>

The EU and structural measures in banking

The global financial crisis highlighted the problem of banks and financial institutions that were too big (or too complex, or too interconnected) to fail, but also sometimes too big to be rescued. It also demonstrated that traditional banking had become enmeshed with speculative and risky financial activities. Unlike in the case of capital requirements or resolution rules for banks, no major work was undertaken by international regulatory bodies with regard to structural measures in the banking sector. Since individual jurisdictions were left free to set their own rules, there was neither uploading nor downloading between the international level and the EU level.

There were, however, some attempts by the EU, and even more by the United States, to crossload (see Mayntz, Chapter 1, this volume) their rules into other jurisdictions through the "extraterritorial" application of the "Volcker Rule" in the United States and "equivalence clauses" in EU legislation. Equivalence clauses stipulate that unless third country rules are equivalent to EU rules, foreign firms providing services in the EU or doing business with EU counterparts will be subject to EU regulation in addition to their home country regulation (for a lawyer's perspective on equivalence, see Ferran 2012). It is a precondition for mutual recognition of rules between two jurisdictions. Equivalence rules were the cornerstone of the new regulatory approach of the EU towards third countries in finance. Although some equivalence clauses had already been included in a couple of EU directives before the crisis (notably, the Financial Conglomerates Directive, see Posner 2009), this trend intensified from 2009 onwards (see Quaglia 2015).

In the United States, the so-called Volcker Rule in the Dodd-Frank Act (2010) was followed by enacting legislation (see Ryan/Ziegler, Chapter 4, this volume). The EU was slower to come up with an equivalent of the Volcker Rule – that is, to lay down rules concerning the structure of the banking sector – because member states had different preferences, rooted in the configuration of their national financial systems. Particularly vulnerable was the "universal bank" model, which was widespread in Germany and France, where banks provide a vast array of financial services. The United Kingdom was first mover in Europe, with the Vickers Report in 2011, which recommended ring-fencing deposit-taking banks (see James, Chapter 6, this volume). Afterwards, France, Germany (see Goldbach/Zimmermann, Chapter 7, this volume) and Belgium adopted new legislation on the structure of the banking sector, unlike other EU countries, which hosted global systemically important banks, namely Italy, the Netherlands, Spain, and Sweden, which did not adopt national structural reforms in the banking sector.

In February 2012, the EU appointed a High-level Expert Group headed by Erkki Liikanen (former governor of the central bank of Finland) to examine structural reforms that would directly affect the structure of individual banks and the market as a whole (High-Level Expert Group 2012). The report recommended that proprietary trading and certain risky trading activities – including market-making, as well as exposures to shadow banking entities, such as hedge funds – ought to be separated from deposit-taking and lending activities. Afterward, the European Commission began consultations in order to put forward a legislative proposal.

The Commission's proposal in January 2014 contained: (i) a *ban* on proprietary trading[7] in financial instruments and commodities; and (ii) a *potential* separation of certain trading activities (including market-making) from the deposit-taking entity, depending on supervisory judgment and/or the breach of certain metrics. Exemptions were provided for financial instruments issued by sovereigns, multilateral development banks, and certain international organizations (The Economist, 1 February 2014).

The legislative proposal differed from the Liikanen Report in two important respects. First, the Commission's proposal contained a Volcker-style prohibition, which also departed from the individual approaches taken by some member states. Indeed, the Commission's proposal included an outright ban on organized proprietary trading instead of requiring it to be assigned to a separate and separately capitalized legal entity. In this respect the Commission proposal resembled the structural reform implemented in the United States (Ryan/Ziegler, Chapter 4, this volume). Although there were no explicit statements by EU policy-makers about using the new US rules as a model from which to borrow some regulatory elements, it seems plausible that there was some emulation.

Second, although the proposal contained provisions that mirrored the Vickers "ring-fencing" approach, they were not – in direct contradiction to Liikanen's recommendation – mandatory. In the implementation of the Regulation, the Commission could grant individual credit institutions derogations from the application of the Regulation if national primary law in their home country was considered to be at least as stringent as the Regulation itself. In other words, the Commission proposal injected a considerable degree of discretion that was absent from the Liikanen report, raising questions about the uniform implementation of the new rules (once approved) throughout the EU (as subsequently noted by Liikanen himself).[8]

---

7 It is, however, difficult to ascertain whether banks are involved in pure speculation or undertake market-making; that is, hold stocks of securities their clients might want to buy.

8 <www.bis.org/review/r140131e.htm>

The proposed legislation was to apply only to Europe's 30 biggest banks; having said that, they represented over 65 per cent of the total banking assets in the EU. This made the scope of the prohibition more limited than the Volcker Rule, which applied to all banks. The proposal was also intended to apply to the European subsidiaries of big foreign banks, if they were deemed to be systemically important in the EU. EU branches of non-EU entities would also fall under the Regulation if they passed the established thresholds (the asset/trading activity test probably centered on the EU branch, not the larger entity).

The proposed Regulation provided for a third-country equivalence regime based on mutual recognition whereby foreign subsidiaries of EU banks and EU branches of foreign banks would be exempted if they were subject to equivalent separation rules. The US Volcker Rule, by contrast, applied to the US branches and subsidiaries of EU and other non-US banks with a presence in the United States.[9] It did not contain equivalence provisions or provisions for substituted compliance, as these provisions are often called in the United States. According to some observers, the Commission planned to use its decision on equivalence as a bargaining chip in order to obtain special exemptions from certain aspects of the Volcker Rule for EU banks operating in the United States (see Ryan/Ziegler, Chapter 4, this volume). As of mid-2015, this Regulation has not been approved, mainly because of disagreements among the member states.

The EU and the regulation of over-the-counter derivatives

Prior to the global financial crisis, a large number of derivatives were traded "over-the-counter" (OTC);[10] in other words, not through exchanges or cleared through central counterparties. This proved to be a major source of risk and uncertainty during the global financial crisis as it made it difficult to determine the interconnection between financial institutions and the exposure of banks in the case of ailing counterparties. As Warren Buffett put it, derivatives had turned into "weapons of mass destruction" (see Helleiner/Pagliari 2010).

The G20 meeting in Pittsburg in September 2009 agreed that "all standardized over-the-counter derivative contracts should be traded on exchanges or electronic trading platforms, where appropriate, and cleared through central coun-

---

9 Only a handful of non-EU banks were likely to be affected by the proposed EU Regulation, among them UBS and JP Morgan Chase (The Economist, 1 February 2014).

10 These are derivatives not traded on stock exchanges or through central counterparties, but instead traded directly between two parties.

terparties. [...] Over-the-counter derivative contracts should be reported to trade repositories" (G20 2009b). Afterwards, work was undertaken mainly by the IOSCO to devise rules for derivatives trading and clearing (see Mayntz, Chapter 3, this volume). This soft law was subsequently downloaded and elaborated further in EU legislation. In this case, as in the case of the structural measures in banking, there was an attempt by the EU and the United States to crossload their rules to other jurisdictions, especially across the Atlantic.

The initial response of the European Commission and the ECB to the global financial crisis was to encourage industry to set up central counterparties in Europe for credit default swaps (CDSs),[11] which are a special type of over-the-counter derivative that caused enormous damage during the global financial crisis. Subsequently, the EU authorities began to discuss legislation, albeit at a slower pace than in the United States because the EU began its regulatory response to the crisis with the other pieces of legislation mentioned above.

In September 2010, the Commission proposed the European Market Infrastructure Regulation (EMIR). It broadly mirrored the reform enshrined in the Dodd-Frank Act to shift transactions onto exchanges and other types of trading platform (Financial Times, 9 May 2011: 16). Unlike the Dodd-Frank Act, however, the Brussels proposal did not deal with how over-the-counter derivatives should be traded, which was an issue tackled separately in the review of the Markets in Financial Instruments Directive, which was also under way. Initially, before being officially proposed by the Commission in September 2010, the European Market Infrastructure Regulation was conceived by the Commission as a "directive", but in summer 2010 it was decided it should be a regulation. This distinction is important, as regulations are enacted into law with immediate effect in EU member states, with no discretion over their interpretation.

The European Market Infrastructure Regulation was intended to ensure the transparency of over-the-counter derivatives transactions and to reduce the risks associated with these products by shifting, where possible, over-the-counter derivatives trading to central counterparties. These central counterparties reduce risks because they act as intermediaries between sellers and buyers of derivative products. They ensure the solvency of their participants by requesting deposits and margin calls. The regulation also involved the creation of harmonized rules for central counterparties and EU supervision of trade repositories. The reporting of all transactions was made mandatory with a view to providing supervisory authorities with the full picture of these markets.

---

11 A credit default swap is a financial swap agreement whereby the seller of the swap will compensate the buyer in the event of a loan default or other credit event.

The debate on the third-country regime under the European Market Infrastructure Regulation was especially complex (see Pagliari 2013; Quaglia 2015). The key issues were: to guarantee legal certainty; to avoid over- or under-laps with similar legislation in third jurisdictions; to ensure an international level playing field for EU central counterparties and trade repositories; and to abide by World Trade Organization (WTO) obligations. During the negotiations, some parties, especially French policy-makers, called for reciprocal provisions – for example, concerning access to data held in repositories outside a regulator's geographic jurisdiction. Others, including the British, objected to the concept of reciprocity with a view to ensuring open markets. They also argued that it could jeopardize EU commitments under the WTO.

As for central counterparties, the crucial issues for the EU concerning their location were to avoid over-reliance on US central counterparties and the ability to access central bank money. The ECB and the Commission wanted at least one central counterparty to be located and regulated in the EU to avoid European dependence on over-the-counter derivatives clearing in the United States (Buckley/Howarth/Quaglia 2012). Moreover, the ECB insisted on a central counterparty to be located in the euro area because of access to central bank liquidity. The City and the ISDA preferred global clearers, which were considered more efficient from the point of view of industry (Quaglia 2014a). Some of these global clearers are located in London and some in the United States. The final text of the Regulation established that recognition of a third-country central counterparty by the European Securities Market Authority (ESMA) would first require an equivalence decision by the Commission. The ESMA should also establish cooperation arrangements with the third-country competent authorities.

As for trade repositories, two issues were at stake for the EU: the treatment of confidential data and market competition. First, after the failure of Lehman Brothers, European regulators had been denied access to trade repositories data in the United States on the basis of confidentiality. The Dodd-Frank Act mandated that American-based swap data repositories obtain indemnification from foreign regulators before sharing information. For all these reason, European policy-makers were keen to establish European trade repositories (Buckley/Howarth/Quaglia 2012). Market competition was also at stake. For example, the American authorities argued in favor of one trade repository per asset class because the Depository Trust and Clearing Corporation (an American post-trade group) was due to launch an interest rate swap data repository in London in late 2012 and had another planned for commodities and foreign exchange (Financial Times, 25 August 2011).

According to the European Market Infrastructure Regulation, authorities were to be granted access to the data of trade repositories (owned by private companies). Recognition of a third-country trade repository was subject to equivalence decisions by the Commission. In addition, the legislation required the putting in place of an international agreement between the Commission and that third country with regard to mutual access to data and exchange of information on over-the-counter derivatives contracts held in trade repositories in order to address the issue of confidentiality. The European Market Infrastructure Regulation was adopted by the EU in July 2012.

As explained by Ryan and Ziegler (Chapter 4, this volume), in May 2012 the United States – to be precise, the CFTC – proposed new legislation on OTC derivatives, which had potential extraterritorial effects and was therefore problematic for the EU. In a letter to the Financial Times (21 June 2012), European Commissioner Michel Barnier criticized the CFTC's "wide interpretation of who is a 'US person'" and thus covered by the CFTC rules, pointing out the "danger" that "many of the requirements would apply to companies in the EU and to trades between the EU and US clients. American rules would take primacy over those in Europe." British policy-makers and the City of London were also worried about the extraterritorial effects of the proposed CFTC rules: London is by far the largest centre of derivatives trading in the EU and one of the largest in the world, together with New York. The European Commissioner shared British concerns and stated explicitly that "[w]e will insist that the interests of the City of London and other European financial centres are respected."

In mid-July 2013, the European Commission and the CFTC agreed on a "Common Path Forward on Derivatives" (2013). The agreement was designed to allow firms to avoid the burden of complying with two different sets of regulations and reflected a compromise. The EU accepted that EU entities would have to register with the CFTC when they met applicable standards, while the CFTC accepted a greater degree of "substituted compliance" for entities to comply with EU requirements in lieu of CFTC rules. Firms trading swaps that were too complex or unique for a clearing house were free to choose which jurisdiction's rules to apply. In February 2014, the CFTC exempted EU trading platforms from all registration requirements. In the end, the CFTC adjusted its rules, toning down their application to third countries.

Banking union[12]

Banking union was proposed by the European heads of government and state in June 2012 to restore confidence in European banking systems weakened by the double whammy of the international financial crisis and the sovereign debt crisis, as well as to break the sovereign debt/bank doom loop that plagued the euro-zone periphery, counteract the growing fragmentation of European financial markets since the outbreak of the international financial crisis, and – in the words of Council President Herman Van Rompuy – "complete" economic and monetary union, thus saving the euro and protecting it better from future shocks (Howarth/Quaglia 2013b; see also Donnelly 2014).

The proposals for banking union amounted to a radical initiative to stabilize the EU's national banking systems that were exposed directly to the sovereign debt crisis by breaking the dangerous link between the high and rising sovereign debt in the euro area's peripheral member states and domestic banks, which had come to hold an increasing amount of this debt. But banking union will also bring about a significant transfer of powers from the national to the EU – to be precise, banking union – level. It can be seen as a necessary response to the "asymmetric" design of EMU (a full monetary union without a full economic/fiscal union).

Indeed, banking union was a crisis-driven attempt to address several important issues that were side-stepped or papered over during the negotiations leading to the Maastricht Treaty, principally the allocation of supervisory responsibilities to the ECB and the creation of a fiscal backstop in the euro area. Other issues, notably the need for a single rule book and the harmonization of deposit guarantee schemes, stemmed from the incomplete nature of the single financial market – despite its heralded re-launch in the early 2000s. Finally, other issues, such as the need for a common deposit guarantee and a resolution fund/authority for the euro area, were highlighted by the global financial crisis and the sovereign debt crisis.

Banking union was to be based on five components: a single rulebook on bank capital and liquidity; a single framework for banking supervision, the Single Supervisory Mechanism (SSM); a single framework for the managed resolution of banks and financial institutions, the Single Resolution Mechanism (SRM); a common deposit guarantee scheme (DGS); and a common backstop for temporary financial support, whereby the European Stability Mechanism (ESM) could be used for this purpose (European Council 2012b, 2012c). From

---

12 This part draws on Howarth and Quaglia (2013, 2014).

June 2012, there were negotiations on four of the five elements of a banking union and, with the exception of the common DGS, agreements were reached by spring 2014.

France was the main proponent of banking union. Its interest stemmed from heavy French bank exposure to the euro periphery and persistent French macroeconomic difficulties, notably on national fiscal policy and high current account deficits. The French supported banking union because they sought reinforced banking supervision, a euro area–wide deposit guarantee and a bank resolution fund that would relieve market worries over unstable banks in the euro-area periphery holding huge quantities of their government's sovereign debt. French interest in banking union also stemmed from a desire to establish a kind of fiscal backstop to the euro area via lender of last resort–style support for banks rather than governments per se. Periphery member states directly hit or threatened by the sovereign debt crisis – namely Greece, Ireland, Portugal, Spain, and Italy – fully supported banking union. These countries called for the setting up of the two core pillars of banking union, namely the SSM and the SRM, given the poor state of their national banking systems and of their public finances.

Germany was recalcitrant towards banking union, especially the SSM, and the SRM. It had a "constrained veto power". It had such veto power because it was the largest economy in the EU and had doubts about banking union, from which it had the least to gain, at least at first sight. Its veto power was constrained by the fact that the euro area (including Germany) needed banking union in order to deal with the sovereign debt crisis and ensure the survival of the euro. In the negotiations on banking union, German policy-makers requested tighter fiscal rules and the imposition of clear conditions for the provision of EU/euro area financial support to ailing states and banks. The main concern of the German authorities was moral hazard: they feared that EU-level support would undermine national macroeconomic policy reform in the countries receiving financial aid. German opposition to the Commission's draft directives on the SSM and SRM stemmed from legal difficulties and the structure of the German banking system and, for the SRM specifically, from concerns over moral hazard both for banks and for sovereign states.

As in the previous negotiations on Economic and Monetary Union, the United Kingdom adopted a wait-and-see approach, though it was by and large supportive of banking union, the SSM and the SRM as means to deal with the sovereign debt crisis in the euro area and ensure financial stability therein. However, it was clear that the United Kingdom did not want to be part of the new institutional arrangements. Several Central and Eastern European Countries that were not in the euro area also took a similar wait-and-see approach, as did Sweden and Denmark.

A Franco-German agreement was necessary for the negotiations on the two main new pillars of banking union – namely the SSM and the SRM – to be successfully completed. A compromise was eventually reached on several issues, even though the final outcome was close to German preferences. The main issues in the negotiations on the SSM and the SRM concerned the centralization of decision-making power, scope, legal basis and, for the SRM, sources of funding. The banking union eventually agreed was "light" compared with the initial declarations and expectations. The proposal for a common DGS was quietly set aside. The SRM that was eventually agreed had a rather cumbersome decision-making process and the Single Resolution Fund, which was of a limited amount, was to be set up gradually by pooling national resolution funds. The ESM would be allowed to directly recapitalize banks subject to a host of conditions.

Overall assessment

The EU's post-crisis regulatory response was based mainly on the downloading of international rules, which it often developed further or significantly amended, as in the case of the Bank Recovery and Resolution Directive and CRD IV, respectively. In a few cases, such as Basel III, the EU was unable to upload its set of preferences to the international level because member states had different preferences (see also Kudrna 2014). In other cases, such as OTC derivatives, the EU attempted to crossload some of its rules to third countries, first and foremost, the United States, which tried to do the same. Finally, there were cases in which the EU established its own rules without downloading from or uploading to the international level; these were, notably, the measures on the structure of the banking sector and banking union.

The main instance of downloading of international rules by the EU concerned the capital and liquidity requirements for banks, namely Basel III, even though there remain some important differences between Basel III and the CRD IV package. The EU and its member states had a disjointed position in the negotiations in the BCBS and some of these disagreements re-emerged during the negotiations on the legislation implementing Basel III in the EU. In downloading Basel III, the EU somewhat watered down the international standards. It is, however, noteworthy that the new capital rules apply to the entire EU banking system, not only to internationally active banks. Hence, the scope of application of Basel rules in the EU is more extensive than in other jurisdictions.

Other instances of downloading of international soft law into EU legislation concerned the rules for bank resolution and OTC derivatives, even though EU legislation went further than what had been agreed at the international level. The unfolding of the sovereign debt crisis in the euro area meant that the EU – to be precise, the euro area – set up a new distinctive regime on resolution, the Single Resolution Mechanism, which complemented the other main components of banking union.

More often than not, the EU presented a disunited front in international regulatory fora. It was not able to upload much, but nor were other jurisdictions, including the United States. Indeed, many international soft rules issued in response to the global financial crisis were brand new, they had to be devised from scratch, and unlike several instances in the past (Quaglia 2014d), they were not uploaded by national jurisdictions. The EU fulfilled most of the G20 commitments it signed up to, implemented internationally agreed rules and often developed them further.

In one important respect the EU attempted to foster international regulatory harmonization: it tried to actively crossload its rules to third jurisdictions through equivalence clauses in most of the EU post-crisis legislation (Quaglia 2015a). Hence, equivalence is both an instrument for the EU to promote the crossloading of its rules and a mechanism to promote mutual recognition between two jurisdictions. Some equivalence clauses were already present in pre-crisis EU legislation (see Posner 2009b), but they were few in number. Post-crisis, the EU used equivalence clauses in several pieces of legislation, such as structural measures in banking and the European Market Infrastructure Regulation, but also in the directive on hedge fund managers and the regulation of credit rating agencies, which are not examined here. Although the wording of equivalence clauses varied across items of EU legislation and was often the focus of heated intra-EU debates, the EU not only requires third-country financial operators to comply with EU rules when they operate in the EU (this is the "national treatment" principle), but, in accordance with the EU's approach to equivalence, third-country financial operators that want to do business either in the EU or with EU counterparts outside the EU can do so only if the legislation in the third countries where they are based is equivalent to EU rules. Such equivalence is decided by the Commission, advised by the European supervisory authorities. The use of equivalence through which the EU has sought to crossload some of its rules to third countries can generate tension with EU counterparts, especially powerful jurisdictions such as the United States, which has often made use of extraterritorial legislation in finance.

The establishment of the banking union will also have important external implications. First, there will be a change in the way in which the euro area – to be precise, the banking union area, which will include euro area member states and opt-in countries – is represented in international fora for banking regulation. In January 2015, the ECB, which had previously sat on the BCBS as an observer, became a full member, together with the Single Supervisory Mechanism (Quaglia 2015b). Hence, the Banking Union will be better equipped to speak with one mouth in relevant international banking fora. Second, the banking union area will be able to project a more cohesive position in international financial negotiations than the EU as a whole in the past, which would augment the ability of banking union countries to upload their rules and supervisory practices. This is because there will be a harmonization of banking rules and supervisory practices in the banking union, which will reduce differences across participating member states, enabling the relevant banking union authorities to speak with one voice (articulate a coherent set of preferences) and not only with one mouth (one representative). Third, banking union might provide a laboratory for the development of new rules, supervisory practices and ideas to be uploaded or crossloaded internationally.

All in all, during and after the global financial crisis, the EU has played the role of "transmission belt" between the national level and the international level. However, this transmission belt has not always worked smoothly, as suggested, for example, by the "distinctive" way in which the EU implemented Basel III. On certain issues, such as the regulation of hedge funds, rating agencies (which are not discussed here, see Quaglia 2014a), and OTC trading, the EU has been a "pace-setter" (in certain cases together with the United States) at the international level and with its own post-crisis legislation. On other issues, such as capital requirements for banks and structural measures for the banking industry, the EU has been more of a foot-dragger. The EU has been reluctant to impose "heavy handed" regulation on banks because it has mainly a bank-based financial system in which banks provide most of the credit to the real economy. Hence, in the post-crisis reform of financial regulation, there has been – at times deliberately overplayed – concern that the tightening up of prudential rules for banks could reduce the flow of credit to the real economy and ultimately economic growth.

References

Bach, David/Abraham Newman, 2007: The European Regulatory State and Global Public Policy: Micro-Institutions, Macro-Influence. In: *Journal of European Public Policy* 14(6), 1–20.

Barnier, Michel, 2012a: The US must not override EU regulators. In: *Financial Times,* 21 June 2012, 11.

Barnier, Michel, 2012b: *Volcker Rule Comment Letter.* <www.sec.gov/comments/s7-41-11/s74111-479.pdf>

BCBS (Basel Committee on Banking Supervision), 2010a: *Basel III: A Global Regulatory Framework for More Resilient Banks and Banking Systems.* Basel: BCBS.

——, 2010b: *Basel III: International Framework for Liquidity Risk Measurement, Standards and Monitoring.* Basel: BCBS.

——, 2010c: *Interim Report Assessing the Macroeconomic Impact of the Transition to Stronger Capital and Liquidity Requirements.* Basel: BCBS.

Buckley, James/David Howarth/Lucia Quaglia, 2012: Internal Market: The Ongoing Struggle to "Protect" Europe from its Money Men. In: *Journal of Common Market Studies* 48(1), 119–141.

Christopoulos, Dimitris/Lucia Quaglia, 2009: Network Constraints in EU Banking Regulation: The Case of the Capital Requirements Directive. In: *Journal of Public Policy* 29(2), 1–22.

Damro, Chad, 2012: Market Power Europe. In: *Journal of European Public Policy* 19(5), 182–199.

Donnelly, Shawn, 2010: *The Regimes of European Integration: Constructing Governance of the Single Market.* Oxford: Oxford University Press.

——, 2014: Power politics and the undersupply of financial stability in Europe. In: *Review of International Political Economy* 21(4), 980–1005.

Drezner, Daniel, 2007: *All Politics is Global: Explaining International Regulatory Regimes.* Princeton: Princeton University Press.

European Commission, 2011a: *Proposal for a Directive on the Access to the Activity of Credit Institutions and the Prudential Supervision of Credit Institutions and Investment Firms 2011/453/EC.* Brussels: European Commission.

——, 2011b: *Proposal for a Regulation on Prudential Requirements for Credit Institutions and Investment Firms 2011/452/EC.* Brussels: European Commission.

——, 2012a: *Proposal for a Directive Establishing a Framework for the Recovery and Resolution of Credit Institutions and Investment Firms and Amending Council Directives 77/91/EEC and 82/891/EC, Directives 2001/24/EC, 2002/47/EC, 2004/25/EC, 2005/56/EC, 2007/36/EC and 2011/35/EC and Regulation (EU) No 1093/2010, COM(2012) 280/3.* Brussels: European Commission.

——, 2012b: *Proposal for a Council Regulation conferring specific tasks on the European Central Bank concerning policies relating to the prudential supervision of credit institutions, COM/2012/0511 final.* Brussels: European Commission.

——, 2012c: *Proposal for a Regulation of the European Parliament and of the Council establishing uniform rules and a uniform procedure for the resolution of credit institutions and certain investment firms in the framework of a Single Resolution Mechanism and a Single Bank Resolution Fund and amending Regulation (EU) No 1093/2010 of the European Parliament and of the Council, COM/2013/0520 final.* Brussels: European Commission.

European Parliament, 2010a: *Resolution on Basel II and revision of the Capital Requirements Directives (CRD 4). Committee of Economic and Monetary Affairs.* Brussels: European Parliament.

——, 2010b: *Resolution on Derivatives Markets: Future Policy Actions.* Brussels: European Parliament.

Ferran, Eilis: Crisis-Driven Regulatory Reform: Where in the World is the EU Going? In: Eilis Ferran (ed.), *The Regulatory Aftermath of the Global Financial Crisis.* Cambridge: Cambridge University Press, 1–110.

FSB (Financial Stability Board), 2011: *Key Attributes Of Effective Resolution Regimes For Financial Institutions.* Basel: FSB.

Greenwood, Justin/Christilla Roederer-Rynning, 2014: The "Europeanization" of the Basel Process: Financial Harmonization between Globalization and Parliamentarization. In: *Regulation and Governance,* Early View, DOI: 10.1111/rego.12063.

G20 (Group of Twenty), 2009a: *The Leaders' Statement. Pittsburgh Summit.* Pittsburgh: G20.

——, 2009b: *The Global Plan for Recovery and Reform. London Summit.* London: G20.

Hardie, Iain/David Howarth (eds.), 2013: *Market-Based Banking and the International Financial Crisis.* Oxford: Oxford University Press.

Helleiner, Eric/Stefano Pagliari, 2010: The End of Self-Regulation? Hedge Funds and Derivatives in Global Financial Governance. In: Eric Helleiner/Stefano Pagliari/Hubert Zimmermann (eds.), *Global Finance in Crisis: The Politics of International Regulatory Change.* London: Routledge, 74–90.

Helleiner, Eric/Stefano Pagliari/Hubert Zimmerman (eds.), 2010: *Global Finance in Crisis: The Politics of International Regulatory Change.* London: Routledge.

Howarth, David/Lucia Quaglia, 2013a: Banking on Stability: The Political Economy of New Capital Requirements in the European Union. In: *Journal of European Integration* 35(3), 333–346.

——, 2013b: Banking Union as Holy Grail: Rebuilding the Single Market in Financial Services, Stabilizing Europe's Banks and "Completing" Economic and Monetary Union. In: *Journal of Common Market Studies* 51(S1), 103–123.

——, 2014: The Steep Road to European Banking Union: Constructing the Single Resolution Mechanism. In: *Journal of Common Market Studies* 52(S1), 125–140.

——, 2015: *The Political Economy of Basel III in Europe,* unpublished manuscript.

IMF (International Monetary Fund), 2011: *United Kingdom: Staff Report for the 2011 Article IV Consultation—Supplementary Information.* IMF Country Report No. 11/220. Washington, DC: IMF.

Kapstein, Ethan, 1989: Resolving the Regulator's Dilemma: International Coordination of Banking Regulations. In: *International Organisation* 43(2), 323–347.

——, 1992: Between Power and Purpose: Central Bankers and the Politics of International Regulation. In: *International Organization* 46(1), 265–287.

Kudrna, Zdenek, 2014: EU Financial Market Regulation: Protecting Distinctive Policy Preferences. In: Gerda Falkner/Patrick Müller (eds.), *EU Policies in a Global Perspective: Shaping or Taking International Regimes?* London: Routledge, 186–204.

Macartney, Huw, 2010: *Variegated Neoliberalism: EU Varieties of Capitalism and International Political Economy.* London: Routledge.

Mayntz, Renate (ed.), 2012: *Crisis and Control: Institutional Change in Financial Market Regulation.* Frankfurt a.M.: Campus.

Moschella, Manuela/Eleni Tsingou (eds.), 2013: *Great Expectations, Slow Transformations: Incremental Change in Financial Governance.* Colchester: ECPR.

Mügge, Daniel, 2010: *Widen the Market, Narrow the Competition: Banker Interests and the Making of a European Capital Market.* Colchester: ECPR.

Pagliari, Stefano, 2013: A Wall Around Europe? The European Regulatory Response to the Global Financial Crisis and the Turn in Transatlantic Relations. In: *Journal of European Integration* 35(4), 391–408.

Porter, Tony, 2005: *Globalization and Finance.* Cambridge: Polity Press.

Posner, Elliot, 2009a: *The Origins of Europe's New Stock Markets.* Cambridge, MA: Harvard University Press.

——, 2009b: Making Rules for Global Finance: Transatlantic Regulatory Cooperation at the Turn of the Millennium. In: *International Organization* 63(4), 665–699.

——, 2010: Sequence as Explanation: The International Politics of Accounting Standards. In: *Review of International Political Economy* 14(4), 639–664.

Quaglia, Lucia, 2010: *Governing Financial Services in the European Union.* London: Routledge.

——, 2014a: *The European Union and Global Financial Regulation.* Oxford: Oxford University Press.

——, 2014b: The European Union, the USA and International Standard Setting in Finance. In: *New Political Economy* 19(3), 427–444.

——, 2014c: The Sources of European Union Influence in International Financial Regulatory Fora. In: *Journal of European Public Policy* 21(3), 327–345.

——, 2015a: The Politics of "Third Country Equivalence" in Post-Crisis Financial Services Regulation in the European Union. In: *West European Politics* 38(1), 167–184.

——, 2015b: *The European Union's Role in International Economic Fora, Paper 5: The Basel Committee on Banking Supervision Policy Department Economic and Scientific Policies.* Brussels: European Parliament. <www.europarl.europa.eu/RegData/etudes/IDAN/2015/542194/IPOL_IDA%282015%29542194_EN.pdf>

Simmons, Beth, 2001: The International Politics of Harmonization: The Case of Capital Market Regulation. In: *International Organization* 55(3), 589–620.

Singer, David, 2004: Capital Rules: The Domestic Politics of International Regulatory Harmonization. In: *International Organization* 58(3), 531–565.

——, 2007: Regulating Capital: *Setting Standards for the International Financial System.* Ithaca: Cornell University Press.

Tsingou, Eleni, 2008: Transnational Private Governance and the Basel Process: Banking Regulation, Private Interests and Basel II. In: Jean-Christoph Graz/Andreas Nölke (eds.), *Transnational Private Governance and its Limits.* London: Routledge, 58–68.

Underhill, Geoffrey, 1997: The Making of the European Financial Area: Global Market Integration and the EU Single Market for Financial Services. In: Geoffrey Underhill (ed.), *The New World Order in International Finance.* London: Macmillan, 101–123.

Underhill, Geoffrey/Xiao Zhang, 2008: Setting the Rules: Private Power, Political Underpinnings, and Legitimacy in Global Monetary and Financial Governance. In: *International Affairs* 84(3), 535–554.

Wood, Duncan, 2005: *Governing Global Banking: The Basel Committee and the Politics of Financial Globalisation.* Aldershot: Ashgate.

Young, Kevin, 2012: Transnational Regulatory Capture? An Empirical Examination of the Transnational Lobbying of the Basel Committee on Banking Supervision. In: *Review of International Political Economy* 19(4), 663–688.

——, 2014: Losing Abroad but Winning at Home: European Financial Industry Groups in Global Financial Governance since the Crisis. In: *Journal of European Public Policy* 21(3), 367–388.

6 The UK in the Multilevel Process of Financial Market Regulation: Global Pace-Setter or National Outlier?

Scott James

Introduction

This chapter examines the UK's role in shaping the regulatory response to the global financial crisis at the national, European and international levels. It makes three principal claims. First, it argues that in key areas of regulatory reform, particularly those related to banking resolution and capital requirements, the UK seeks to perform the role of global pace-setter. Its leading role in international institutions such as the Financial Stability Board (FSB) has, consequently, enabled it to "punch above its weight" in uploading its preferences and shaping new global regulatory standards. Second, at the European level, by contrast, the UK's role is complicated by domestic "euroscepticism" and diminishing influence in Brussels. It therefore displays a more mixed picture of successes and failures, leaving UK regulators facing higher adaptational costs of downloading EU financial legislation with respect to capital requirements, alternative investment funds, derivatives trading and bank resolution. Third, the UK's role in multilevel regulatory processes cannot be understood without analyzing the domestic political context. Through the structural reforms outlined by the Independent Commission on Banking (ICB) aimed at ringfencing domestic retail banks, the UK has been at the forefront of efforts to address problems of moral hazard and institutions that are "too big to fail". Although at first glance the Vickers reforms risk leaving the UK as a global outlier, regulators have been careful to ensure that they do not undermine the competitiveness of London as the world's leading international financial centre.

The chapter is informed by an extensive review of publicly available documents and media coverage of EU and UK financial regulation, and private interviews conducted with UK and EU policy-makers and financial services practitioners during 2013/14 under the Chatham House Rule. I am indebted to their help and assistance and any errors are entirely my own.

The UK's regulatory response to the financial crisis has been shaped by powerful multilevel dynamics at the national, European and international levels. Its reform efforts at each level are intrinsically linked, giving rise to a two- or three-level game (Putnam 1988) in which regulators negotiate reforms in different institutional arenas simultaneously and seek to leverage their influence by exploiting political pressures emanating from other levels.

The UK recognizes that it is in its economic interest to perform the role of "pace-setter" at the international level. Any new regulatory framework will have a disproportionate impact on the UK economy, given the size of its financial services sector and the fact that it hosts one of the world's leading international financial centres. It therefore has a clear incentive to seek to upload its regulatory preferences in order to minimize the adaptational costs of downloading: in other words, to maximize the institutional "goodness of fit". This section provides a brief overview of the UK's role in shaping the emergent post-crisis regulatory agenda.

The UK's capacity to shape Europe's response to the financial crisis has been more mixed. The euro-zone crisis and subsequent attempts to forge a banking union have reignited parliamentary and public euroscepticism at home, increasing the uncertainty surrounding the UK's relationship with Europe and reducing the autonomy of UK negotiators in Brussels. Where the UK has sought allies with other member states it has succeeded in opposing protectionist impulses, notably with regard to equivalence rules for third-country access. But at other times the reputational damage caused by the veto of the EU Fiscal Treaty in 2011 has left the UK isolated, culminating in it's being outvoted on financial services legislation for the first time over the cap on bankers' bonuses. Table 6-1 provides a brief overview of the UK's negotiating position and current implementation of key EU financial services regulations.

Regulation of bank capital requirements

The UK government's preferences on bank capital requirements have undergone a dramatic shift over the previous two years, rooted in regulators' experience of and learning from the financial crisis. Historically, the UK has been a cheerleader for global financial deregulation and as a leading member of a broader deregulatory "market-making" coalition of like-minded states (Quaglia 2012). But the fiscal burden of bailing out two of its largest banks sent shockwaves through the political establishment. UK regulators concluded that it was uniquely vulnerable due to its financial sector being too big to save and that the international regulatory framework for bank capital was fundamentally broken. In response, regulators acted swiftly at home by forcing banks to deleverage, while at the international level they allied with US and Swiss counterparts in pushing for much higher capital levels and stricter capital definitions. On banking regulation the UK has therefore become one of the most hawkish members of the "market-shaping" coalition of states in favor of much stricter statutory regulation.

The change of government in May 2010 heralded no notable shift in the UK government's preferences as the need to urgently address bank capital was shared by all the main political parties. This strengthened the hand of UK regulators who commanded a disproportionate share of the chairmanships of key sub-committees, enabling them to punch above their weight in shaping the new accord. The former Deputy Governor of the Bank of England, Paul Tucker, played a leading role in formulating international guidance on banking resolution as chair of the FSB Resolution Steering Group: he also chaired the Basel Committee on Payments and Settlement Systems (CPSS) and was co-chair of the Steering Group established jointly by the CPSS and the International Organisation of Securities Commissions (IOSCO). Similarly as chair of the UK Financial Services Authority (FSA), Lord Adair Turner chaired the FSB Standing Committee on Supervisory and Regulatory Cooperation and led the FSB's work on tightening regulation of the shadow banking sector. The appointment in July 2013 of Mark Carney as the new Governor of the Bank of England, who has chaired the FSB since 2011, has further strengthened the UK's capacity for shaping global regulatory standards.

Much of the intellectual driving force behind the Basel negotiations was the US Federal Reserve and the Bank of England/Financial Services Authority (FSA). In the final agreement, UK regulators accepted the need for a long implementation phase as the price for securing an outcome close to their ideal position. Their success in doing so consequently reverberated at the European and domestic level as regulators were adamant that there should be no subsequent dilution of the Basel proposals.

A rather different story emerges at the European level. The recently-agreed EU Capital Requirements Directive IV (CRD IV) provides a useful illustration of how domestic factors have shaped the UK's European negotiating position. Contrary to the common misconception that the UK government simply defends the interests of its financial services sector, the UK has been a leader in championing both higher capital requirements and narrow definitions of capital. The UK resisted attempts by France and Germany to dilute capital definitions by allowing "silent participation" (state support for banks, such as the German Landesbanken) and "double counting" (of capital held by the insurance subsidiaries of [mainly French] banks) in the calculation of regulatory capital. It also fought unsuccessfully to have a binding leverage ratio and strict liquidity standards included in CRD4, and the UK was subsequently outvoted in March 2013 over Parliament's amendment to impose bonus caps on bankers' pay.

Howarth and Quaglia (2013) argue that this reflects the distinctive nature of bank capital in different national financial systems and the fact that since the crisis UK regulators have unilaterally forced the largest banks to strengthen their capital position. It therefore makes sense strategically to try to "externalize" British capital rules by uploading them to the European level in order to create a level playing field around the highest common denominator.

However, this economic interest–based account presents only a partial explanation. First, it is not clear why the UK persisted in its determination to impose higher capital standards on its own banks once it became apparent that the EU's proposals would be significantly weaker. This led to a prolonged battle which the UK government fought to oppose "maximum harmonization": that is, the Commission's proposal for CRD4 to legislate for a maximum level of capital requirements. In line with the Basel 3 recommendations, the UK sought the flexibility to impose higher capital requirements on its banks than the EU demanded (Financial Times 2012). Second, economic explanations struggle to explain the misalignment of preferences between the UK government and the UK banking industry. Rather than trying to protect the competitive advantage of the City of London, the government was pursuing an autonomous agenda in defiance of the industry's opposition. Instead, many in the City allied themselves with pan-European groups to actively lobby in favor of maximum harmonization because it viewed the UK's desire for higher capital rules as damaging to the City's competitiveness and it favoured regulatory convergence through a Single Rule Book.[1]

Any explanation of the UK's opposition to maximum harmonization must account for the importance of domestic politics in the formulation of the UK government's preferences (James, forthcoming). This gave rise to two principal concerns.[2] First, the government's position reflected the reality of coalition politics that had set in train a domestic regulatory reform process (the Independent Commission on Banking), the outcome of which was a call for the imposition of higher capital requirements than those proposed by the European Commission. A failure to implement these recommendations risked undermining the carefully crafted compromise on banking reform between the ruling Conservatives and Liberal Democrats. Second, the UK had recently introduced new macroprudential supervisory structures, the centrepiece of which was a powerful

---

1 Private interviews, 2013.
2 Private interviews, 2013

new Financial Policy Committee (FPC) with the capacity to vary capital rules in order to address systemic risk, such as cyclical economic bubbles. Maximum harmonization risked seriously blunting the committee's powers before it was even operational. These factors led UK negotiators to seek to retain their autonomy to regulate the domestic banking system as they saw fit.

Banking structural reform

Rather than waiting for international or European agreement on banking structural reform to download, the UK has pursued its own autonomous agenda. This has been driven by two factors. First, the UK was perceived as uniquely vulnerable to a future financial crisis on account of the size of its financial sector. The turmoil of the financial crisis and the fiscal burden of bailing out two of the UK's largest banks had sent shockwaves through the political establishment and there was a realization that having to do so again would be catastrophic for the City's reputation.[3] Political leaders therefore viewed the protection of taxpayers as a priority. Second, the UK's banking reform process is reflects the nature of coalition politics and the need to find a mutually acceptable solution between the ruling parties on one of the most potentially divisive issues. The decision in June 2010 to establish an Independent Commission on Banking (ICB), headed by the former chairman of the Office of Fair Trading Sir John Vickers, suited both parties: the Conservatives were able to put off a decision on banking reform for 18 months and thus avoid damaging any economic recovery, while the Liberal Democrats favoured an independent process that would help to insulate the process from industry lobbying.[4] It also made economic sense as it allowed time for the outcome of EU and international-level rules to become clearer before settling on reforms.

The terms of reference given to the ICB by the Treasury go a considerable way to helping us to understand the nature of the reforms eventually proposed (ICB 2010). First, the commission was tasked with making recommendations on structural and non-structural measures that would promote both stability and competition in banking. The nature of the dilemma between these two objectives inevitably forced it to prioritize one over the other: it did so by focusing its efforts on addressing the stability dimension.[5] Second, the ICB's mandate

---

3 Private interviews, 2013.
4 Private interviews, 2013.
5 Private interviews, 2013.

combined the aim of "reducing the likelihood and impact of firm failure" with the need to mitigate problems of moral hazard and banks that are "too big to fail". The contradiction between these two objectives meant that John Vickers had to simultaneously propose structural reforms designed to secure the right incentives within the industry, while also seeking to control behaviour arising from the wrong incentives (Kay 2011). These tensions are reflected in the rationale expounded for the ringfencing of UK retail banking activities. Ostensibly, it serves the purpose of making it easier for both ringfenced and non-ringfenced entities to fail without having a catastrophic impact on bank lending or a run on retail deposits. However, the ICB made clear that ringfencing can work properly only if combined with a more effective global or EU banking resolution regime: in this context ringfencing serves a form of *ex ante* separation, making it easier to wind up banks methodically. Nonetheless, there remains a nagging doubt that ringfencing may perversely exacerbate problems of moral hazard within the retail entity by making it easier to bail out and thus signalling that government would do so (Lilico 2012).

The recommendations outlined in the ICB's Final Report in September 2011 constitute a carefully crafted compromise between industry (which sought to defend the universal banking model) and some high profile figures (notably Mervyn King, Governor of the Bank of England, and Vince Cable, Business Secretary) calling for a full split (see Table 6-1). The proposals also sought to skilfully balance the competing demands of domestic stability and international competitiveness (Kapstein 1989) by refraining from changes that would give a clear competitive advantage to foreign banks. For example, the ringfencing of all UK retail banking activities includes both British or foreign-owned firms, thereby preventing the latter from gaining a competitive advantage and undermining the economic case for large UK banks moving their headquarters abroad. On capital the largest retail banks will be required to hold CET1 equal to 10 percent of risk-weighted assets, putting UK banks on par with those in Switzerland (Figure 6-1). This goes against the received wisdom of international regulators as Basel 3 raised capital requirements for all banks, but particularly for certain areas of investment banking. However, two factors serve to mitigate the effects of these tougher requirements. First, to compensate for the fact that smaller banks are disproportionately affected by higher capital rules, the "ringfence buffer" will vary between 0 and 3 percent, depending on size of bank. For the largest UK banks the additional buffer was also in line with expectations of the ratio recommended by international regulators for global SIFIs. Second, the Commission was keen to avoid putting the UK's non-ringfenced banking activities at a competitive disadvantage by ensuring that there are no additional capital requirements above and beyond those in Basel 3 and CRD4. Contro-

Table 6-1   ICB key recommendations

Ringfencing	– UK banks' retail activities – defined as deposits, small business lending and payment systems – to be placed in a ringfenced subsidiary
	– No longer permitted to engage in trading of derivatives and securities, provide services to other financial companies or services to customers outside the EEA
	– Ringfenced entity to have independent governance, be legally separate and operationally separable, and economic links to the rest of the corporate group no more substantial than those for third parties
Capital requirements	– Additional core equity tier 1 (CET1) "ringfence buffer" of up to 3% of risk-weighted assets for ringfenced banks, on top of the 7% requirements in Basel 3 and CRD4 (CET1 of 4.5% + capital conservation buffer of 2.5%): total CET1 capital for ringfenced part is 10%
	– No additional capital requirements above and beyond those in Basel 3 and CRD4 for non-ringfenced entity
	– Leverage ratio (equity to assets) of 4%, above Basel 3 requirement of 3%
Loss absorbancy	– Primary Loss Absorbing Capacity (PLAC): both parts of the bank must hold additional loss-absorbing capital of 7–10% in the form of bail-in bonds or contingent convertible bonds (cocos), on top of the 10% CET1 requirement
	– Depositor Preference: depositors to be made senior to bondholders

versially, however, it did propose a higher leverage ratio of 4 percent, above the international/EU minimum.

In understanding the logic behind the Vickers reforms, it is useful to consider the reform options that were not adopted. The ICB ruled out the option of maintaining the status quo with respect to bank structures. Although industry defenders of the universal banking model criticized Vickers for increasing the costs of raising capital, the report makes clear that the bulk of the cost of ringfencing is the higher costs banks will incur in capitalizing their investment operations without access to large retail deposits or the implicit state guarantee that they enjoy (Kay 2011). At the opposite end of the spectrum, it is noteworthy that in the run-up to the 2010 election the Conservatives favoured a UK version of the US Volcker Rule restricting banks from proprietary trading on their own accounts (Financial Times 2010). Similarly, during 2010/11 two key figures – Vince Cable and Mervyn King – sought to shape the agenda by repeatedly calling for a full split between banks' retail and investment operations along the lines of the Glass-Steagall Act in the US. However, John Vickers argued that market-making (banks holding bonds and shares to sell to clients) and proprietary trading (banks taking their own positions in securities for their own gain) are almost indistinguishable and so any attempt to try to police the boundary would consume too much time and energy. In addition, it risked

Figure 6-1   Core Equity Tier 1 capital requirements for UK ringfenced banks

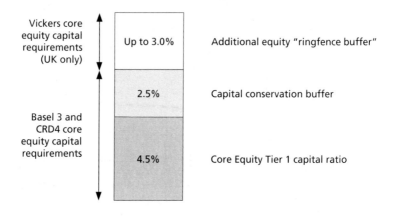

encouraging proprietary trading to move to less regulated parts of the financial system (Bloomberg 2013).

The Commission also considered non-structural alternatives to ringfencing, such as simply imposing a CET1 ratio of 20 percent across the board, but favoured lower requirements combined with structural reforms in order to facilitate other objectives, such as bank resolution. Curiously, however, John Vickers has since suggested that, in an ideal world, CET1 capital ratios should be doubled to 20 percent and the leverage ratio to 10 percent (Financial Times 2013a). This fits with more recent international trends towards strengthening capital levels through the imposition of higher leverage ratios (the US, for example, plans a 6 percent leverage ratio) in response to mounting concerns about how banks have met the Basel 3 CET1 requirements and yet remained highly leveraged. Finally, the option of ringfencing investment banking operations, as proposed by the EU Liikanen Expert Group, was ruled out as too costly. More fundamentally it would also contradict the overarching objective to make it easier for large banks to fail as it would seek to make investment banks "safer" (ICB 2011).

At first glance the UK would appear to be an outlier on banking reform. Its proposals for capital requirements put the UK with Switzerland and parts of Asia in having one of the toughest regulatory regimes in the world, while the structural reforms to be achieved through ringfencing are unmatched in any other major financial centre. This reform agenda has been driven primarily by domestic dynamics: the need to design regulation appropriate to the UK's unique vulnerability and in response to parliamentary pressure for action. However, this claim needs to be qualified on at least three important grounds. First, an emphasis on the national distinctiveness of structural reforms ignores the extent to which they are overlapping and complementary. For example, the IMF notes that if the Liikanen proposals are implemented in the UK alongside the Vickers reforms, then it will establish a tougher capital regime for both ring-fenced retail banks and their non-ringfenced trading affiliates, thereby strengthening the resilience of the whole group (IMF 2013: 23). Similarly, Paul Tucker has recently suggested that the EU Banking Resolution and Recovery Directive will effectively supersede the UK ringfencing requirements anyway (Financial Times 2013c). Finally, in implementing these reforms the government has been careful to amend or remove anything that threatens the UK's pre-eminent position as an international financial centre: most significantly, the Banking Reform Bill, which implements the Vickers Report, reduces the leverage ratio from 4 percent to 3 percent in order to align it with the Basel 3 Agreement and CRD IV.

Regulation of bank recovery and resolution

As home to a number of the world's largest financial institutions – notably HSBC and Barclays – the UK has been a first mover in the field of banking recovery and resolution. During 2009/10 regulators conducted a pilot project to develop Recovery and Resolution Plans (RRPs) with four – later six – large UK banks. In August 2011 the FSA published its plans for a new framework. This requires banks, building societies and investment firms to prepare (by late 2012) and maintain RRPs, which identify options to recover financial strength and viability should a firm come under severe stress (PRA 2013).

For this reason it also had a keen interest in reaching agreement on international guidelines on "living wills" for G-SIBs. In this they made common cause with the United States, enabling the Bank of England to leverage its influence at the global level by forming a close partnership with the Federal Reserve and the Federal Deposit Insurance Corporation (FDIC). In December 2012, the UK and US authorities published a joint paper on resolution strategies that endorsed the "single point of entry" (SPOE) approach to bank resolution. The Bank of England supported this strategy because many UK banks had begun to organize along the lines of a holding company structure and because of the extent of British bank holdings in the US. Trilateral negotiations were later initiated with FINMA, the Swiss Financial Market Supervisory Authority, reflecting the fact that US, UK and Swiss officials dominated many of the key working groups on the issue. Particularly important was the fact that the chair of the FSB Resolution Steering Group for most of this period was Paul Tucker, Deputy Governor of the Bank of England. It was this group that developed the first set of international standards for cross-border resolution which was approved by the G20 leaders at the Cannes Summit in 2011.

Having played a leading international role, the UK therefore had a direct stake in the outcome of negotiations in Brussels to implement these guidelines through EU legislation. The Bank Recovery and Resolution Directive (BRRD) is intended to reduce the risk to taxpayers of future bank failures and contribute to financial stability by setting out common rules for the "bail-in" of a failing bank, enabling national authorities to recapitalize a bank by writing-down liabilities and/or converting them to equity. It also establishes a network of national funds to cover resolution costs, guarantee deposits and lend to each other in an emergency.

In early 2013 the UK appeared isolated in opposing plans for mandatory pre-financed national resolution funds to pay for bank resolution costs and covering at least 1 percent of deposits. It had already levied a temporary £2.5 billion bank levy on bank balance sheets, requiring any new insurance scheme to be funded from borrowing or a higher levy. UK regulators also argued that the unused funds will serve as a drag on growth, risk creating moral hazard in banks and reduce the credibility of the bail-in tools. By contrast, most other member states, including traditional UK allies such as Sweden, agreed in principle on the need for national resolution funds or already had them in place (Financial Times 2013d). The final outcome was far from ideal but acceptable to the UK authorities: national regulators will establish resolution funds or introduce corresponding levies, which over the next decade should raise the equivalent of 1 percent of covered deposits (Financial Times 2013e).

The second area of disagreement concerned depositor preference. Brussels initially proposed that almost all creditors, including depositors, should share the pain equally if losses are imposed, with guarantee schemes reimbursing deposits under 100,000 euros. However, their position later shifted in line with Germany favouring US-style depositor preference, ensuring uninsured deposits are bailed-in last. The UK allied with France in opposing an overly prescriptive interpretation of depositor preference, demanding greater national flexibility to spare some creditors when using bail-in (Financial Times 2013f). On the whole the UK achieved its objective as the final compromise accepted the need for national discretion to recapitalize banks with public money, either after stress tests or during a systemic crisis, albeit subject to EU approval.

Regulation of market infrastructure

Unlike banking regulation, the UK's role in shaping post-crisis regulation of shadow banking activities (notably of market infrastructure and alternative investment fund managers) has been much less effective, despite having a disproportionately large stake in the outcome. Broadly speaking, this reflects a widely held view among UK regulators that the causes of the global financial crisis lay principally in the banking sector. It therefore sees little value in increasing the statutory regulation of shadow banking at the EU level, preferring to strengthen non-binding international guidelines instead. As with banking, this has led the UK to ally more often than not with the US, against France and Germany, the key difference being that the UK forms part of the market-making – rather than market-shaping – coalition (Quaglia 2012).

Prior to the global financial crisis, a high volume of derivatives were traded over-the-counter (OTC) rather than being cleared through central counterparties (CCPs). In September 2009, leaders at the G20 Pittsburg summit agreed that all over-the-counter derivative contracts should be traded on exchanges or electronic trading platforms, cleared through central counterparties, and reported to trade repositories (G20 2009a). UK regulators and the City of London were broadly content with this agreement and supported its translation into non-binding rules by IOSCO on the grounds that it would contribute further to market transparency.

It was in the interests of the US and UK for debate about the regulation of shadow banking to take place at the global level, for three reasons. First, regulators sought to secure international agreement in order to maintain a level playing field, addressing the concerns of the industry that increased regulation could push jobs away from London and New York (Helleiner/Pagliari 2010). Second, the US and UK wished to upload their own preferences for enhanced transparency and oversight at the global level as a way of deflecting calls for more stringent regulation at the European level (Fioretos 2010). The UK in particular has historically punched above its weight in the G20, FSB and ISOCO as it chairs many of the international-level committees tasked with drafting proposals. Finally, an additional safeguard is provided by the fact that the decision-making process in these informal global institutions tends to be consensus-based, preventing other countries – notably France and Germany – from tabling more stringent international standards (Prabhaker 2013).

The UK and London-based industry was less sure-footed when it came to the European level. With respect to OTCs, the Commission soon proposed to give the G20 agreement a legislative footing through a new European Market Infrastructure Regulation (EMIR). While there was broad consensus amongst national governments around the two main pillars (central clearing and report-ing), disagreement remained over specific elements linked to national sensitivi-ties, rooted in competitiveness concerns. For the UK there were two main areas of contention: open access and liquidity rules.

The UK, Netherlands and Sweden argued that the regulation should cover all derivatives, including those traded on stock exchanges, and strongly supported the Commission's moves to promote open access: exchanges would have to allow clients to use any central clearing party (CCP); and clearing houses would be obliged to accept any trade executed at another venue. Germany and Poland op-posed this "interoperability" as their stock exchanges operated vertical silo struc-tures incorporating trading and post-trading services, so had most to lose from open access rules. After considerable lobbying Germany was eventually success-ful in getting the Commission to back down and limited the scope of the direc-tive to unregulated OTC derivatives, in line with G20 commitments. In addition, although the final agreement gives CCPs access rights to transactions traded in a venue of execution, it does not imply full interoperability (Buckley et al. 2012).

On liquidity the UK opposed French moves to tighten rules for CCPs: in particular, the proposal that CCPs should have access to central bank liquidity in the currency of the trade being cleared, and that CCPs should be located in the euro zone and clear euro trades in order to access ECB liquidity. This threat-ened to damage London clearing houses, which are the largest in Europe: LCH. Clearnet and Ice Clear Europe. The UK did succeed in ensuring that the final text stated that CCP liquidity could come from a central bank and/or a credit-worthy commercial bank liquidity (Buckley et al. 2012). However, the victory proved short-lived as in 2011 the ECB published a paper proposing that clearing houses should be based in the euro zone if they handle more than 5 percent of the market in euro-denominated products. This was a serious blow to the UK which promptly took the case to the European Court of Justice on the grounds that this would create a two-tier single market. In March 2015 the ECJ ruled in the UK's favour in a further notable legal victory on financial regulation.

Regulation of alternative investment fund managers

The UK played a similarly high stakes game with respect to the regulation of the so-called "alternative" investment fund management (AIFM) sector: that is, pri-vate equity, venture capital and hedge funds. Again, it has more often than not allied with US to try to contain political pressure for action by seeking to upload the issue to the international level: a strategy that has largely failed.

New regulatory initiatives have been driven by France and Germany. For example, at the G8 summit in Heiligendamm in 2007 Germany called for greater transparency and oversight of hedge funds through mandatory registration in a global database and a greater supervisory role for the FSF. The US and UK were, however, willing to support only unbinding declarations of intention, while the EU also recorded its opposition to increased regulation. A compromise was agreed to strengthen the existing "indirect supervisory approach", publicly endorsed by all EU leaders in 2007 (Ecofin 2007). Soon afterwards, Angela Merkel signaled a shift of strategy, pledging to renew her push for EU regulation in the belief that agreement would strengthen Europe's position at the international level (Zimmerman 2010: 128).

A second turning point came in autumn 2008 at the international level. The G20 Summit in Washington in November 2008 acknowledged the limits of the self-governance regime and invited the industry to "bring forward proposals for a set of unified best practices" (G20 2008: 4). This was followed in April 2009 by the London Summit which called for direct regulation of hedge funds for the first time, with managers to be registered with national authorities and required the disclosure of appropriate information to allow the assessment of systemic risks (G20 2009b). The US and UK were at the forefront of the G20's "alarmed discovery" of the issue (Lutton 2008: 168). The crisis had shifted the terms of the regulatory debate decisively in favor of those pushing for direct regulation or "market-shaping" legislation (Quaglia 2010).

At the European level agreement on the Alternative Investment Fund Managers' Directive (AIFMD) was reached in November 2010 and marked the EU's earliest legislative response to the financial crisis. By contrast with CRD4, however, it was clear to most observers that the UK's primary motive for doing so was economic self-interest. As home to nearly 85 percent of the European hedge fund industry (TheCityUK 2012) and 13 percent of global investments in private equity (TheCityUK 2010), the UK would be impacted disproportionately by the new directive and so regulators sought to minimize the perceived adaptational cost of downloading.

The UK's initial strategy of seeking to render EU-level initiatives redundant by uploading the issue to the international level backfired. Instead, the Commission responded to the G20 agreement by issuing a Communication in early 2009 which pledged to introduce a harmonized regulatory and supervisory framework for the AIFM sector as a matter of priority (European Commission 2009: 5). Ironically this was justified as necessary to meet the political commitments made by the G20 to mitigate the risks to financial instability by extending regulation and oversight to all systemically important financial institutions, instruments and markets (G20 2009). Under pressure from France and Germany, and to secure the support of the Socialist group in the European Parliament for his re-appointment, Commission President Manuel Barroso intervened to ensure that a draft directive on the regulation of the alternative fund management industry was published by April 2009.[6] The draft was rushed out without the usual preparatory work and sought to create a single harmonized regulation covering all alternative investment funds. Although the early EU passport proposal was welcomed by the industry, last-minute amendments imposed stringent requirements on third-country access, disclosure, leverage and depositary banks (Woll 2012).

In response the predominantly UK-based private equity and hedge fund industry launched a concerted lobbying campaign in an attempt to amend the draft directive (Buckley/Howarth 2011). Although the UK and hedge fund industry supported plans for an EU passport, a particular priority was to secure agreement on less prescriptive third-country standards, supported by Ireland, the Czech Republic, Malta, Sweden and Austria. US intervention proved critical in paving the way for eventual agreement. US Treasury Secretary Timothy Geithner made his concerns about third-country access clear in two letters in 2010. Although there was no threat of retaliation, the industry also warned that EU funds could face reprisals in Congress in response to discrimination against US funds (Woll 2012).

The final deal was brokered by the FSA during the final stages of the trialogue negotiations in July 2010 based on a weaker definition of regulatory "equivalence" closer to the UK position. The outcome was a significant improvement on the original Commission proposal as the UK succeeded in securing the removal of the most controversial or unworkable provisions in alliance with the Netherlands and the Nordic states. On the specifics of the directive, there was a broad consensus that the UK secured a higher *de minimis* exemption for private equity and in contributing to the relaxation of the third-country provisions: specifically, the continuation of the private placement regime until 2018 and relaxed equivalence rules for non-EU domiciled funds. In return it accepted a delay in the introduction of EU passports for non-EU funds. The leverage, transparency and disclosure rules were also far less prescriptive than initially proposed, although the UK was less satisfied with the outcome on the depositary rules and remuneration restrictions. The larger philosophical defeat, however, was failing to prevent the EU from designing a one-size-fits-all piece of legislation to cover a range of highly diverse financial sectors.

---

6 Private interview, 2014.

Conclusion

The chapter concludes that the UK's role in shaping the post-crisis financial regulatory agenda has been an important one. However, its record in securing favourable regulatory outcomes has varied depending on the nature of the institutional context and the policy issue. At the international level, for instance, the UK has sought to play the role of global pace-setter, particularly in relation to banking resolution and capital requirements. Its leading position in largely technocratic international institutions such as the Financial Stability Board (FSB) has consequently enabled it to "punch above its weight" in uploading its preferences and shaping new global regulatory standards. By contrast, the UK's influence in the more politicized environment of the EU is greatly diminished on account of declining engagement in Brussels, fuelled by increasing euroscepticism in Parliament and the government's pledge to hold an in/out referendum on EU membership in 2017. This has left UK regulators exposed and consequently facing higher adaptational costs with respect to EU legislation on capital requirements, alternative investment funds, derivatives trading and bank resolution. Its capacity for pace-setting therefore remains conditional on alliance-building with like-minded states, most often with the US and Switzerland (at the international level), and with the Netherlands and the Nordic states (at the EU level). The durable nature of the transatlantic alliance, which contrasts with the ad hoc or "promiscuous bilateralism" of its European relationships (Smith/Tsatsas 2002), goes some way to explaining its mixed fortunes in the three-level game.

The nature of the policy issue also proved critical. The UK has been most successful where it has been able to take the moral high ground by distancing itself from the preferences of the City of London and pushing for much tougher regulatory standards, such as on bank capital requirements. By contrast, where the UK is seen to be more explicitly defending its economic self-interest, for example with regard to private equity and derivatives, its moral authority and powers of political persuasion are much weaker.

Finally, the account of the UK banking reform process demonstrates that although EU and international negotiations have provided a backdrop, the principal drivers of structural reform remain domestic. These domestic pressures have at times given rise to a series of contradictory objectives, such as those that the ICB was forced to reconcile. They have also caused the UK to pursue its own autonomous agenda on structural reform, giving rise to claims that it has become a global outlier. In this sense the journey to ringfencing has been a historically contingent process, the outcome of which was determined by the particular configuration of (mainly) domestic political forces – actors, institutions and ideas – at a particular point in time.

References

Bloomberg, 2013: UK should shun "difficult" Volcker Rule, says John Vickers. In: *Bloomberg*, 16 January 2013. <www.bloomberg.com/news/2013-01-16/u-k-should-shun-difficult-volcker-rule-says-john-vickers.html> (accessed 14 November 2013)

Buckley, James/David Howarth, 2011: Internal Market: Regulating the so-called "Vultures of Capitalism". In: *Journal of Common Market Studies* 49 (Annual Review), 123–143.

Buckley, James/David Howarth/Lucia Quaglia, 2012: Internal Market: The Ongoing Struggle to "Protect" Europe from Its Money Men. In: *Journal of Common Market Studies* 50 (Annual Review), 99–115.

Economic and Financial Affairs (Ecofin), 2007: *Council of the European Union Press Release: 2798th Council Meeting, 8 May 2007.* Brussels: Council of the European Union.

European Commission, 2009: *Driving European recovery. Communication for the Spring European Council, Brussels, COM(2009) 114 final, 4 March 2009.* Brussels: Commission of the European Communities.

Financial Times, 2010: Cable weighs "crude" surgery on banks. In: *Financial Times,* 8 September 2010.

——, 2012: UK fights Brussels over bank capital rules. In: *Financial Times,* 1 April 2012.

——, 2013a: Vickers calls for doubling of bank capital levels. In: *Financial Times,* 8 September 2013.

——, 2013b: Tough UK bank break-up threat revived by coalition. In: *Financial Times,* 1 October 2013.

——, 2013c: Paul Tucker signals all banks will need to go beyond ringfencing. In: *Financial Times,* 8 October 2013.

——, 2013d: UK Treasury fears £9bn bank crisis fund. In: *Financial Times,* 30 April 2013.

——, 2013e: EU reaches landmark deal on failed banks. In: *Financial Times,* 12 December 2013.

——, 2013f: Cyprus bailout trauma clouds EU bank bail-in plans. In: *Financial Times,* 12 May 2013.

Fioretos, Orfeo, 2010: Capitalist diversity and the international regulation of hedge funds. In: *Review of International Political Economy* 17(4), 696–723.

G20 (Group of Twenty), 2008: *Declaration from the Washington Summit,* 15 November 2008. Toronto: University of Toronto.
<www.g20.utoronto.ca/2008/2008declaration1115.html>

——, 2009a: *The Leaders' Statement, Pittsburgh Summit,* 25 September 2009. Pittsburgh: G20. <https://g20.org/wp-content/uploads/2014/12/Pittsburgh_Declaration_0.pdf>

——, 2009b: *Communiqué from the London Summit,* 2 April 2009. London: G20.
<www.imf.org/external/np/sec/pr/2009/pdf/g20_040209.pdf>

Helleiner, Eric/Stefano Pagliari, 2010: Between The Storms: Patterns in Global Financial Governance, 2001–2007. In: Geoffrey Underhill/Jasper Blom/Daniel Mügge (eds.), *Global Financial Integration Thirty Years On: From Reform to Crisis.* Cambridge: Cambridge University Press, 42–57.

Howarth, David/Lucia Quaglia, 2013: Banking on Stability: The Political Economy of New Capital Requirements in the European Union. In: *Journal of European Integration* 35(3), 333–346.

Independent Commission on Banking (ICB), 2010: *Terms of Reference, The National Archives*. London: ICB. <http://bankingcommission.independent.gov.uk/terms-of-reference> (accessed 6 June 2013)

——, 2011: *Final Report, Recommendations*, 12 September 2011. London: ICB.

International Monetary Fund (IMF), 2013: *Creating a Safer Financial System: Will the Volcker, Vickers, and Liikanen Structural Measures Help?* IMF Staff Discussion Note, 14 May 2013. Washington, DC: IMF.

James, Scott (forthcoming): The Domestic Politics of Financial Regulation: Informal Ratification Games and the EU Capital Requirement Negotiations. Forthcoming in: *New Political Economy.*

Kapstein, Ethan B., 1989: Resolving the regulator's dilemma: International coordination of banking regulations. In: *International Organization* 43(2), 323–347.

Kay, John, 2011: The nightmare of taking on "too big to fail". In: *Financial Times,* 12 April 2011.

Lilico, Andrew, 2012: The FSA is largely to blame for slow lending growth. In: *The Telegraph,* Andrew Lilico Blog, 14 August 2012. <http://blogs.telegraph.co.uk/finance/andrewlilico/100019481/the-fsa-is-largely-to-blame-for-slow-lending-growth> (accessed 7 November 2013)

Lutton, David John, 2008: The European Union, Financial Crises and the Regulation of Hedge Funds: A Policy Cul-de-Sac or a Policy Window? In: *Journal of Contemporary European Research* 4(3), 167–178.

Prabhakar, Rahul, 2013: *Varieties of Regulation: How States Pursue and Set International Financial Standards.* The Global Economic Governance Programme (GEG) Working Paper 2013/86, June 2013. Oxford: University of Oxford.

Prudential Regulation Authority (PRA), 2013: *Supervisory tools: Recovery and Resolution Plans.* London: PRA. <www.bankofengland.co.uk/pra/Pages/publications/recoveryandresolution.aspx> (accessed 11 November 2013)

Putnam, Robert D., 1988: Diplomacy and Domestic Politics: The Logic of Two-Level Games. In: *International Organization* 42(3), 427–460.

Quaglia, Lucia, 2010: Completing the single market in financial services: The politics of competing advocacy coalitions. In: *Journal of European Public Policy* 17(7), 1007–1023.

——, 2012: The "Old" and "New" Politics of Financial Services Regulation in the European Union. In: *New Political Economy* 17(4), 515–535.

Smith, Julie/Mariana Tsatsas, 2002: *The New Bilateralism: The UK's Relations in the EU.* London: Royal Institute of International Affairs.

TheCityUK, 2010: *Private Equity 2010*, August. London: TheCityUK.

——, 2012: *Hedge Funds 2012*, March. London: TheCityUK.

Woll, Cornelia, 2012: Lobbying under Pressure: The Effect of Salience on European Union Hedge Fund Regulation. In: *Journal of Common Market Studies* 51(3), 555–572.

Zimmerman, Hubert, 2010: Varieties of Global Financial Governance? British and German Approaches to Financial Market Regulation. In: Eric Helleiner/Stefano Pagliari/Hubert Zimmerman (eds.), *Global Finance in Crisis: The Politics of International Regulatory Change.* London: Routledge, 121–136.

7   Germany in the Context of the Multilevel Reform Process

Roman Goldbach and Hubert Zimmermann

Introduction

Overshadowed by the dramatic events in the sovereign debt markets of the eurozone, the reform of financial regulation in Germany has received relatively little public and scholarly attention over the past few years. After the escalation of the financial crisis in 2008, German policy-makers proclaimed a comprehensive overhaul of financial regulation at the international, European, and national levels a core political project for the years to come (Zimmermann 2009). There was a lasting cross-party consensus that in the future no financial product and no financial actor should remain unregulated. In a prior assessment of the pattern of regulatory reform in Germany until 2011, Stefan Handke and Hubert Zimmermann depicted the relatively slow and hesitant pattern of reform in Germany, despite all political declarations and the obvious need for comprehensive regulatory steps (Handke/Zimmermann 2012). Based on the empirical case studies of financial market supervision, bank restructuring, and deposit insurance reform, they argued that a pattern of institutional layering and drift was the most accurate description of the regulatory process in Germany (see also Zimmermann 2013). The limited extent of regulatory interventions in the financial system was due mainly to entrenched resistance by political actors, in particular the *Länder* governments. However, it was obvious in 2011 that the gestation and implementation of many reform efforts at the international and European levels was still at quite an early stage.

This raises the question of whether additional and possibly more radical reforms have trickled down in the meantime from the international and European levels, and have changed the dynamics of regulatory reform in Germany. Has the piecemeal implementation of international rules that was observable in 2011 changed the content of such rules, leading to more regulatory divergence instead of creating a degree of convergence that minimizes the potential of regulatory arbitrage by financial market actors? The Financial Times recently lamented, in a summary of regulatory efforts since Lehman, that global unity was increasingly breaking down, even in the case of already agreed measures, such as the capital standards contained in Basel III. The newspaper quoted a senior bank executive, who declared: "It's a bloody nightmare. The regulators have no respect for one another at all. Each country is looking after itself" (FT, 2 April 2012: 7). This increases compliance costs for financial actors and, even worse, augments the risk of another financial crisis, given the expansion of the shadow banking sector. Many commentators identified Germany as one of the main culprits in this respect (Wall Street Journal, 28 July 2010). German politics of regulatory reform are important not only because of this alleged role as roadblock, particularly on Basel III, but also because the country undisputedly has a major influence on European financial reform. The overall success of the efforts to make the global financial system more stable hinges on European and American policy convergence.

This chapter looks at Germany's place in the multilevel dynamic of global financial regulation. What has shaped Germany's performance in the implementation of international initiatives? What role has the country played in pursuing its own preferences at international and European levels and what explains the emphasis on particular reforms to the exclusion of others? We argue that Germany has privileged those regulatory reforms that shield the traditional bank-based structure of its financial system and that may help the state to reassert its authority in setting the basic rules of the game. International initiatives that threaten to erode the institutional equilibrium in the German financial system and the competitiveness of traditional structures have been resisted. The attempts to upload German reforms to the international level have mostly failed. However, by influencing the transposition of international rules into European and national laws, and by uploading their own blueprints to the European level, the Germans have managed – up until now – to pursue their own preferences to a significant extent. Like the other chapters in this book, we will look at selected regulatory measures, specifically the attempts to separate commercial and investment banking, the new rules regarding the restructuring of banks, the treatment of OTC derivatives, and the implementation of Basel III.

Banking regulation: Coping with the global pressure for Basel III

In banking regulation, the German authorities have constantly slowed and blocked progress on the development and adoption of global rules, particularly Basel III, and, subsequently, their European adoption, CRD IV, and CRR (Capital Requirements Regulation; for details on the content of these international and European standards see Mayntz and Quaglia in this volume). In terms of uploading, the Germans have attempted to pursue specific interests in a two-stage process: first, in the attempt to water down the content of Basel III rules and to delay their adoption/implementation schedules in the Basel Committee on Banking Supervision (BCBS); second, in coalition with the French authorities, by altering the EU adoption of these rules.

A number of studies have described how the Basel III rules left continental European banks relatively worse off vis-à-vis the banks of the United States, the United Kingdom, and other jurisdictions (see, for example, Young 2014: 372–375). It is, thus, not surprising that the United States and the United Kingdom pressed for higher capital standards and wanted short implementation periods, while Germany, France, and Japan called for revisions that took into consideration state banks and smaller regional banks (Goldbach/Kerwer 2012: 251–252). The conflict over the costs of the reform also split the members of the EU into two opposing camps, with the United Kingdom in one, and most of Continental Europe in the other. This also explains why there was no agreed EU position on these matters.

Basel III negotiations

Already during the Basel II negotiations, German authorities had fought for the recognition of specific features of its banking sector, in particular its publicly-owned banks (Goldbach 2015: 85–134).[1] Public sector banks play a crucial role in the national economy because they account for about half of all lending to German companies (FT, 7 September 2010: 17). The veto of German politicians and regulators had already complicated and prolonged Basel II deliberations substantially and resulted in the inclusion of specific internal ratings-based risk calculation models, specific treatment for small and medium-sized

---

1 Germany has a peculiar three-pillar banking system, which consists of private commercial banks, public sector savings banks and their associated *Landesbanken*, and cooperative banks (FSB 2014: 36; Busch 2009).

enterprises (SMEs), and several small bank–specific options (Goldbach 2015: 85–134). The same German dynamic – in which the public sector and other small banks lobbied the *Bundestag's* finance committee, which, in turn forced regulators to renegotiate on those banks' behalf – was repeated in the context of Basel III. This time, however, German negotiators achieved much more limited success. This can be ascribed to the global negotiating circumstances in the Basel Committee: against the background of the most severe financial crisis in six decades, policy-makers were under intense time pressure to adopt Basel III – the cornerstone of global reform efforts. A particularly strong push for the Basel III reforms was exercised by the US and UK authorities, which had initiated substantial domestic reforms and now aimed to level the international playing field by globally harmonizing regulatory change. The US/UK-led push in combination with public pressure for reform made it difficult for German and other European countries to realize their specific preferences – in contrast to what was possible during the extensive Basel II negotiations.

In July 2010, when the Governors and Heads of Supervision (GHOS, the body to which the BCBS is subordinated) agreed on the basic elements of the new Basel III rules, Germany was alone among the 27 members in saying it could not agree to tighter definitions of capital (FT, 7 September 2010: 17). The opposition was rooted in German public sector banks' heavy reliance on so-called "silent participations", which were defined as unsuitable for the top-quality capital category of tier 1 core capital under Basel III. The VÖB, the association of public sector banks, warned of "dramatic consequences" for the German economy (FT, 7 September 2010: 17).

Thus, German banks and authorities had to get it right once public scrutiny had ebbed away. Following the consultative Basel III paper of December 2009, and, furthermore, since the final agreement on the new Basel II.5 and Basel III standards in October 2010 (and the revision in June 2011), attempts to get regulators to soften adoption and implementation were very successful (see, for example, Howarth/Quaglia 2013b; Bloomberg 2014; The Economist 2013). Scholars and journalists have already pointed to the general trend of postponing actual reform by means of lengthy transition periods from initially end-2012 to January 1, 2019 (Howarth/Quaglia 2013b; The Economist 2013; Young 2013; Goldbach/Kerwer 2012), which Young (2013) has identified as a distinct new strategy on the part of the financial industry. Beyond this general phenomenon, political and industry pressure have resulted in major ex post reversals in almost all areas of regulatory change.

The list of reversals begins with the setting of the minimum capital requirements at a considerably lower level than initially envisioned. The finally agreed 8 percent (10.5 percent including the capital conservation buffer) was the result of opposition from continental European regulators and politicians – Germany even threatened to veto the agreement (Bloomberg 2013a; Howarth/Quaglia 2013b: 11). According to Young (2014: 374), a coalition of the United States, the United Kingdom, and Switzerland favored 9 percent, but Germany and France opposed this and aimed for 6 percent. The 2010 negotiations led to a watering down of the initial proposal. As a result, 8 percent became the ratio, while the new rules were to be phased in from January 2013 through to January 2019.[2]

The Germans were also successful in watering down the rules during extensive rounds of refinement. Thus, the ex post reversals continued with the revisions of the liquidity framework, which weakened the Liquidity Coverage Ratio (LCR), the new element that forces banks to have liquid assets available according to predefined guidelines (The Economist 2013; Bloomberg 2013b). In addition to several other substantial technical easements (Goldbach 2015: 157–158), the calculation of the LCR rules now allow all investment-grade corporate bonds. This helps universal banks with a large amount of corporate deposits and corporate credit lines, in particular French and German ones.[3] The latter were expected to struggle to meet the draft standards by 2015 (FT, 8 January 2013: 15). Moreover, regulators postponed the deadline of meeting the requirements. Banks now have to meet merely 60 percent of the LCR obligations by 2015, while the full extent will be phased in annually through 2019, increasing by 10 percentage points each year.

Furthermore, the minimum leverage ratio also became subject to substantial revisions (Howarth/Quaglia 2013b: 12). French and German banks, regulators, and politicians were particularly aggressive in demanding these changes, as their banks' leverage ratios tend to be substantially lower than those of their US counterparts (Howarth/Quaglia 2013b; The Economist 2014). As a result of the European pressure, transition periods were lengthened and the formula for calculating them diluted.

This is politically relevant, as "[a] rough calculation suggests that [the leverage ratio requirements] have been loosened just enough to allow most big European banks to pass the 3 percent test. Without the committee's help as many

2 Moreover, the definition of capital was watered down: American banks were allowed to continue counting some mortgage-linked assets as equity, European banks their minority stakes in other financial firms, and Japanese institutes their deferred tax benefits. As Bloomberg (2013a) reported, "[t]he last crisis showed that such assets failed to provide a buffer against losses."

3 The revision extends the range of corporate debt that banks can use, allowing securities with a credit rating of as low as BBB– to be eligible for the LCR. The 2010 version of the rule stipulated that such debt must have a rating of at least AA–; banks would also be allowed to use highly rated residential mortgage-backed securities and some equities (Bloomberg 2013b; The Economist 2013).

as three-quarters of Europe's big banks might have failed the test" (The Economist 2014). Moreover, there is still plenty of room for further dilution, as the BCBS "will carefully monitor the impact of these disclosure requirements. The final calibration of the leverage ratio, and any further adjustments to its definition, will be completed by 2017, with a view to migrating to a Pillar 1 (minimum capital requirement) treatment on 1 January 2018" (BCBS 2014). In other words, German, French, and other interests succeeded in keeping the ratio in Pillar 2 and in ensuring a potential further softening at a later stage (the Pillar 2 approach refers to the qualitative supervisory assessment of a bank's leverage, in contrast to a Pillar 1 approach, according to which banks have to meet the quantitative target set; Pillar 2 approaches grant more room for lenient supervision).

Finally, in coalition with the French government, the German Chancellor's Office successfully pushed for the lifting of limits on the double counting of capital in banks' insurance subsidiaries, a model widespread in Germany and particularly common in France (FT, 23 January 2012: 2). This was initiated by a joint paper of the German and French finance ministers, Wolfgang Schäuble and François Baroin.

Reopening the Basel III package in the EU negotiations on CRD IV

These adaptations were substantial, but lagged far behind what had been possible during the Basel II negotiations and failed to meet many of the German actors' preferences. They faced an altered strategic setting in global regulation: first, there was less room for securing specific German interests in Basel; second, European regulations grew in relevance due to their direct application in German law and regulation. As a consequence, German actors adapted their strategies to reduce their disadvantages from the global Basel III standards. In the past, the jurisdictional adoption and implementation of the soft-law Basel standards had repeatedly opened the door for competitiveness-boosting lenient regulation and supervision (Chey 2006; Walter 2007). German actors thus had two opportunities to change the effect of Basel III rules on them: uploading their policy preferences into the EU rules that would eventually be binding for German authorities, as well as downloading those rules in a lenient manner in the context of German regulatory implementation and supervision.

In contrast to Germany's Basel II strategy,[4] its authorities this time pursued a renegotiation of crucial Basel III issues within the EU context. Another reason for this new strategy, in addition to the disappointing Basel contents, is the changing legal approach of the EU. It adopted the standards through the third renewal of the Capital Requirements Directive (CRD IV), but also adopted important Basel III elements through a Capital Requirements Regulation (CRR; see Quaglia, this volume).[5] It has direct effect in EU member states and reduces the room for lenient regulatory implementation in national jurisdictions.[6]

Also, in mid-2011, the savings and cooperative banks changed their previously broadly supportive view of Basel III and started to lobby against the unchanged transposition of the Basel rules into European and German law (Handelsblatt 2011). Representatives of SMEs, German cities and counties joined the critical chorus. These concerns were taken up by the Upper Chamber, the *Bundesrat,* which, in a statement of February 10, 2012, supported all the points made by the actors just cited. The chamber argued that Basel III should be implemented in Europe by way of a directive instead of a directly applicable regulation. This would give national legislative authorities the chance to influence the implementation process. It also argued for the exclusion of banks under a certain size from the leverage ratio and other onerous standards.

This new government strategy was successfully pursued in liaison with the French government. They effectively lowered capital requirements for continental European banks through the watering down of what counts as core tier 1 capital under the CRR (Young 2014: 380–381). Several hybrid capital forms, in particular German banks' favored silent participations, are now allowed (up to a limit and only under restrictive conditions), minority interests are recognized, investments in unconsolidated financial firms are allowed and so on.

Likewise, success could be celebrated with regard to the leverage ratio (Howarth/Quaglia 2013a; Young 2014: 381–382). As a result of the Franco-German pressure, the European Commission has extended the deadline for mandatory reporting of the leverage ratio and has left open many issues in the CRR, which the European Banking Authority (EBA) is expected to amend once more information is available.

---

4 Shortly before closing the Basel II deal, German regulators pushed for a direct EU adoption of Basel II as developed in the BCBS without much adaptation. The reason was that German negotiators had achieved an agreement strongly in line with their political and economic interests. They wanted to avoid new deliberations at the EU level, where Germany had a weaker negotiating position due to the EU's qualified majority voting (Bundestag Finance Committee 2003).

5 While the former includes the stipulations regarding the supervisory structure of the national authorities, the latter encompasses all regulations that affect banks in the EU directly.

6 This is part of the political goal of achieving a single rulebook for EU banking regulation.

Particularly lenient adaptations were also achieved with regard to LCR implementation in the EU. Easement for trade finance transactions was introduced through the possibility of fully accounting them under the EU LCR. Furthermore, the EBA received authority to construct the list of eligible instruments, subject to European and national specificities (Young 2014: 382–383).

Regulatory adoption, supervision, and additional measures

The formal transposition of the Basel III standards into German law took place on January 1, 2014. German authorities' possibilities in pursuing individual regulatory strategies are limited due to the increasingly invasive EU reach through the direct regulatory force of the CRR, as well as the EBA's far-reaching authority (see Quaglia, this volume). In other words, the CRR narrowed the room for maneuver and forced a substantial alteration of the German banking act (*Kreditwesengesetz*; Bundesbank 2013). More specifically, many paragraphs have been replaced with reference to the CRR.

Nevertheless, the possibilities of cosmetic compliance in the form of lenient implementation and supervision are abundant (Goldbach 2015: 85–134). One particularly complex and important example is the treatment of hybrid capital in German public and community banks: according to the 13 criteria to be met by assets counted as core capital, silent participations would not count in this category. However, the EU "substance over form" approach allows room for maneuver: the German Bundesbank has stated that specific exceptions in favor of German capital instruments will therefore remain eligible as core capital, although in a "clearly limited amount" (Bundesbank 2013: 59). Thus, the capability to pursue regulatory boosting of German banks' competitiveness is limited. However, the precise degree of faithful adoption remains to be seen, in the context of the application of the rules, the exact application of the optional capital buffers, and the reviews of the leverage ratio and LCR at the European level.

Bank resolution and the eurozone banking union

Germany was among the first countries to undertake a comprehensive reform of its rules for the restructuring of failed banks. The main reason was the painful experience with failed banks, such as IKB or Hypo Real Estate, which forced a costly state-sponsored bail-out. The restructuring process was complicated by rules protecting the rights of private stakeholders who demanded compensation for all their losses. A new law was deemed necessary that ensured that shareholders and creditors of a failing institution would share the cost with the taxpayer (Bertinchamp 2010). The CDU/CSU and FDP coalition in power between 2009 and 2013 accorded a high priority to this project. Interestingly, they based their plans on a blueprint presented by SPD ministers Peer Steinbrück and Brigitte Zypries (Justice) during the reign of the Grand Coalition of 2005–2009. In March 2010, a key issues paper formulated the core provisions of the government's ideas: the creation of an orderly procedure for the restructuring and wind-down of troubled banks, a bank levy to establish a privately financed safety net for future emergencies, and new rules on the pay and conduct of employees of financial institutions (BMF 2010). The burden on the state and the taxpayer would be reduced, while private shareholders would participate in the cost of failed investment strategies. Troubled banks would first attempt their own restructuring process, under the supervision of an administrator. If this process failed, the German supervisory authority BaFin would be allowed to transfer assets to a "good bank", which could be sold. Investors would be left with the rest, a "bad bank". In addition to this procedure, a bank levy was introduced. Banks were expected to pay parts of their profits into a restructuring fund with a target size of 70 billion euros. The German bank levy and the resolution provisions were among the first in the OECD. They preceded the "Key Attributes of Effective Resolution Regimes for Financial Institutions", that were issued by the FSB in 2011, and they anticipated important aspects of these recommendations (FSB 2011; see also Mayntz, this volume). In a recent interview, the head of BaFin, Elke König, said that Germany had been able to shape the international debate to an important degree, not least because BaFin headed the FSB working group on those questions (Bafin 2014). However, we found no further evidence that Germany was particularly active at the international level (for the role of the United States as "pacesetter" in this area, see the chapter by Ryan and Ziegler, this volume).

The German banking industry, notably Deutsche Bank and the Bundesverband deutscher Banken (the association of German private banks) strongly attacked the bank tax, as well as new rules on the pay of top executives, alleging that the law went far beyond internationally envisioned rules. But their lobbying effort was futile. In October 2010, the law passed the *Bundestag*, with the SPD abstaining. The *Bundesrat* had to vote on the law, too, and some *Länder* governments objected to the fact that the bank tax would also fall on small cooperative banks, which had survived the crisis unscathed. The *Länder* managed to have their demands satisfied in the implementing legislation: large banks would have to pay a higher percentage of their annual profits, whereas small banks were exempted. Since January 2011, the Law on the Restructuration and Orderly

Dismantling of Credit Institutions *(Restrukturierungsgesetz)* has been in force. Its basic philosophy was a reaffirmation of the official German interpretation of the financial crisis, which held that the three-pillar system of German banks was not to blame for the difficulties and that its structure had to be preserved. In essence, the law strengthened this pattern notwithstanding the pressure towards convergence resulting from international and European interdependence. The law was among the first of its kind in Europe, and Germany hoped that it provided a blueprint for similar resolution mechanisms in other countries.

However, contrary to Germany's intentions, the euro crisis forced the Europeanisation of this mechanism. In June 2012, the members of the eurozone agreed to create a banking union (Quaglia 2014). In September 2012, the European Commission published a blueprint arguing for a European resolution authority which would work together with national regulators. National bailout funds were to be Europeanized. Under the Commission's proposal, a "single resolution board" would carry out restructurings of all eurozone banks that experienced financial problems. A shared fund financed by contributions from banks would finance the process, which was to be dominated by the Commission (see Quaglia, this volume).

Germany had initially signaled its approval of a banking union broadly along these lines but now back-pedaled and announced that with its proposals the Commission had overstepped its authority. According to the German authorities, the Commission should not have powers to decide on winding down banks under current treaties; decision-making in the resolution board should give member states, especially the larger ones, veto rights; and the single resolution fund should not use money built up by national funds (Wall Street Journal 2013). Reflecting sharp protests by German banks, the governing parties CDU/CSU and FDP, though open to a European resolution regime, also were strictly against a joint fund that would be created by using the money of national funds. According to them, the funds should originate from the European Stability Mechanism, but only once there was a working European banking supervision (Joint Statement 2012). Until then, national governments were to be responsible. There also should be no common deposit guarantee. And in accordance with the long-standing opposition to the loss of policy control over the vast savings and cooperative banking sector, Germany wanted to limit European oversight to only the biggest banks in Germany (Deutsche Bank 2012). This stance was opposed by the few large banks falling under a potential European regime, but they were easily outweighed by the savings and cooperative banks (Bundesverband 2012). Overall, the German government wanted to push the Europeanization of banking resolution to the distant future, possibly after a change of the European treaties (Gordon/Ringe 2014: 30).

Due to these numerous complaints, negotiations came to a standstill. Most observers did not expect progress until the results of the October 2013 federal elections in Germany were in (Businessweek 2013). The SPD had pronounced its support for a European resolution authority while being adamantly against the use of taxpayer's money for the restructuring of banks. This meant excluding the ESM from the procedure (Rinke/Sobolewski 2013).

When it became clear that Germany would be governed by a Grand Coalition after the 2013 elections, the lingering resistance against a European restructuring authority came to an end. The SPD would now formally become a leading force in German regulatory policy-making and its support for a European resolution authority was well known. In fact, during its opposition years, the SPD had already been the major policy entrepreneur in Germany in this area. Due to the unreliability of Merkel's coalition partners – the FDP and the CSU – the SPD was needed to get various euro rescue measures approved by the parliament. As compensation, the SPD demanded that the government be more proactive in financial regulation (Zimmermann 2014). In their coalition talks, both sides agreed on the need for a European solution. The CDU/CSU gave up its insistence that a network of national resolution authorities rather than a single resolution mechanism should determine bank resolutions. The SPD agreed to the use of the ESM. However, it was supposed to come into play only as an instrument of last resort once the ECB had started the common supervision of European banks (DGAP-Medientreff 2013).

Based on this understanding between the governing parties, Germany managed to upload its preferences: the Single Resolution Board would resolve only the banks that were directly supervised by the ECB, that is, the 130 biggest European banks. During a transition period national funds would still be responsible; afterwards mutualization would happen according to a separate treaty. The Germans also managed to obtain their preferences regarding who should bear the cost of bailouts. First, shareholders, creditors, and big depositors will be liable, followed by the new EU bank rescue fund. Only after these sources are exhausted would taxpayers in the bank's home country have to contribute financial support, and only after that would the European Stability Mechanism (ESM) be used, under strict conditions. Its crucial role in the euro crisis permitted Germany to decisively influence the shape of the future European resolution regime. There was a clear spill-over from the increasing clout of Germany in the policy to save the euro, and its influence in shaping financial regulation in the EU. The downside was that the Europeanization of bank restructuring was forced on Germany by the functional necessities of preserving the common currency.

The German debate on ring-fencing

Among the most frequently cited structural causes of the escalation of the financial crisis were the ramifications of the 1999 repeal in the United States of the Glass-Steagall Act of 1933, which had separated commercial from investment banking. Trades by universal banks with their own assets (proprietary trading) were seen as core factors in the pre-crisis process of amassing risky positions, leading to "taxpayer-sponsored" bailouts. However, despite the prevalence of universal banks in Germany and the fact that the most serious cases of bank failure had resulted from proprietary trading, the introduction of such a separation was not seriously discussed in Germany in the immediate aftermath of the crisis. This contrasts with the international arena: the so-called Volcker Rule was proposed in the United States very early in the regulatory process and became part of the 2010 Dodd-Frank Act (see Ryan and Ziegler, this volume); the Vickers Report, which separated retail-banking from the rest of banking activities, was published in Britain in 2011 (see James, this volume); and already in 2009 the OECD advocated in a report the separation of risky activities via a holding model (Blundell-Wignall/Wehinger/Slovik 2009). Despite such international initiatives, the German government remained inactive on this issue and concentrated on other regulatory measures.

However, in late 2011 the international impetus was picked up by Germany's Social Democrats who suddenly began to advocate the topic strongly (Steinberg/Somnitz 2012). In an interview with Der Spiegel in October 2011, SPD Chairman Sigmar Gabriel, referring to the OECD, advocated the separation of investment from commercial banking (Der Spiegel 2011; SZ 2011). Although the proposal was picked up by the media, the CDU/CSU/FDP government balked at the suggestion, although it refrained from rejecting it outright. In response to a long parliamentary questionnaire prepared by SPD MPs soon afterwards, the government responded in a non-committal way, referring to the initiatives under way at the European level, which preempted the need for a national response (Bundestag 2012). However, the SPD continued to push the idea. In September 2012, former finance minister and chancellor candidate Peer Steinbrück published an SPD memorandum on regulatory reform, in which he demanded a strict separation of client-based services and proprietary trading in larger banks (Steinbrück 2012). One month later, the Liikanen report, which advocated a strong separation of retail and trading units in banks, was published by the European Commission, prompting widespread opposition among German banks, which vowed to defend Germany's universal banking system (VÖB 2012).

This acted as a wake-up call for the government, which hurriedly started to draft its own law. However, modeled on a French precedent, a relatively soft

version was being prepared, allegedly with the help of Deutsche Bank (Handelsblatt 2012a). In January 2013, the Finance Ministry published the draft bill.
Unlike the Liikanen report, the German draft foresaw no complete separation of
commercial and investment units, and suggested the creation of common holdings with separate capital. In particular, so-called "market-making" deals – deals
undertaken on behalf of clients – were to be excluded from the separation. In
addition, the threshold above which banks were eligible for the provisions was so
high that they would apply only to the very largest institutions, essentially only
Deutsche Bank (BBVA 2014). Press reports speculated that the main objective
of the initiative was to deprive the SPD of an election issue for the 2013 campaign (FT 2013a). In fact, the SPD heavily criticized the proposal as being far
too timid (Handelsblatt 2012a). The European Commission joined in this criti-
cism and asked France and Germany not to fall short of the more comprehensive
reforms envisioned by the Liikanen report (Handelsblatt 2012b).

According to the Financial Times, the rationale behind the soft German version was primarily to preserve the structures of Germany's universal banking
system (FT, 31 January 2013: 4). Despite the limited scope of the plan, German
banks commented that they were unhappy with it (FT 2013a, 2013b), especially because of a requirement to move lending to hedge funds, private equity and
high-frequency traders to the separated parts. Even smaller banks argued that
the provision of the whole range of banking services for clients was necessary for
their survival. But these protests have to be taken with a grain of salt. According
to the Financial Times, the German (and French) "pre-emptive version" was not
seen as particularly threatening by bankers in their countries (FT 2014). Dombret et al. (2014) have shown that proprietary trading proper has played almost
no role in German banks since the crisis.

The relatively speedy drafting of the law was due in all likelihood to the
attempt to influence the European decision-making process that followed the
publication of the report. During the first reading of the law in the *Bundestag*,
Wolfgang Schäuble expressed this intention quite clearly:

The French and German governments have agreed to propose to our national legislatures to execute the relatively uncontroversial parts of the Liikanen report in national laws in anticipation
of European rules. We do not want to replace these rules, but rather speed them up. Furthermore, we want to further a process in which any European regulation draws to a certain extent
on the national experiences of France and Germany.   (Schäuble 2013, authors' translation)

He justified the retention of market-making activities with the need to preserve the global competitiveness of German banks and for adequate provision
of banking services for the German economy. In a hearing of the *Bundestag*
Finance Committee, experts criticized that restricting the law exclusively to proprietary trading and very big banks would lead to a situation such as the one

in France where, allegedly, less than 1 percent of all trading activities would be covered. They also warned that the German law would conflict with the regulation the Commission was preparing because market-making activities would be separated in the EU proposal (Bundestag 2013).

Despite such criticisms, the *Trennbankengesetz* passed the *Bundestag* in May 2013 with few changes, and one month later it was also approved by the *Bundesrat*. In the Coalition Treaty, the Grand Coalition committed itself to the goals of the Liikanen group, as long as these were not detrimental to the credit conditions on German corporate financial markets (Koalitionsvertrag 2013). However, when the European Commission in early 2014 unveiled its draft legislation on ring-fencing it became obvious that French and German lobbying had succeeded in watering down substantially the provisions of the Liikanen report (FT 2014). In particular, the separation of market-making was now left to discretionary political decisions. Despite this, the draft still went further than the French and German versions, prompting critical comments from the finance ministers of these countries (Financial Regulation 2014). They also set in motion another round of lobbying by the banking industry and big business to limit the scope of the regulation. Currently, it seems that the legislative process has stalled and, if adopted, the Commission proposal will continue to be mitigated substantially (FT, 24 November 2014: 16).

This case study is an example of German resistance to one of the most prominent regulatory consequences of the crisis in "Anglo-Saxon" countries. Only when the Social Democrats discovered the issue and when the Liikanen proposals threatened to impose a fairly strict version on Germany, did the government move. Teaming up with France, Germany managed to dilute the Liikanen reforms and forced the Commission to settle on a substantially watered-down regulation, successfully uploading its preferences. The case also demonstrates a pattern of German inactivity in the international arena which, however, is then remedied by recourse to the strategy of influencing European regulation and trying to internationalize the resulting standards. Another example of the latter strategy is the German attempt to internationalize a unilateral ban on naked short selling that was put in place temporarily in May 2010. Shortly afterwards, BaFin declared that the ban would be made permanent, while the IMF and many governments, even in the eurozone, criticized German unilateralism (Moosa 2013). Nonetheless, in July 2010, Germany passed a law regulating so-called harmful naked short selling,[7] However, Germany pressed on with its efforts to achieve a Europe-wide ban. In mid-2011, other European countries,

---

7 Naked short selling essentially involves placing a bet that a stock or bond will rise or fall without the trader actually owning the asset on which the bet has been placed.

affected by the turmoil, joined Germany. A corresponding regulation was published by the EU in November 2012, setting the stage for a wider global debate.

Passivity and symbolic politics in the regulation of OTC derivatives

German actors' activity was much lower in the area of OTC derivatives than in the other cases discussed in this chapter. This comes as no surprise given the much smaller importance of OTC derivatives markets for the German economy, the less well connected channels of political influence available to OTC advocates, and the lesser importance of non-banking financial activities. Thus, German authorities have, with the exception of the symbolic measure of banning naked transactions on credit default swaps related to sovereign bonds, left the field to other jurisdictions. Notably, the EU's laws (EMIR, see Quaglia this volume) set the framework for German regulation. The EU, in turn, reacted to the lead exercised by US supervisors, which – under Congressional pressure – had to implement the Dodd-Frank measures in regulating derivatives (Pagliari 2013: 160–178).

In response to the G20's call for regulation of derivatives, the reforms of widely discredited OTC derivatives did progress on a two-lane track. First, the centralization of most OTC contracts, combined with a regulatory framework to oversee the necessary market infrastructure (for simplicity's sake, we refer to these measures as "clearing reforms"). Second, the introduction of additional capital requirements for those OTC derivatives that are still traded bilaterally (requirements reforms).

Silent deliberations at the international and European levels

The central aims of European Market Infrastructure Regulation (EMIR) are to enhance transparency with regard to the opaque derivatives markets and to establish public regulation and supervision. In closely following the G20's 2009 Pittsburgh agreement, EMIR mandates the trading of derivatives on electronic platforms through central counterparties (CCP) and the reporting of all contracts to trade repositories. Thus, the aim of EMIR is to transform many OTC contracts into standardized, centrally registered, and cleared derivatives.

The second piece of legislation concerns the remaining, bilaterally cleared derivatives (which even after the reforms, at least for now, means the majority of derivatives). These rules essentially stipulate how to manage the related operational, liquidity, and credit risks, as well as how much capital or collateral has to be put aside as security. They remain under negotiation in the Committee on Payment and Settlement Systems (CPSS) and the International Organization of Securities Commissions (IOSCO), as well as in the context of the EBA's development of regulatory and implementation standards for EMIR (Bundesbank 2012).

In both initiatives, the German authorities have been far less politically active. High government intervention in both cases was almost absent. A systemic database research of all articles between January 2009 and November 2014 of the Financial Times, the Wall Street Journal, and the German Börsen-Zeitung did not reveal any significant, publicly visible German activity in the EU or the IOSCO-CPSS. BaFin and the Bundesbank cooperated in IOSCO and CPSS, but did not engage in publicly visible political negotiations. Likewise, EU deliberations on EMIR were also less publicly debated.

One exception, where some political engagement was in play, concerns the responsibilities of industrial end-users of derivatives contracts. In contrast to Dodd-Frank legislation, the initial EMIR drafts envisioned an encompassing clearing duty for all non-financial counterparties. Heavy industry pressure, in particular from the German-based airline Lufthansa, resulted in the inclusion of thresholds for these firms, below which central clearing is waived (see Article 11, EMIR; Börsen-Zeitung 2009, 2010, 2012b).

With regard to the margins requirement initiative, the German authorities seem to have pushed for higher margins and tougher rules (Börsen-Zeitung, 2012a). However, again there is little indication of any pronounced engagement in these matters by politicians or regulators.

Limited freedom in downloading

The opportunity to change regulations before adoption is rather limited, because EMIR has direct legal force in the EU member states and gives limited freedom to national supervisors. Thus, EU Regulation 648/2012 (EMIR) on OTC derivatives, central counterparties (CCPs) and trade repositories entered into force on August 16, 2012. The German EMIR Implementation Act *(EMIR-Ausführungsgesetz)* entered into force on February 16, 2013. The law is complemented by several technical standards that ESMA and EBA have developed or will publish in the future. The potential for technical influence in the EU administrative processes of its new financial supervisory structure is an important subject of future investigation.

Likewise, limited room for maneuver is available in the downloading of capital requirements regulations for non-centrally cleared derivatives, which became effective through EMIR and CRR.

Symbolic politics of crossloading

As already mentioned, the strongest German stance in the regulation of OTC derivatives was one of symbolic politics. Germany's solo banning of naked selling of credit default swaps (see Pagliari 2013: 168–177) was a symbolic act to accommodate government factions that were opposed to the eurozone bailout fund, with Germany as the main financial contributor. As Pagliari (2013: 177) explains:

The need to achieve consent from a reluctant Bundestag created pressures upon the German government to demonstrate a commitment to tackle the sources of the crisis, including the role of "speculation" in the derivatives markets. Ralph Brinkhaus, a lawmaker from Merkel's party, described this regulatory measure as "symbolic politics": "Sometimes it's important, alongside facts, also to send signals."

In sum, the German authorities' engagement in OTC derivatives regulation was less publicly visible. This can be attributed to the relatively lesser economic and political influence that this sub-sector wields in Germany. At the same time, the EU's positions were broadly in line with most of those of the main German stakeholder, the Frankfurt stock exchange Deutsche Börse Group. Several technical aspects, however, with substantial economic and political implications, might still become subject to intense debate in the context of finalizing legislation. The technical and implementation standards that the European authorities are to decide in the coming years present considerable opportunities for pushing specific interests.

Conclusion

As has been mentioned, the regulatory processes traced in this chapter constitute only a small part of the regulatory reforms undertaken by Germany after the financial crisis. Further measures include the reform of banking supervision, the pursuit of a financial transaction tax, changes in the deposit insurance regime, new rules for shadow banks and hedge funds, and consumer protection measures. For a comprehensive evaluation of the dynamics of Germany's participation in the multilevel regulation of financial markets, in-depth studies of other regulatory reforms will be necessary. However, two patterns seem to hold for the broader set of measures: first, the relatively limited success of uploading in the first (international) phase of post-crisis regulation and, second, greater – yet also limited – success in the European arena.

With regard to the first pattern, namely limited influence in the negotiation of global standards, the German authorities faced a similar strategic setting in most of the cases under review. Despite often quite early activity in the international arena, they found little space for securing specific German interests. This was due mainly to the dominance of the United States and the United Kingdom in international negotiations and to Germany's peculiar interests stemming from the structure of its banking system, which tended to isolate the Germans on the international stage. Moreover, the growing relevance of European regulations with direct application in German law and regulation further limited opportunities to influence the regulatory process. Thus, policy-makers adapted their strategies to negotiations in the EU, where the global deals of BCBS, FSB, IOSCO and so on were reopened to integrate specific national interests. However, the majority voting procedures in the EU constrain Germany's capacity to integrate peculiar interests into laws and regulations. Therefore, in sum, the influence on global standards (which become EU regulations) has decreased.

Nevertheless, with regard to the second pattern – the stronger influence on some of the issues lost at the international stage via EU negotiations – Germany's key role in the euro crisis enabled it to recapture negotiating power. On issues such as the banking union, which was a direct outcome of the policies to stabilize the euro, Germany was able to use not only its political and economic weight but also the argument of domestic constraints. The unpopularity of the bailout measures among the German population and many members of the German parliament, as well as the fact that financial markets were seen as one of the main causes of the crisis, made it necessary for the government to present tangible results in financial regulation as justification for the rescue of eurozone banks and governments (Zimmermann 2014). The SPD's position in the upper chamber, the *Bundesrat,* and its key role in the euro crisis gave it strong clout as policy entrepreneur in financial regulation, whereas the FDP, as the natural ally of the financial industry, was mostly sidelined. Germany's stronger influence in uploading policies to the European level was less obvious in the attempts to prevent the downloading of international initiatives, which it opposed. Although the characteristics of the German federal system that are closely reflected in the structure of the banking system rendered it very resistant to change from the outside and remained important in shaping defensive and offensive moves, it often had to bend to the spillover dynamics of increasingly Europeanized financial markets.

In sum, the German authorities have adapted to changed international and European conditions. However, the defense of specific German ways of organizing the regulation of financial markets has become more difficult in the context of global and European harmonization. German policy-makers and financial firms will face substantial challenges in further adapting to this new multilevel environment.

References

BaFin (Bundesanstalt für Finanzdienstleistungsaufsicht), 2014: Interview mit Dr. Elke König. In: *BaFin Journal*, Dezember 2014, 32–33. <www.bafin.de/SharedDocs/Downloads/DE/BaFinJournal/2014/bj_1412.pdf?__blob=publicationFile&v=6>

BBVA (Banco Bilbao Vizcaya Argentaria), 2014: *Regulatory Watch: European Commission's Proposal on Structural Reforms*, 12 February 2014. Madrid: BBVA. <www.bbvaresearch.com/wp-content/uploads/2014/05/140212_RegulatoryWatch_ECproposalonSR.pdf>

BCBS (Basel Committee on Banking Supervision), 2014: *Amendments to Basel III's leverage ratio issued by the Basel Committee*. Technical report, 12 January 2014. Basel: Bank for International Settlements. <www.bis.org/press/p140112a.htm>

Bertinchamp, Axel, 2010: Restructuring Act: Background and Content. In: *BaFin Quarterly* Q4/10, 5–7.

Bloomberg, 2013a: Basel Becomes Babel as Conflicting Rules Undermine Safety. In: *Bloomberg Online*, 3 January 2013. <www.bloomberg.com/news/2013-01-03/basel-becomes-babel-as-conflicting-rules-undermine-safety.html>

——, 2013b: Banks Win 4-Year Delay as Basel Liquidity Rule Loosened. In: *Bloomberg Online*, 7 January 2013. <www.bloomberg.com/news/2013-01-06/banks-win-watered-down-liquidity-rule-after-basel-group-deal.html>

——, 2014: Deutsche Bank Attacks Basel Plan's Threat to Repo Market. In: *Bloomberg Online*, 29 April 2014. <www.bloomberg.com/news/2014-04-29/deutsche-bank-attacks-basel-plan-s-threat-to-repo-market.html>

Blundell-Wignall, Adrian/Gert Wehinger/Patrick Slovik, 2009: The Elephant in the Room: The Need to Deal with What Banks Do. In: *OECD Journal: Financial Market Trends* 2/2009, 11–35.

BMF (Bundesministerium für Finanzen), 2010: *Key Issues Paper: Preventing Crises with Banks Paying their Due*. Key Issues Paper, 31 March 2010. Berlin: BMF. <www.bundesfinanzministerium.de/Content/EN/Standardartikel/Topics/Financial_markets/Articles/2010-08-16-Key-issues-paper-Preventing-crises-with-banks.html?__act=renderPdf&__iDocId=199384>

Börsen-Zeitung, 2009: Derivatehandel – Interview mit Stephan Gemkow: Derivate-Regulierung nur für Banken. In: *Börsen-Zeitung* No. 193, 8 October 2009, 11.

——, 2010: OTC-Derivate-Regulierung praxistauglich gestalten. In: *Börsen-Zeitung* No. 241, 14 December 2010, 4.

——, 2012a: Derivate-Clearing bereitet der Aufsicht Sorgen. In: *Börsen-Zeitung* No. 107, 6 June 2012, 3.

——, 2012b: Derivate-Regeln werden konkreter. In: *Börsen-Zeitung* No. 188, 28 September 2012, 3.

Bundesbank, 2012: *Die neuen CPSS-IOSCO-Prinzipien für Finanzmarktinfrastrukturen.* Monatsbericht 07/2012. Frankfurt a.M.: Bundesbank, 39–51. <www.bundesbank.de/Redaktion/DE/Down-loads/Veroeffentlichungen/Monatsberichtsaufsaetze/2012/2012_07_cpss_iosco.pdf?__blob=publicationFile>

——, 2013: *Die Umsetzung von Basel III in europäisches und nationales Recht.* Monatsbericht 06/2013. Frankfurt a.M.: Bundesbank, 57–73. <www.bundesbank.de/Redaktion/DE/Down-loads/Veroeffentlichungen/Monatsberichtsaufsaetze/2013/2013_06_umsetzung_basel_3.pdf?__blob=publicationFile>

Bundestag, 2012: *17. Wahlperiode, Drucksache 17/8935, 7 March 2012.* Berlin: Bundestag. <http://dipbt.bundestag.de/doc/btd/17/089/1708935.pdf>

——, 2013: *17. Wahlperiode, Protokoll 17/138, Finanzausschuss, 22 April 2013.* Berlin: Bundestag. <www.bundesgerichtshof.de/SharedDocs/Down-loads/DE/Bibliothek/Gesetzesmaterialien/17_wp/Abschirmung_Risiken/wortproto.pdf?__blob=publicationFile>

Bundestag Finance Committee, 2003: *Minutes of the 18. Finance Committee Meeting (Nonpublic) in Legislative Period 15, 21 May 2003.* Berlin: Bundestag.

Bundesverband, 2012: *VÖB sieht EU-Pläne zur Bankenunion skeptisch.* Press Release, 12 September 2012. Berlin: Bundesverband Öffentlicher Banken Deutschlands. <www.voeb.de/de/pressezentrum/pressemitteilungen/pressemitteilung_2012_052.html>

Busch, Andreas, 2009: *Banking Regulation and Globalization.* Oxford: Oxford University Press.

Businessweek, 2013: *EU Stumbles towards Bank Plan Deadline amid German Resistance.* <www.businessweek.com/news/2013-11-14/Germany-digs-in-against-risk-sharing-in-eu-bank-failure-debate#p1>

Chey, Hyoung-Kyu, 2006: Explaining Cosmetic Compliance with International Regulatory Regimes: The Implementation of the Basle Accord in Japan, 1998–2003. In: *New Political Economy* 11, 271–289.

Deutsche Bank, 2012: *Banking Union: Germany on the Brakes.* German Policy Watch, 20 September 2012. Frankfurt a.M.: Deutsche Bank. <www.dbresearch.com>

DGAP-Medientreff, 2013: *ROUNDUP: Union und SPD einig über Regeln für Bankenabwicklung und ESM Hilfe.* Berlin, 27 November 2013. München: EQS Group AG. <www.dgap-medientreff.de/news/technologie/roundup-union-und-spd-einig-uber-regeln-fur-bankenabwicklung-und-esm-hilfe-425479>

Dombret, Andreas/Thilo Liebig/Ingrid Stein, 2014: Trennbankensystem – ein Weg zu mehr Finanzstabilität in Deutschland? In: *Perspektiven der Wirtschaftspolitik* 15, 41–55.

Economist, The, 2013: Go with the flow. Global regulators soften their stance on liquidity. In: *The Economist,* 13 January 2013. <www.economist.com/news/finance-and-economics/21569405-global-regulators-soften-their-stance-liquidity-go-flow>

Economist, The, 2014: Leavened. Regulators go easy on Europe's overstretched banks. In: *The Enonomist,* 18 January 2014. <www.economist.com/news/finance-and-economics/21594344-regulators-go-easy-europes-overstretched-banks-leavened>

FSB (Financial Stability Board), 2011: *Key Attributes of Effective Resolution Regimes for Financial Institutions.* Bank for International Settlements, October 2011. Basel: FSB. <www.financialstabilityboard.org/wp-content/uploads/r_111104cc.pdf?page_moved=1>

——, 2014: *Implementing OTC Derivatives Market Reforms. Bank for International Settlements.* Basel: FSB. <www.financialstabilityboard.org/2010/10/fsb-report-on-implementing-otc-derivatives-market-reforms/?page_moved=1>

Financial Regulation, 2014: *A European Glass-Steagall to preserve the single market,* 31 March 2014. <www.financialregulationintl.com/financialindustry/a-european-glasssteagall-to-preserve-the-single-market-98368.htm>

FT (Financial Times), 2013a: DZ Bank hits out at proposed reforms. In: *Financial Times Online,* 6 March 2013. <www.ft.com/cms/s/0/47122a26-8669-11e2-8f47-00144feabdc0.html#axzz3OKDBTZO7>

——, 2013b: EU agrees to cap bankers' bonuses. In: *Financial Times Online,* 28 February 2013. <www.ft.com/intl/cms/s/0/c6a5a6aa-8173-11e2-904c-00144feabdc0.html#axzz3OKDBTZO7>

——, 2014: "Barnier rule" looks like a shadow of what it set out to be. In: *Financial Times Online,* 6 January 2014. <www.ft.com/intl/cms/s/0/0880ca58-76d5-11e3-807e-00144feabdc0.html>

Goldbach, Roman, 2015: *Global Governance and Regulatory Failure. The Political Economy of Banking.* Basingstoke: Palgrave Macmillan.

Goldbach, Roman/Dieter Kerwer, 2012: New Capital Rules? Reforming Basel Banking Standards after the Financial Crisis. In: Renate Mayntz (ed.), *Crisis and Control: Institutional Change in Financial Market Regulation.* Frankfurt a.M.: Campus, 245–260.

Gordon, Jeffrey N./Wolf Georg Ringe, 2014: *Bank Resolution in the European Banking Union. A Transatlantic Perspective on What it Would Take.* University of Oxford Legal Research Paper Series 18/2014. Oxford: Oxford University.

Handelsblatt, 2011a: Sparkassen proben den Aufstand. In: *Handelsblatt Online,* 9 August 2011. <www.handelsblatt.com/unternehmen/banken/heinrich-haasis-im-gespraech-sparkassen-proben-den-aufstand-seite-all/4477060-all.html>

——, 2012b: Steinbrück ist Schäubles "Lex Deutsche Bank" zu lasch. In: *Handelsblatt Online,* 31 January 2013. <www.handelsblatt.com/politik/deutschland/trennbanken-vorschlag-steinbrueck-ist-schaeubles-lex-deutsche-bank-zu-lasch-seite-all/7717006-all.html>

——, 2012b: EU-Kommissar Barnier kritisiert deutsche Zurückhaltung. In: *Handelsblatt Online,* 28 March 2012. <www.handelsblatt.com/politik/international/aufspaltung-von-grossbanken-eu-kommissar-barnier-kritisiert-deutsche-zurueckhaltung-/7997558.html>

Handke, Stefan/Hubert Zimmermann, 2012: Institutional Change in German Financial Regulation. In: Renate Mayntz (ed.), *Crisis and Control: Institutional Change in Financial Market Regulation.* Frankfurt a.M.: Campus, 119–142.

Howarth, David/Lucia Quaglia, 2013a: Banking on Stability: The Political Economy of New Capital Requirements in the European Union. In: *Journal of European Integration* 35, 333–346.

Howarth, David/Lucia Quaglia, 2013b: *The Comparative Political Economy of Basel III in Europe*. Conference Paper. SPERI-Conference at the University of Sheffield, Sheffield, July 2013.

Joint Statement, 2012: *Joint Statement of the Ministers of Finance of Finland, the Netherlands and Germany*. Press Release, 25 September 2012. Berlin: BMF. <www.bundesfinanzministerium.de/Content/EN/Pressemitteilungen/2011/2011-11-25-Joint-Statement.html>

Koalitionsvertrag, 2013: *Deutschlands Zukunft gestalten. Koalitionsvertrag zwischen CDU, CSU und SPD. 18. Legislaturperiode*, 27 November 2013. Berlin: CDU, CSU, SPD.

Moosa, Imad, 2013: The Regulation of Shirt-Selling: A Pragmatic View. In: *Journal of Banking Regulation* 13, 211–227.

Pagliari, Stefano, 2013: *Public Salience and International Financial Regulation. Explaining the International Regulation of OTC Derivatives, Rating Agencies, and Hedge Funds*. Ph.D. Thesis. Waterloo, ON: University of Waterloo.

Quaglia, Lucia, 2014: *The European Union and Global Financial Regulation*. Oxford: Oxford University Press.

Rinke, Andreas/Matthias Sobolewski, 2013: Exclusive: German parties reach deal on banking union. In: *Reuters Online*, 9 November 2013. <www.reuters.com/article/2013/11/09/us-europe-banks-germany-idUSBRE9A808320131109>

Schäuble, Wolfgang, 2013: *Dr. Wolfgang Schäuble anlässlich der 1. Lesung des Trennbankengesetzes im Deutschen Bundestag*. Speech, 15 March 2013. Berlin: BMF. <www.bundesfinanzministerium.de/Content/DE/Reden/2013/2013-03-15-bundestag-finanzmarktpolitik-textfassung.html>

Spiegel, Der, 2011: Ende einer Epoche. Gespräch mit Sigmar Gabriel. In: *Der Spiegel* No. 42, 22–24. <www.spiegel.de/spiegel/print/d-81015400.html>

Steinberg, Philipp/Caroline Somnitz, 2012: Wege zu einer stärkeren Trennung von Investment- und Geschäftsbanking. In: *Wirtschaftsdienst* No. 6, 384–391.

Steinbrück, Peer, 2012: *Vertrauen zurückgewinnen. Ein neuer Anlauf zur Bändigung der Finanzmärkte*. Discussion Paper, 25 September 2012. <www.peer-steinbrueck.de/wp-content/uploads/2012/09/Steinbrueck_Vertrauen_zurueckgewinnen_final.pdf>

SZ (Süddeutsche Zeitung), 2011: Entweder sparen oder spekulieren. In: *Süddeutsche Zeitung Online*, 18 October 2011. <www.sueddeutsche.de/geld/regulierung-der-finanzmaerkte-entweder-sparen-oder-spekulieren-1.1167091>

VÖB (Bundesverband Öffentlicher Banken Deutschlands), 2012: *Statement of Christian Brand, President of the Federation of Public Banks, at a Breakfast for the Press*, Brussels, 6 December 2012. Berlin: VÖB. <voeb.de/down-load/statement-pressefruehstueck-2012>

Wall Street Journal, 2013: Germany Objects to EU Proposal for Restructuring Banks. In: *Wall Street Journal Online*, 10 July 2013. <online.wsj.com/news/articles/SB10001424127887324425204578597213438213952>

Walter, Andrew, 2007: Do voluntary standards work among governments? The Experience of International Financial Standards in East Asia. In: Dana L. Brown/Ngaire Woods (eds.), *Making Global Self-Regulation Effective in Developing Countries*. Oxford: Oxford University Press, 32–61.

Young, Kevin, 2013: Financial industry groups' adaptation to the post-crisis regulatory environment: Changing approaches to the policy cycle. In: *Regulation & Governance* 7, 460–480.

Young, Kevin, 2014: Losing abroad but winning at home: European financial industry groups in global financial governance since the crisis. In: *Journal of European Public Policy* 21, 367–388.

Zimmermann, Hubert, 2009: Varieties of Global Financial Governance? British and German Approaches to Financial Market Regulation. In: Eric Helleiner/Stefano Pagliari/Hubert Zimmermann (eds.), *Global Finance in Crisis: The Politics of International Regulatory Change*. London: Routledge, 121–136.

——, 2013: The Uneasy Promise of Deposit Insurance: Financial Globalisation and the Protection of Savers. In: *Competition & Change* 17, 265–282.

——, 2014: A Grand Coalition for the Euro: The Second Merkel Cabinet, the Euro Crisis and the Elections of 2013. In: *German Politics* 23, 322–336.

8 The Multilevel Dynamics of Regulatory Reform

Arthur Benz and Renate Mayntz

The problem of coordination

Problem situations that extend beyond the borders of single states, such as pollution and climate change, have always called for collective international problem-solving. As Fritz W. Scharpf maintains, "the theoretical tools for analyzing the conditions under which such solutions are likely to succeed are reasonably well developed" (Scharpf 1997: 520). In reality, however, collective international action tends to encounter serious obstacles. This was also true when the recent financial crisis induced policy-makers at different political levels to try to reform a regulatory regime that had been incapable of preventing it. Given the internationalization of the financial system and persisting economic competition between different countries, coordinated action to design an effective system of financial market regulation inevitably gave rise to distributive conflicts. Depending on the structure of national economies and the relative size and importance of their banking sector, some national governments prefer stricter regulation than others. Moreover, due to the variety of financial market actors and financial instruments and the acceleration of financial transactions, the regulation of financial markets poses a particularly difficult coordination problem. In addition to the complexity of the issue, the public perception of the crisis led to the politicization of decisions formerly dealt with mainly by experts. Public pressure forced policy-makers to take action. Governments appeared, in principle, willing to re-regulate, providing that other governments did so as well. The dilemma of collective action thus posed was reinforced by the fact that the reform process had to take place in a multilevel system, including actors from the national, European, and international levels, and requiring both horizontal and vertical coordination.

The regulatory changes that we have observed did not result from a master process of combined horizontal and vertical coordination. What we have observed is in fact a case of policy coordination across territorial levels, although these levels do not constitute a coherent governance structure, nor do we find a well-established institutional framework linking the different arenas of action. Levels demarcate scopes of action rather than jurisdictions, and relations between levels are defined in functional terms rather than by formal rules. The multilevel action system of regulatory reform is not a classic multilevel governance system.

Theoretical approaches

Although more than two decades of research on multilevel governance has resulted in a wide range of literature (for an overview, see: Bache/Flinders 2004; Piattoni 2010; Stephenson 2013), none of the available theoretical approaches worked out in this context deals with multilevel action systems of the kind dealt with here. The multilevel action system in financial market regulation differs from the two-level policy systems to which most studies on multilevel governance refer. One exception is the theory of European integration suggested by Liesbet Hooghe and Gary Marks (2001). They consider that integration comprises simultaneous processes of delegation of power by member-state governments to the EU and a regionalization of authority inside member states. However, while the authors explain this process as a result of functional requirements and identity claims of communities (Hooghe/Marks 2009), they do not discuss its consequences for policy-making. Other studies focusing on coordination or reform in multilevel systems consider only two levels, involving the interplay of international and domestic, European and national or federal and regional politics. Robert Putnam, for instance, explicitly characterizes the substance of his "linkage theory" as a "two-level game" of domestic and international politics (Putnam 1988). In a similar vein, Fritz W. Scharpf's theory of joint decision-making covers two-level interactions between the European Parliament and representatives of member states in the Council, or between the federal and *Länder* governments in German federalism (Scharpf 1988, 2011). This also applies to studies explaining exits from the Joint Decision Trap (Falkner 2011; Héritier 1999), theories of intergovernmental relations in federal states (Painter 1991; Simeon 2006) or intergovernmentalist approaches explaining amendments of EU treaties (Christiansen et al. 2002; Moravcsik 1998). A more extended conception of multilevel policy-making is indicated by scholars who have pointed out strategies applied by regional or local governments to by-pass the national or state level in order to pursue their interests (for example, Leuprecht/Lazar

2007: 4), or who studied the "paradiplomacy" of regions in federal or regional-ized states (Aldecoa/Keating 1999). In the EU, scholars observed that the European Commission tends to get into direct contact with regional governments in order to implement its regional policies (Keating/Hooghe 2001). However, beyond the conclusion that a structure of multiple, loosely connected arenas has arisen (Benz/Eberlein 1999; Benz 2000; Hooghe 1996), these studies have not led to a theory of multilevel decision-making in which the top-most level has no formal powers.

The coexistence of a variety of international bodies in a given policy field is dealt with in the international relations literature, but typically from a strategic-interaction viewpoint. The classical "modes of coordination" described in these studies – mutual adjustment, negotiation, persuasion – appear as single-level, intergovernmental processes. Where not treaties but only soft law or policy recommendations are produced in international negotiations, a different dynamic operates in decision-making. In this literature, although the interaction with lower political levels is not ignored, scholars are interested mainly in identifying national preferences or preference formation (Aspinwall 2007; Kim 2014; Moravcsik 1998) or focus on constraints caused by domestic institutions (for example, Lütz 2011), but not on processes of "uploading" national preferences to the next higher political level. The rare studies concerned with compliance and implementation of higher level "soft law" deal with the strategies to cope with a "clash" of global and national regulation, which is resolved either by veto points or by networks favoring cross-national mutual adjustment (Farrell/Newmann 2014).

Regarding rules and norms that emerge at a level beyond the nation-state and the EU, a third body of literature has some relevance. It has emerged under the broad heading of "global governance" and includes different theoretical approaches trying to account for the emergence of transnational institutions, norms or international law and policies. One line of reasoning refers to the "soft power" of states or international organizations or the role of ideas, discourses and norms. Using Robert Nye's concept as point of departure (Nye 1990, 2005), scholars have tried to sort out whether rules or norms can be established in the global context by persuasion or the attraction of best practices (for a summary, see Solomon 2014). In a similar vein, the concept of transgovernmentalism has been used to explain global norms or standards resulting from deliberation in a stratified architecture of networks, including not only governments but also bureaucracies, private actors and experts (Baker 2009). Again focusing on horizontal relations, these studies do not emphasize the multilevel aspect. The same holds true for "constructivist" approaches in international relations explaining the emergence of order, norms or rules as a result of arguing processes or communicative action (Deitelhoff 2006; Risse 2000). While many publications have tried to clarify conceptual and methodological issues, few have addressed institutional conditions of normative reasoning or the implementation of ideas or arguments taking the national level into account (Checkel 1997). Critical reviews of the global governance concept point out that "[o]ne effect of the crises of the early twenty-first century is that the state has made a major comeback as the principal stakeholder and actor in the unfolding process of economic reform" (Higgott 2012: 24). Like most international relations theories, these research perspectives have remained in the classical two-level context.

The multilevel action system of regulatory reform

When the recent financial crisis broke out, there existed no coherent structure of financial market governance extending from the national to the international level. As policy at all levels shifted from coping with the crisis to regulatory reform, an action system formed that included institutions at all political levels. As shown in detail in Chapters 1 to 3 (in this volume), the *international level* of the emerging action system of regulatory reform is populated by a wide variety of institutions, including a classic international organization, the IMF, a negotiation forum such as the G20, and technical expert bodies established to deal with specific issues and based on "epistemic communities" sharing normative and causal beliefs (Haas 1992: 3). These institutions have different mandates and different memberships, and their policy domains overlap. In the course of the reform process, the transformed G20, together with another transformed forum, the FSB, evolved into closely collaborating core actors, or network coordinators. However, these "nodal actors" (Viola, Chapter 2) are unable to make binding decisions, which raises the question of whether we can in fact speak of the international as a separate *level* in the way the concept of level is usually understood in the literature on multilevel systems. In any case, as Lora Viola argues in Chapter 2, we have observed new types of international bodies coming to dominate international policy-making: bodies that provide fora for necessary international coordination without formally impinging on the autonomy of established jurisdictions. The emergence and role of such bodies make for a new type of multilevel system different from systems of joint decision-making such as the EU and federal states. In the process of regulatory reform, international institutions have formulated a reform agenda for the international financial system, developed templates for legislation at lower political levels, and given impetus to the reform process.

The *European level* in the action system of regulatory reform concerns a specific region. After 2008, Europe and North America have been the regions most strongly affected by the financial crisis. However, conditions for policy coordination are quite different in both regions. In North America no comparable level of policy coordination exists; in fact, the United States stands for a hegemonic power in this region. In Europe, the EU has evolved into a jurisdiction with variable territorial boundaries for financial market regulation, partly including all 28 member states of the Union, partly the 19 members of the euro zone. The EU can regulate only with the approval of a qualified majority of member-state governments; it is a classical two-level system, embedded in an unorthodox multilevel action system. In the process of regulatory reform, the EU played the role of a mediator: EU decisions have been shaped by the preferences of – different coalitions of – member states, but they have also taken into account the reform plans of dominant non-EU countries, such as the United States, and the standards and principles formulated by international bodies. Once cast in the form of directives and regulations, the resulting EU policy has shaped regulatory reform in the member states.

At the *national level*, policies are developed in the respective constitutional frameworks. The research summarized in this volume covers three nation-states representing decisive political players in financial market regulation. However, these states also stand for the heterogeneity that obtains at the national level, with respect to both constitutional frameworks of politics and policy-making and the financial system (Lütz 2002).[1] Germany and the United States are federal governments, although of distinct types, while the United Kingdom can be regarded as a unitary government for the purposes of this study. The presidential system in the United States divides power between the legislative and the executive, whereas these powers are fused in the parliamentary systems of the United Kingdom and Germany. Party systems differ in these three countries, having developed towards an increasing pluralism in Germany and in the United Kingdom, but not in the United States, where party dualism has intensified. Regarding the economy, the liberal market model is characteristic of the United States and the United Kingdom, whereas Germany has moved stepwise from the coordinated market model towards liberalization in the wake of European integration. In the United Kingdom, a process of deindustrialization has made the financial sector the dominant branch, whereas the economies in the United States and Germany have remained more diversified in both regional and sectoral terms. As is evident in Chapters 5 to 7, these differences affect the policy

---

1 See also the literature on comparative government (Lijphart 2012) and on varieties of capitalism (Hall/Soskice 2001).

preferences pursued by governments in negotiations at higher political levels, and their willingness to abide by international agreements and rules. There is, then, heterogeneity at both the international and the national level of the multilevel action system engaged in the reform of financial market regulation. In addition, the system is asymmetric in so far as we find a regional level only in Europe, whereas the United States can be considered the dominant actor and hegemon in North America. Consequently, the relations between levels differ for the countries included in this project.

In contrast to multilevel systems described in research on European governance and federal systems, there is no formal hierarchy linking all levels. Hierarchical relations exist only between the EU and its member states in those policy fields in which the European legislature has the power to pass regulations. The EU, however, is not an independent top level in a classic two-level system; it is embedded in the wider context of the multilevel system and subject to both the guidance of international bodies and horizontal shaping forces from the United States. The international bodies claim guidance power for the regulatory changes they recommend, but the EU and national governments can act independently. Except for the IMF, which has not been a core actor in the reform process, the international bodies engaged in regulatory reform are negotiation platforms rather than supra-national institutions, and decisions are made by officials (and sometimes representatives of private organizations). True, there is interdependence between the decisions taken at the different levels, but it is not the shared power characteristic of policy-making in federal systems and the EU. Higher level decisions are made in a bottom-up manner by delegated national representatives (or executives). Where delegates (agents) of lower level units (principals) negotiate collective decisions, this links two levels in the form of two-level games. But being "member driven" does not mean that national preferences are simply "uploaded": lower level preferences are positions to be negotiated at the next higher level. Negotiation is a crucial form of interaction in our action system, and while it is negotiation among particularistic (national) interests, it is also negotiation in light of the need for coordination.

Underlying the linkage constituted by interaction among regulators at different political levels is a causal interdependence between different elements of the differentiated financial system that are the targets of regulation. As pointed out by Viola in Chapter 2, the complexity of the financial system is reflected in the equally complex structure of its governance. Because different parts of the financial system are "regulated" (in different ways at different levels) by different institutions, it is imperative that they coordinate their actions. As shown in Chapter 3, the FSB has come to operate as the focal coordinator in the reform process, linking activities both between levels and horizontally at the international level.

Complementing the goal-setting activities of the G20, the FSB has developed strategies to make reform effective. In this way, the governance structure of financial markets has over time become more coherent, without a significant reallocation of formal authority.

These, then, are the features that characterize the multilevel action system of regulatory reform: the lowest or national level consists of countries with widely different power and institutional make-up. For a significant part, but not for all of them there exists a regional level with some decision-making powers; the EU can also act as broker in relation to powerful independent states. The top level, finally, consists of a fragmented set of international institutions without a competent supra-national actor at its center and hence without the power to make binding decisions. Under these particular conditions, policy coordination results mainly from processes of negotiation between actors representing governments, central banks or business organizations at a higher decision-making level. These negotiations aim at agreements, but more often than not, they merely set standards or end up with proposals for (regional and national) jurisdictions. Institutional rules often allow actors to opt for exit. Commitments are stronger when negotiations are guided by emerging norms of cooperation, but in many instances of multilevel interaction, exchange of information or mutual observation links actors and policy-making processes without resulting in effective coordination.

The dynamics of interaction in multilevel regulatory reform

While the different coordination mechanisms highlighted in the theoretical approaches discussed above point to certain aspects of the dynamics we have observed in this study, none of them can serve as a model for the multilevel action system of regulatory reform. In this system there is hierarchy and joint decision-making, but only in some fields of European policy-making; there has been mutual adjustment, as between the United States and the EU, and there has been intergovernmental negotiation. Instead of positing ex ante a complex analytical model that fits our case, we used a relatively simple conceptual framework of different kinds of vertical and horizontal interaction among the actors in our multilevel system to emphasize the dynamics of interaction. As stated in the introductory chapter, we sought to identify, in addition to autonomous national and European reforms, processes crudely called "downloading", "uploading", and "crossloading".

"Downloading" means a transfer of policy from a higher to a lower level, either voluntary or compulsory. Voluntary downloading consists of the specification of, and compliance with, higher level recommendations and policy proposals at lower levels. Given the internationalized character of finance and the corresponding international expansion of the financial crisis that had started in the United States, it is not surprising that reform needs were soon articulated and reform initiatives taken at the international level. But since core international actors could at best produce "soft law" there could be no compulsory downloading from the international level. While we have found instances where national governments have voluntarily anticipated a higher level ruling, putting off independent national action, voluntary adoption of international templates has been limited where lower level preferences had not been sufficiently taken into account in their development. The transposition of Basel III into the EU directive CRD (Capital Requirements Directive) IV and the – collectively binding – Bank Recovery and Resolution Directive (BRRD) are exemplary cases of voluntary downloading from the international level, demonstrating that the "transposition" of proposed higher level rulings into lower level law may include – even major – modifications. Processes of downloading in our type of multilevel system have always been embedded in, and accompanied by, negotiation.

As "uploading" we designated actions designed to promote a specific policy move at a higher political level, thus shaping a collective decision or commitment. Such uploading is carried out by actors representing their government or organization in policy-making at a higher level. These actors do not behave simply as agents. National delegates to European and international bodies are typically "experts" in their field – but experts with a national passport. As such they are aware of how a global, transnational problem arising in financial markets or in the real economy affects the financial system or economy of their own countries. Accordingly, they show a two-pronged orientation ("mixed-motives") in multilevel policy-making: while determined to safeguard national interests, they are also aiming at solving collective problems in coordinated action with other national or international partners. Their effort to shape higher-level decisions according to national preferences – that is, to upload national preferences – is always tempered by the knowledge that the solution of the collective action problem is also in the national interest.

As we have seen in the preceding chapters, policy preferences can be either pro-active or defensive (Kudrna 2013: 201). In both cases, representatives of countries can try to form coalitions to further their aim. The United States, for example, sought support from the United Kingdom in pushing its preference for stricter standards at the Basel Committee on Banking Supervision (BCBS), whereas Germany and France formed a defensive coalition, asking for lower capital requirements or at least an extension of the implementation period. In either case, the preferred decision must be argued to be in the collective interest.

Successful pro-active strategies can make a national government, or the EU, not only an agenda-setter at a higher level, but also a pace-setter, whether through imitation by others or through a binding collective decision. Agenda-setting can also merge into the attempt to establish regulatory hegemony, such as the United States enjoyed before the recent crisis. The intensity with which a problem defined as transnational affects a given country is a strong motivator of pro-active uploading. Not surprisingly, the United States and the United Kingdom, which had been particularly affected by the crisis, became immediately active players in regulatory reform. Assisted by the fact that they were represented by high-ranking officials with superior expertise in bodies such as the BCBS and the FSB, these two countries managed to become pace-setters on various occasions.

Pro-active uploading can also be motivated by the desire to push a domestically contested preference considered to be superior at a higher level. This strategy is familiar from two-level constellations. Though we found no instance where this strategy has visibly been pursued, Kudrna, Müller and Falkner have described it for the EU as a version of "policy import", labelled as "harmonizing globally to harmonize internally" (Kudrna/Müller/Falkner 2014: 1113), and found instances in various policy fields, including financial market regulation (for example, the Commission's initiative to transfer international accounting standards into EU legislation; Kudrna 2013: 201).

Uploading always implies the risk of failure. Thus national initiatives to introduce a financial transaction tax or to have naked short-selling prohibited at the international or at least the European level have failed. Successful uploading depends on a number of conditions. First is the choice of the appropriate arena. Appropriate means both that it is an arena competent to deal with the issue, and that its sponsor has access to it. The importance of access for delegates of a specific country, or the competent branch of government – for example, finance ministry, central bank, supervisory authority – has been demonstrated empirically by Lall (2015). A second condition is the likelihood of finding support at the higher level, given the preferences of the negotiating partners. Finally, timing is important. Interventions at a time when a policy proposal has already found majority consent are deemed to fail.

As indicated by the choice of the term, uploading is generally understood to be a bottom-up process. There are, however, instances of collective learning "from below" when a higher level body takes up an initiative tried out independently by a country. International bodies, in particular those including specialists and experts, often profit from observing experimental policy-making that has proved successful in individual nation states (Bednar 2011; Sabel/Zeitlin 2008). In financial market reform, due to time pressure and the mobilization of policy-makers at all levels at the same time, there has been little "learning from below". In contrast, what we have called "crossloading", a horizontal process, has played an unexpectedly important role. In the literature on policy transfer or policy diffusion (Berry/Berry 1999; Evans 2009; Holzinger et al. 2007), the harmonization of policies or policy learning by unilateral or mutual adjustment between governments has been extensively discussed. In the reform of financial market regulation, we found not only horizontal policy transfer by imitation or in a process of coalition building, but also by legal constraint. In the first case, a government adopts a regulation which it has observed in another country and assessed as an appropriate problem solution. This happened in the case of reforms of the structure of the banking sector in Germany, the United States and the United Kingdom. Voluntary crossloading can also result from information processing; the EU reform agenda "crossloaded" much of the US legal framework expressed in the Dodd-Frank Act. Compulsory crossloading by legal constraint can take place when a government exploits the advantage of moving first, forcing financial institutions with other national passports to comply. The "equivalence clauses" in EU legislation and the "extra-territorial" application of the "Volcker Rule", which countries had to accept due to their dependence on the US economy, are examples of this form of crossloading.

Policy transfer both by imitation and by legal constraint are the consequence of independent action by a nation state or the EU, the fourth type of action we distinguished. In contrast to joint decision systems, which rule out independent action, independent action has been a driving force of policy reforms in the multilevel action system of financial market regulation. True, the capability for independent action can slow down reform if a government abstains from participating in coordinated action or remains inactive, as is exemplified by the German government's refusal to separate commercial and investment banking. But where no hierarchical relations exist, as in sovereign states and in certain policy fields in the EU, independent action often has the effect of setting at least the agenda, if not the pace of international reform. Both the United Kingdom and the United States were willing to act independently in reforming their financial systems, partly trying to upload their preferences (as in Basel III), partly being copied, and partly constraining other countries to follow suit.

The empirical analysis presented in Chapters 3 to 7 has shown that the four types of action that formed our analytical framework – downloading, uploading, crossloading, and independent action – are intimately linked empirically. This does not hold only for crossloading potentially following from independent action; it also holds for uploading and downloading. Where higher level regulations are typically the result of negotiation between the representatives of lower level units, downloading tends to follow uploading; it is an independent process only where binding law can be produced by true supra-national actors.

The dynamics of the reform process were set and kept in motion by various driving forces, operating at the different levels of policy-making. It appears that international institutions responded immediately to the perceived global nature of the crisis, while national responses varied according to the nature and extent of being directly affected. National responses were clearly affected by domestic politics; this holds both for independent national reform initiatives and for attempts to initiate a policy at the international level. In the wake of the crisis, financial market regulation became highly politicized at all political levels. However, party politics did not play a significant role beyond the national level, where they did in fact shape policy preferences. At the European level, where the rise of a European party system has been discovered (Hix et al. 2007), the potential impact of party politics was moderated by a shift to intergovernmental negotiations. When the European Parliament participated in legislation, the pressure of the crisis overshadowed the influence of parties. At the international level, interests of specialized institutions and policy experts (such as central bank governors) predominated.

Not only the role played by party politics in the reform process has been limited. The empirical analyses in Chapters 3 to 7 demonstrate that the reforms set in motion emerged to a considerable extent outside democratic procedures and institutions. Certainly, binding regulations passed the legitimized legislative bodies at the national and European levels, and members of national governments acting at the different levels are accountable to parliaments and hence to voters. However, the dynamics of policy-making were driven by other processes, whereas democratic institutions have often slowed these processes down. As pointed out in the introductory chapter, we did not choose the issue of democratic legitimation as a prominent perspective, but it is evident that despite widespread public attention, democratic procedures involving – in fact – the demos, and not only elected politicians and executives, have played a subordinate role in the process of regulatory reform. At all levels, expert officials and executive politicians have dominated decision-making. A shift towards executive politics has also been observed in other fields, especially in European policy-making. However, in the case of financial market regulatory reform, the "democratic deficit" is not simply an effect of the multilevel governance structure in which it evolved, but reflects specific features of the particular reform challenge: its sudden impact, dramatic consequences, and the perceived time pressure under which reformers operated. It is not by accident that we have chosen to speak of a multilevel *action* system of financial reform.

The shift towards executive politics accords with another characteristic of the reform process, namely the absence of a notable influence of civil society organizations or NGOs, as they are often labelled. In recent decades, these organizations have emerged as important players in the EU (Kohler-Koch/Quittkat 2013), in international politics, and international organizations (Zürn 2010: 56). Regarding democratic legitimacy, scholars have often viewed them as important representatives of public interests or as defenders of minority rights. We did not systematically inquire into NGOs in financial market reform, but the authors of Chapters 3 to 7 did not find them to be relevant in their analyses.

Business associations and particular financial industry interests certainly had more capacities than NGOs to access policy-making at the different levels and to exploit the access points. If they could not achieve substantial change in favor of their interests, they lobbied for a delayed introduction of regulations. There has obviously been much interaction between governments and higher level bodies, on one hand, and business associations or industry, on the other, but it has mostly remained under-cover, intransparent, and invisible. As Kevin Young (2013) reported, the crisis in financial markets shattered established networks of interest intermediation and weakened the capacity of these private actors to veto regulation. Therefore, they changed strategies and tried to influence agendas, or the timing of implementation of new regulations. Apparently, the dynamics of the multilevel action system and the complexity of its structure have reduced the impact of lobbying.

Patterns of multilevel interaction in the reform of financial market regulation

The dynamics of the reform process was set and kept in motion by various driving forces operating at the different levels of policy-making. They met opposing forces, which also surfaced at different locations in the multilevel action system. The aggregated effect of driving and constraining forces cannot be simply determined by adding them up. The impact of one or the other very much depended on the sequence in which they occurred (Héritier 2007). Moreover, a political system consisting of multiple arenas provides opportunities to circumvent constraints in one arena by proceeding in another, as it can give rise to power in one arena blocking or delaying reform processes in another (Benz 2013). Sequences can create a self-enforcing reform dynamics, as they can lead to a cycle of innovative action and counter-reaction, ending with only gradual change.

The process of regulatory reform triggered by the financial crisis did not follow a master plan. Different parts of the financial system – units like banks or rating agencies and transactions like over-the-counter trade – became the object of separate reform initiatives. As already stated in the introductory chapter, political responses to the crisis first addressed the less complex problems, with the more complicated issues being left for later decisions. The level of uncertainty in defining the specific collective action problem increased accordingly, and so did the challenge of coordination. In order to identify different patterns of multilevel interaction that together constitute the dynamics of the reform process we have singled out four specific reform issues for closer analysis in Chapters 3 to 7. In this section, we present the sequence of steps in the evolving reforms.[2]

Whether these reforms follow the ideal-typical model of policy formation or the famous garbage can model (Cohen/March/Olsen 1972), we have tried to identify in each case the political level at which the analytically distinguishable steps took place. The first step is the articulation of a reform demand, based on the definition of a collective action problem. The next step is the first formulation of a proposal for solving the problem. This initiative may generate reactions or responses, either supporting the proposal or modifying it with the aim of watering it down or ratcheting it up. This step typically involves extensive communication and negotiation among the involved actors. Elaboration of a new standard, rule or other kind of intervention goes along with attempts to form coalitions or to veto a decision. We have followed through the different reform processes to the regulation finally adopted, or at any rate to the point at which the decision process had arrived by the fall of 2014. Whether the new regulation is in fact implemented and the process of policy-making ends in a change of the behavior of market actors lies beyond the scope of this study.

Capital requirements (Basel III)

Regulation of capital requirements for banks turned out to be a primary objective of governments and prudential banking regulators. It was related to a clearly defined collective action problem. All governments and the experts they called on agreed that one standard of minimum capital requirement is needed in order to avoid a race to the bottom in the financial market. Within this framework, there was cognitive certainty and consensus that something needs to be done, although there was no consensus on how much capital requirements should be increased. Disputes also surfaced concerning the regulation of bankers' performance-based payments. In the end, the bonus system and level of compensation – that is, the problematic incentives for bankers – have not really changed. However, banks now have to have higher capital ratios.

---

2 Except when literature is referenced, the analysis in this section is based entirely on the information provided in the various chapters of this volume, and has been checked by the respective authors.

The certainty and consensus on the need for capital standards developed through a longer practice of coordination in this policy area. This started with the first Basel Accord of 1988 and continued with negotiations on the second Accord of 2004. During this period, experts from central banks and regulatory agencies set the agenda focused on capital standards and negotiated in well-established procedures in the BCBS. In general, the US Federal Reserve Board took the lead as a pace-setter, often in concert with the Bank of England, and uploaded its preferences on capital standards successfully to the Committee. This pattern prevailed during the Basel III process. Again the Federal Reserve Board and the Federal Deposit Insurance Corporation (FDIC) successfully uploaded their goals (for instance on common equity ratios) or US rules – for example, surcharge for SIFIs – to the international level, again in close cooperation with UK representatives and supported by the Swiss and Dutch delegations. This coalition overcame resistance from French and German representatives, both confronted by interests representing a banking sector that traditionally has been closely linked to the state or (as in Germany) to regional governments. Acting as a first mover, the US delegation set the agenda for a considerable change in capital standards and supplementary leverage ratios. Against this strong player, supported by a coalition of some European countries and in particular the United Kingdom, the EU was not in a position to pursue its own policy. Due to the divide between the United Kingdom, on one hand, and Germany and France on the other, the Union was not able to define common preferences, all the more so because it participated not as a full member of the BCBS until the Banking Union was established. In the negotiations, Basel III emerged as a compromise between the US and UK proposals and the efforts of France and Germany to relax the proposed rules. This compromise was negotiated despite extensive lobbying by the financial industry aimed at watering down the rules.

Thus, the negotiations at the international level helped to avoid threatening deadlocks that could have occurred both in the EU and in Germany's federal system. More importantly, the interplay of the different levels generated change that would have been impossible under the conditions of the joint-decision system in federal Germany, where the most powerful *Länder* defended the savings and cooperative banking sectors. When decision-making on legislation in the EU started, policy-making was hampered by the divergent interests of Germany and the United Kingdom. However, both had to take the Basel agreement, negotiated at the international level, as the point of departure.

While the US Federal Reserve Board and the FDIC implemented more stringent standards compared with the minimum agreed at the international level ("gold plating"), legislation in the EU had to accommodate the contradictory demands of member-state governments. The European Commission softened

Figure 8-1   Capital requirements (Basel III)

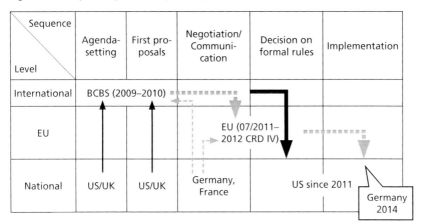

Note: black arrows: change towards tighter regulation; dashed arrows: watering down, constraining change.

its definition of Core Tier I capital relative to the Basel III recommendations and on liquidity, and it adopted the less prescriptive definition of liquid assets. Concerning a minimum leverage ratio, French and German banks, regulators and politicians aggressively demanded reduced standards. At the European level, governments of both countries were in a better position to pursue their interests than at the international level. In particular, Germany's authorities pushed for a renegotiation of crucial Basel III issues within the EU context (in particular, the Capital Requirements Directive – CRD IV) and succeeded in effectively lowering capital requirements for continental European banks. However, they also adopted important Basel III elements through the Capital Requirements Regulation (CRR). Once again, the result was a compromise. The final version of the CRD IV package signified a victory for the UK government, which, however, lost the battle in Brussels about the legally binding cap imposed on bankers' bonuses. Hence in the downloading of Basel III in the EU, the international standards were somewhat watered down.

Finally, in applying the new regulation of the EU, German regulatory agencies responsible for supervising banks, partly under pressure from the financial industry, further lowered the standards agreed upon in the BCBS, in clear contrast to US agencies, which strictly implemented the standards and tightened control or review processes (for example, Comprehensive Capital Analysis and Review). As Goldbach and Zimmermann report (Chapter 7), German regulators used discretionary powers left to them by EU regulation to adjust implementation to the particular demands of national banks. While policy-making at the international level ended with convergence on tightened soft law, European legislation and national implementation in nation-states resulted in considerable policy divergences, compared with this standard.

To sum up, the process aimed at tighter regulation of bank capital started at the international level, where the United States and the United Kingdom profited from their proactive strategy to upload their policies. Against this powerful move, neither the – internally divided – EU nor the coalition of Germany and France were capable to veto reform or slow down the reform dynamics. In the end, a combination of problem-oriented negotiations in the BCBS and bargaining in the EU joint decision system resulted in significant change in regulation, which may not meet the highest expectations and failed to fully harmonize national rules, but produced considerable effects.

Resolution and recovery of systemically important financial institutions

Coping with the failure of "systemically important financial institutions" (SIFI) became an issue at the international level in 2009, after national governments – in particular the German and US governments – had reacted to the pending collapse of big banks with independent action. Apparently, the bank crisis occurring in 2008 shaped the agenda of governments and made resolution and recovery a high priority. However, the issue was soon uploaded to the international level, where it was discussed at G20 conferences and in committees (FSB, BCBS). Moreover, it was adopted by international organizations, including the IMF, the OECD and the UN expert-commission on "Reforms of the International Monetary and Financial System" headed by Joseph Stiglitz.

In the United States, the FDIC and the Federal Reserve Board set the pace by demanding higher standards for globally systemically important banks. Both organizations pushed for a common standard on minimum levels of loss absorbing capacity for these banks, and changed the rules for an orderly resolution of failed banks. They also succeeded in uploading their policy to the international level due to their authority resulting from the size and interconnectedness of the US financial market, the expertise and capacities of these organizations in resolving banks and dealing with large capital funds, and their negotiation mandate established in the Dodd-Frank Act. Moreover, their delegates hold important positions in the FSB and the BCBS, and the FDIC worked in close contact with its British counterpart, the FSA. Bilateral relationships of US regulators also included Swiss and German authorities supervising financial markets.

The German government was probably a particularly important partner for the United States because it took early steps towards a comprehensive reform of the rules for restructuring failed banks. Painful experiences with failed banks caused an intense media response, protests by anti-globalization groups, and legal proceedings. These events compelled the German government to take bold steps: despite the protests of the banking industry and the resistance of some *Länder* governments, a law that passed the German Federal Parliament in October 2010 introduced a bank levy and procedures for resolving failed banks. These measures anticipated recommendations that were later elaborated by the FSB. In parallel with Germany, the United Kingdom was also among the first movers in Europe. Here, however, the governing parties, wanting to avoid conflicts, first established an advisory commission before passing legislation. In 2011, the FSA published a new Recovery and Resolution Framework. Delegates from the United Kingdom also played leading roles in international bodies, and the British government joined Germany in efforts to influence EU legislation.

In parallel with the various national initiatives, negotiations on how to deal with systemically relevant banks took place at the international level. Here the orchestrating role of the G20 became obvious. While international organizations such as the IMF and the UN discussed the problems of financial markets in parallel, G20 leaders initiated coordinated action of the major international finance institutions, calling on, among others, the FSB and the BCBS to identify the globally systemically important banks. The "Resolution Regimes Steering Group" of the FSB developed the first set of international standards for cross-border resolution (Key Attributes of an Effective Resolution Regime), based on US rules and policies more than on the example of European countries. Endorsed at the G20 summit in November 2011, these principles subsequently shaped EU legislation.

With its Bank Recovery and Resolution Directive (BRRD), the EU followed recommendations of the FSB and the G20, but transposed them into law with some leeway for national governments. European legislation occurred in a context that not only consisted of the US standards that could not be ignored in Europe, but also of the efforts of the UK and German governments to upload their policies and existing regulation to the European level. In particular, the United Kingdom had a strong interest in making the EU adopt the guidelines that had been elaborated by the FSA. In the end, the European directive appeared to be acceptable, although not ideal, from a British point of view. One reason for this had to do with Germany's resistance to delegate power to supervise all banks to the European Central Bank, and to Europeanize the German bank levy. Germany thus prevented a common deposit guarantee scheme from being included in the European Banking Union.

The driving forces for reform in this case came from national governments, who acted under the immediate pressure of the 2008 bank crisis. However, the problem had also been recognized at the international level, where efforts to

Figure 8-2   Resolution of systemically important financial institutions

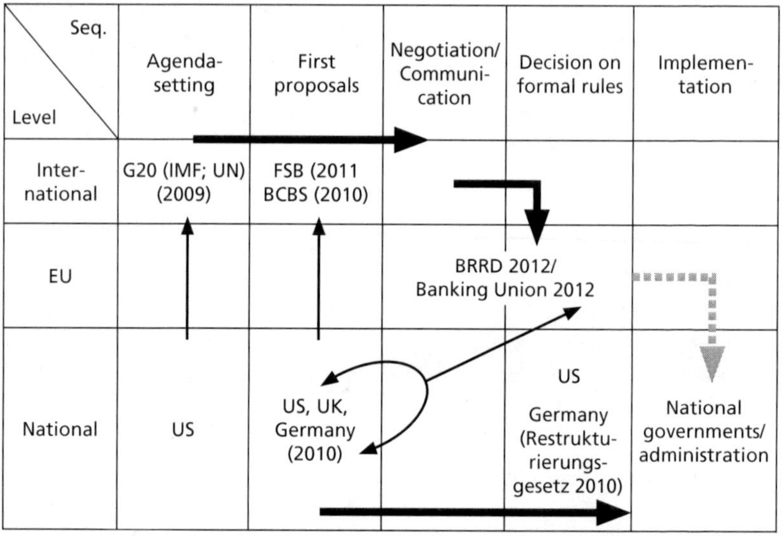

Seq. / Level	Agenda-setting	First proposals	Negotiation/ Communi-cation	Decision on formal rules	Implemen-tation
Inter-national	G20 (IMF; UN) (2009)	FSB (2011 BCBS (2010)			
EU			BRRD 2012/ Banking Union 2012		
National	US	US, UK, Germany (2010)		US Germany (Restruktu-rierungs-gesetz 2010)	National governments/ administration

Note: black arrows: change towards tighter regulation; dashed arrows: watering down, constraining change.

arrive at an agreed solution were made in the interplay of different arenas and organizations. The reform of bank resolution achieved a certain degree of harmonization, although it also watered down initiatives, regulatory models and recommendations elaborated by independent international bodies.

OTC derivatives trading

According to widespread belief, the extended use of derivatives and OTC trading, as well as the rise of the shadow banking system ranked among the main causes of the crisis in global financial markets (Morgan 2012). There was hardly any doubt that serious deficits in the regulation of new financial products led to market failure. However, defining the collective action problem to be addressed by regulation precisely turned out to be difficult. Disputes emerged concerning the cause and scope of the problem: some regarded "alternative" forms of private debt financing generally as causes of the crisis, others only the extension and acceleration of the trading of these products. Opinions differed as to whether the crisis was due to the behavior of banks, a lack of regulation and supervision by regulatory authorities, or the volatility of the world economy. As to the scope of the problem, there was disagreement on whether it concerned all banks or only specific financial institutions. Depending on the answers to these questions, the suggestions for remedies of the problem varied. Even if policy-makers and their experts had agreed on the goal of regulation, they disagreed on the ways to achieve this goal and on the appropriate means. In fact, there was not even consensus on whether derivatives traded outside the stock exchange or their unregulated spread in global markets should be considered a collective action problem at all that required coordinated action at the international level.

Coordinated measures to regulate OTC derivatives started later than policies addressing the structure or the capital requirements of banks. The first actions at the international level surfaced when in 2009 the G20 summit at Pittsburgh discussed the issue. In line with its orchestrating role, the conference of heads of government mandated the IOSCO to elaborate solutions. The soft law resulting from this work was subsequently downloaded to the EU level.

At the international level, this process was again initiated and driven by the United States as the pace-setter. The Dodd-Frank Act delegated significant remedial powers to the Commodity Futures Trading Commission (CFTC) and the Securities and Exchange Commission (SEC). In view of the global dimension of the problem, these two institutions pushed for coordinated policies at the international level and actively uploaded US policies to international norm-setting bodies. They also tried to crossload US rules to the EU and other jurisdictions, partly by bilateral negotiations, and partly by extending US regulation to international corporations operating on its territory. The outcome of this strategy was mixed. The European Commission sought an agreement with US regulators. Both preferred more transparency in financial trades and proposed the standardization of contracts, and the inclusion of central counterparties (CCP) in trades instead of bilateral OTC. The G20 endorsed this policy. However, conflicts between the United States and the EU on the territorial scope of regulation and monitoring delayed the reform, as did the reactions of banks and the financial industry generally.

Coordination problems arose when the EU objected to the definition of addressees of derivative regulation in US law as too extensive and causing widespread extraterritorial effects. Consequently, despite similar approaches to regulation, an overall harmonization of rules failed, with negative effects for trades cutting across jurisdictions. Another obstacle to international coordination resulted from activities of business organizations. While major American banks and swap dealers anticipated reforms and adjusted their business accordingly, international organizations of financial institutions objected to the CFTC's policy and slowed down the reform process. In the EU, regulation was also influenced by internal conflicts, in particular the conflict between the ECB and the United Kingdom regarding the location of CCP. Moreover, whereas the United King-

Figure 8-3   OTC trade of derivatives

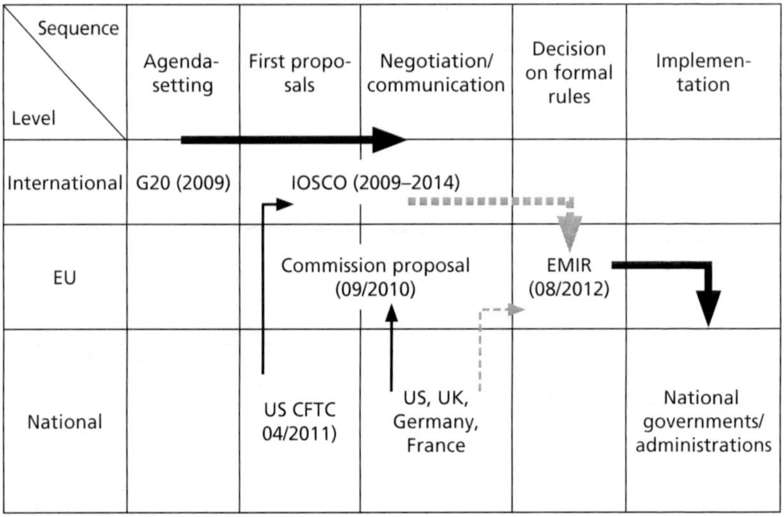

Sequence / Level	Agenda-setting	First proposals	Negotiation/ communication	Decision on formal rules	Implementation
International	G20 (2009)	IOSCO (2009–2014)			
EU		Commission proposal (09/2010)		EMIR (08/2012)	
National		US CFTC 04/2011)	US, UK, Germany, France		National governments/ administrations

Note: black arrows: change towards tighter regulation; dashed arrows: watering down, constraining change.

dom favored the new regulation covering all derivatives, Germany successfully lobbied to limit its coverage to OTC derivatives. Nevertheless, although Germany was not very supportive of effective regulation in this policy area, it did not counteract European legislation initiated by the Commission to meet the G20 summit commitments and to attain convergence with US rules.

International soft law, finally, was downloaded from the EU level to the national level. The European Market Infrastructure Regulation (EMIR) turned into binding law what had been initiated and elaborated at the international level, or resulted from horizontal crossloading between the United States and the EU. This law covers OTC derivatives, central counterparties (CCPs), and trade repositories, but does not ensure "interoperability" of CCPs nor regulate derivatives in general, including those traded on stock exchanges, as preferred by the United Kingdom. As in other policy areas, downloading of international agreements to the EU ended with adjustments due to the different interests of member states.

In sum, protracted negotiations moving back and forth between national governments (in particular the United States), the EU, and international bodies led to a reform process with a more diffuse profile than in some other areas of financial market regulation. Besides, the effects appear more limited, conforming to theories predicting gradual change. The disagreement on the collective action problem at the international level, in combination with the more effective countervailing power of the financial industry and divergent interests of the United States and the EU, seem to account for this outcome.

Bank structure

Efforts to regulate or re-regulate bank structure appeared on the agenda of national governments soon after the bank crisis erupted in 2008. The United States introduced the so-called Volcker Rule, separating, once more, commercial banking from investment banking, and especially from proprietary trading relying on high-risk products. The United Kingdom favored "ring-fencing" of risky trades by means of organizational separation in banks. Compared with the regulation of specific activities of banks, the international regulation of their structure was confronted by differences in national banking systems, which raised stronger resistance.

Due to public pressure in the wake of the 2008 crisis, regulation of bank structure ranged high on the agenda of the US and UK governments. In 2010, the United States enacted the Volcker Rule provisions as part of the Dodd-Frank Act, reversing the deregulatory trend of the late 1990s by prohibiting proprietary trading by banks. In both countries, bank structure was a pressing issue in the context of stabilizing the financial market, in contrast to Germany, where the government continued to defend German universal banks. While the United States implemented its unique approach autonomously without any efforts to up- or crossload its policy, the United Kingdom followed suit by establishing the Independent Banking Commission, which recommended the ring-fencing of banks' retail activities and thus prepared the Banking Reform Act, passed in 2013. In Germany, a new law of May 2013 required the assignment of lending to hedge funds, private equity funds and high-frequency traders to separate parts of a bank. In contrast to the UK law, no legal separation of these units was required. This modest change made it possible to maintain universal banks.

Thus, in policies aimed at regulating banking structures, national governments' decisions trumped attempts at international coordination. There have been some efforts to crossload policies. For instance, the EU and the United States tried to transfer their rules to other jurisdictions: the EU by using an "equivalence clause" aimed at inducing other states to introduce corresponding rules, and the United States by applying the Volcker Rule to non-US banks. Beyond that, the EU tried to achieve convergence in Europe based on the recommendations of the Liikanen report. Apparently, the Commission's legislative proposal following this report was influenced by the British ring-fencing approach and the Volcker Rule. At the same time, it was watered down under

Figure 8-4   Bank structure reform

Sequence / Level	Agenda-setting	First proposals	Negotiation/ communi-cation	Decision on formal rules	Implemen-tation
International					
EU		Liikanen group (2012–2014)	Commission proposal (01/2014)		
National	US (Dodd-Frank Act 2010)	US, UK (Vickers Commission 06/2010–09/2011)		US (2010), UK (2013), Germany (2013)	National authorities

Note: black arrows: change towards tighter regulation.

pressure from Germany and France, and leaves national governments consider-able discretion.

Germany reacted rather late to the problem of bank structure. Instead, it favored a tax on financial transactions (a "Tobin tax") and launched an initiative together with the French government. This move had some effect at the European, but not at the international level. In the EU, discussion of this issue started in 2011, but so far without results. Nation-states are still reluctant to delegate powers to determine taxes to external bodies. For this reason, attempts to upload the proposal to the international level did not succeed. In the EU, a group of 11 member states engaged in negotiations on a coordinated introduction of a financial transaction tax, but could not conclude the agreement envisaged for the end of 2014. They rejected a draft elaborated by the European Commission. As a consequence, the issue has shifted back to the national level.

National governments did not address banking structure as a collective prob-lem; rather they proceeded with independent action and did not try to upload the issue to the international level. Compared with coordinated international policy, which certainly would have ended with compromises, they preferred to adjust regulation to the perceived needs and particular conditions of the do-mestic banking sector. Divergent interests inside states and the EU also made coordination difficult. In the United States, the various regulatory agencies had to come to an agreement and therefore were in no position to act with a unanimous voice at the international level. The EU was divided, with the United Kingdom, Germany and France pursuing diverging policies. The German government was confronted by *Länder* governments and powerful banks, both of which fought against making far-reaching changes in bank structure.

Regarding the results of efforts to reform bank structure, it seems that competitive policy-making at the national level has generated significant change in some countries at least. Market competition might well compel other governments to adjust their rules, producing more convergence in the end. To date, however, there are scant indications of crossloading policies. Apparently, varieties of national business structures ("varieties of capitalism") impact strongly on the regulation of business organization. Compared with the other fields of regulation considered in this volume, the case of bank structure suggests that without moving up to the international level, constraints due to European joint decision-making, and comparable problems of coordination between different actors at the national level, cannot be counteracted, and therefore limit the scope of coordinated reform.

Reform processes in a multilevel system: Concluding observations

The impact of the financial crisis was strongly felt at the national level, but it was widely recognized as a collective problem, calling for a collective response at higher political levels. Reform initiatives accordingly started both at the national and the international level, often in parallel. This is presumably a feature of the specific case: a global crisis calling for immediate and internationally coordinated action. The vertically and horizontally differentiated structure of financial market governance existing at the time did not permit an immediate and coordinated policy response. Instead, different parts of the equally differentiated financial system became the object of separate, only loosely coupled reforms.

We selected four of these reforms for closer analysis. As it turned out, the processes in the four issue areas did not follow the same model, although there were some commonalities. In all cases, national policy preferences were the decisive drivers – both in promoting and in resisting reform initiatives – in a policy process spanning several political levels. None of the countries covered in this study had a general preference either for soft or for strict reform in all areas; policy preferences were issue-specific, and dependent on domestic politics and the relative importance, and shape, of national financial systems. As international institutions, recognizing the need for a coordinated international response, put the reform of financial market regulation on their agenda, national reform proposals were "uploaded" to higher political levels. In this bottom-up process, power inequalities between countries played a significant role, giving right of way especially to US reform proposals, while minor powers such as Germany exerted influence more by foot-dragging and resistance than by pro-active uploading. As the comparison of the four reform sequences makes evident, not all reform issues were recognized as a collective problem to be taken up at the international level. A prominent example is the regulation of bank structures, where national governments defended their particular models. Other lower level initiatives such as the introduction of a Tobin tax and the prohibition of naked short-selling also failed to make it to the international level. Apparently, international bodies cannot autonomously define a policy agenda, and uploading of policies to the international level fails if national governments see their basic powers or interests at risk. Independent action by individual governments tends to be limited to issues that can be dealt with nationally without having significant side-effects for other countries – a rare situation given the "globalized" nature of the present financial system. In compensation, the different forms of "crossloading" played an unexpectedly important role in the overall reform process, again reflecting the structure of the international financial system.

Straightforward downloading did not play a major role in the reform process. Non-binding higher level rules were often watered down, but sometimes there was "gold-plating" instead; both occurred with regard to bank capital (Basel III). Because higher level (EU and international) decisions were the result of negotiation between high-ranking and expert representatives of nation-states, uploading and downloading proved to be intimately connected. The EU apparently was not an independent driving force in the reform process, but neither did it simply serve as transmission belt between the international and the national level, having to navigate between the reform proposals of international bodies, contrasting member preferences, and the demands of the United States, the still powerful former hegemon of financial market regulation. EU member states that failed to shape policy at the international level tried to upload their preferences to the EU. In this way, the EU transposed into law recommendations of international bodies that met with different reactions from its member states; ultimately, member states complied more with EU rules than they would have complied with non-binding Basel III rules and FSB recommendations and principles.

The multilevel action system of regulatory reform differs significantly from classic two-level, joint-decision policy systems. However, it does not seem feasible to formulate a new mode of coordination, characterizing the whole array of vertical and horizontal interactions we observed. True, we dealt only with an action system that emerged ad hoc in response to a specific crisis, not with a policy process in an established multilevel governance structure. Of course there could, in principle, be other cases of a similar kind; the historical specificity of a given case does not preclude the identification of a more general pattern. But while we have found instances of the different modes of action coordination discussed in the literature – hierarchy, joint decision-making, policy learning, mutual adjustment, and intergovernmental bargaining – they co-existed and intermingled in a scarcely predictable form, and did not combine to constitute a new mode of coordination. Looked at in its entirety, even that part of the regulatory reform looked at in this study is too complex to be represented by a single structural model. The hope of discovering a new theoretical template, a mode of coordination that integrates the diverse coordination mechanisms, forming a new generalizable model, is vain.

What we discovered, however, is a dynamic of interaction between levels and between bodies at the different levels that, without being coordinated, shaped agendas, policy proposals, preferences of negotiating actors, and decisions, and ultimately led to policy changes. The loosely coupled action system with its overlapping venues of policy-making constituted a variable opportunity structure for the strategic interaction of policy-makers, which were the main driving forces of change.

One of the questions posed in this study referred to the impact of the specific character of the action system of regulatory reform on the direction of change: have multilevel dynamics pushed the reform process forward, or have they dampened the reform impetus? Where, as in our case, not binding decisions are to be produced at the top level in a given multilevel system, but only recommendations and at best soft law, the outcome will predictably be compromise, rather than blockade as in joint-decision traps (Scharpf 1988; Falkner 2011); the obvious downside of such a multilevel system is, of course, implementation. As not only Wilson and Grant (2012: 249) point out, "there was no fundamental reform of the financial system." But financial market regulation has changed. The chapters in this volume justify the conclusion that the interaction of the different action arenas has induced a dynamic that stimulated policy change. This change evolved incrementally and did not follow a master plan, but the different steps and different measures accumulated to reduce at least some risks of market failure. The change achieved appears modest if the financial crisis is regarded as a window of opportunity for radical reform (Moschella/Tsingou 2013: 194), but it goes beyond what theories of veto players or historical institutionalism can explain. Rather than creating more veto points and patterns of bargaining ending in a race to the bottom, the dynamic of multilevel action in financial market regulation has activated, and partly created, a set of overlapping and interdependent arenas. While national policy-making was constrained by institutional conditions, reform impulses arose in particular venues, and change agents engaged in one arena influenced policy-making in others. In the movement of reform proposals across countries and levels, proposed changes were watered down, but never utterly blocked. The multilevel dynamic has both dampened and pushed reform of financial market regulation, but overall it worked towards tighter regulation in a number of policy fields.

References

Aldecoa, Francisco/Michael Keating (eds.), 1999: *Paradiplomacy in action: The foreign relations of subnational governments.* London: Frank Cass.

Aspinwall, Mark, 2007: Government preferences on European integration: An empirical test of five theories. In: *British Journal of Political Science* 37(2), 89–114.

Bache, Ian/Matthew Flinders (eds.), 2004: *Multi-level Governance.* Oxford: Oxford University Press.

Baker, Andrew, 2009: Deliberative Equality and the Transgovernmental Politics of the Global Financial Architecture. In: *Global Governance* 15, 198–215.

Bednar, Jenna, 2011: Nudging Federalism toward Productive Experimentation. In: *Regional and Federal Studies* 21(4), 503–521.

Benz, Arthur, 2000: Two types of Multi-level Governance: Intergovernmental Relations in German and EU Regional Policy. In: *Regional and Federal Studies* 10(3), 21–44.

——, 2013: Balancing Rigidity and Flexibility: Constitutional Dynamics in Federal Systems. In: *West European Politics* 36(4), 726–749.

Benz, Arthur/Burkhard Eberlein, 1999: The Europeanization of Regional Policies: Patterns of Multi-Level Governance. In: *Journal of European Public Policy* 6(2), 328–348.

Berry, Frances S./William D. Berry, 1999: Innovation and Diffusion Models in Policy Research. In: Paul A. Sabatier (ed.), *Theories of the Policy Process.* Boulder: Westview Press, 169–200.

Checkel, Jeffrey T., 1997: International Norms and Domestic Politics: Bridging the Rationalist-Constructivist Divide. In: *European Journal of International Relations* 3(4), 473–495.

Christiansen, Thomas/Gerda Falkner/Knut Erik Jørgensen, 2002: Theorizing EU treaty reform: Beyond diplomacy and bargaining. In: *Journal of European Public Policy* 9(1), 12–32.

Cohen, Michael D./James G. March/Johan P. Olsen, 1972: A Garbage Can Model of Organizational Choice. In: *Administrative Science Quarterly* 17(1), 1–25.

Deitelhoff, Nicole, 2006: *Überzeugung in der Politik. Grundzüge einer Diskurstheorie internationalen Regierens.* Frankfurt a.M.: Suhrkamp.

Evans, Mark (ed.), 2009: New Directions in the Study of Policy Transfer. In: *Policy Studies* 30(3), 237–241.

Falkner, Gerda (ed.), 2011: *The EU's Decision Traps. Comparing Policies.* Oxford: Oxford University Press.

Farrell, Henry/Abraham L. Newman, 2014: Domestic Institutions beyond the Nation-State: Charting the New Interdependence Approach. In: *World Politics* 66(2), 331–363.

Haas, Peter M., 1992: Introduction: Epistemic Communities and International Policy Coordination. In: *International Organization* 46(1), 1–35.

Hall, Peter A./David Soskice (eds.), 2001: *Varieties of Capitalism: The Institutional Foundations of Comparative Advantage*. Oxford: Oxford University Press.

Héritier, Adrienne, 1999: *Policy-Making and Diversity in Europe. Escaping Deadlock*. Cambridge: Cambridge University Press.

——, 2007: *Explaining Institutional Change in Europe*. Oxford: Oxford University Press.

Higgott, Richard, 2012: The Theory and Practice of Global Economic Governance in the Early Twenty-First Century: The Limits of Multilateralism. In: Wyn Grant (ed.), *The Consequences of the Global Financial Crisis*. Oxford: Oxford University Press, 15–33.

Hix, Simon/Abdul G. Noury/Gérard Roland, 2007: *Democratic Politics in the European Parliament*. Cambridge: Cambridge University Press.

Holzinger, Katharina/Helge Jörgens/Christoph Knill (eds.), 2007: *Transfer, Diffusion und Konvergenz von Politiken*. PVS-Sonderheft 38. Wiesbaden: VS Verlag für Sozialwissenschaften.

Hooghe, Liesbet,1996: *Cohesion Policy and European Integration*. Oxford: Clarendon Press.

Hooghe, Liesbet/Gary Marks, 2001: *Multi-Level Governance and European Integration*. Lanham: Rowman & Littlefield Publishers.

——, 2009: A Postfunctionalist Theory of European Integration: From Permissive Consensus to Constraining Dissensus. In: *British Journal of Political Science* 39(1), 1–23.

Keating, Michael/Liesbet Hooghe, 2001: By-Passing the Nation State? Regions in the EU Policy Process. In: Jeremy Richardson (ed.), *European Union: Power and Policy-Making*. London: Routledge, 216–229.

Kim, Min-hyung, 2014: Theorizing National Preference Formation. In: *Cambridge Review of International Affairs,* published online, 19 August 2014, DOI:10.1080/09557571.2014.936362.

Kohler-Koch, Beate/Christine Quittkat, 2013: *De-Mystification of Participatory Democracy. EU Governance and Civil Society*. Oxford: Oxford University Press.

Kudrna, Zdenek, 2013: EU financial market regulation: Protecting distinct policy preferences. In: Gerda Falkner/Patrick Müller (eds.), *EU Policies in a Global Perspective: Shaping or Taking International Regimes?* London: Routledge, 186–205.

Kudrna, Zdenek/Patrick Müller/Gerda Falkner, 2014: EU–global interactions: Policy export, import, promotion and protection. In: *Journal of European Public Policy* 21(8), 1102–1119.

Lall, Ranjit, 2015: Timing as a source of regulatory influence: A technical elite network analysis of global finance. In: *Regulation & Governance* 9(2), 125–143.

Leuprecht, Christian/Harvey Lazar, 2007: From Multilevel to "Multi-order" Governance? In: Christian Leuprecht/Harvey Lazar (eds.), *Spheres of Governance*. Montreal: McGill-Queen's University Press, 1–21.

Lijphart, Arend, 2012: *Patterns of Democracy: Government Forms and Performance in Thirty-six Countries*. Third Edition. New Haven: Yale University Press.

Lütz, Susanne, 2002: *Der Staat und die Globalisierung von Finanzmärkten: Regulative Politik in Deutschland, Großbritannien und den USA*. Frankfurt a.M.: Campus.

Lütz, Susanne, 2011: Back to the future? The domestic sources of transatlantic regulation. In: *Review of International Political Economy* 18(4), iii–xxi.

Moravcsik, Andrew, 1998: *The Choice for Europe. Social Purpose and State Power from Messina to Maastricht.* London: UCL Press.

Morgan, Glenn, 2012: Constructing Financial Markets: Reforming Over-the-Counter Derivatives Markets in the Aftermath of the Financial Crisis. In: Wyn Grant (ed.), *The Consequences of the Global Financial Crisis.* Oxford: Oxford University Press, 67–87.

Moschella, Manuella/Eleni Tsingou, 2013: Conclusions: Too little, too slow? In: Manuella Moschella/Eleni Tsingou (ed.), *Great expectations, slow transformations. Incremental change in post-crisis regulation.* Colcester: ECPR Press, 193–215.

Nye, Robert, 1990: Soft Power. In: *Foreign Policy* 80, 153–171.

——, 2005: *Soft Power: The Means to Success in World Politics.* New York: Public Affairs.

Painter, Martin, 1991: Intergovernmental Relations in Canada: An Institutional Analysis. In: *Canadian Journal of Political Science,* 24(2), 269–288.

Piattoni, Simona, 2010: *The Theory of Multi-Level Governance: Conceptual, Empirical, and Normative Challenges.* Oxford: Oxford University Press.

Putnam, Robert D., 1988: Diplomacy and Domestic Politics: The Logic of Two-level Games. In: *International Organization* 42(3), 427–460.

Risse, Thomas, 2000: "Let's Argue!": Communicative Action in World Politics. In: *International Organization* 54(1), 1–39.

Sabel, Charles F./Jonathan Zeitlin, 2008: Learning from Difference: The New Architecture of Experimentalist Governance in the EU. In: *European Law Journal* 14(2), 271–327.

Scharpf, Fritz W., 1988: The Joint Decision Trap: Lessons from German Federalism and European Integration. In: *Public Administration* 66(3), 239–278.

——, 1997: Introduction: The Problem-solving Capacity of Multi-level Governance. In: *Journal of Public Policy,* 4(4), 520–538.

——, 2011: The JDT Model: Context and Extensions. In: Gerda Falkner (ed.), *The EU's Decision Traps: Comparing Policies.* Oxford: Oxford University Press, 217–236.

Simeon, Richard, 2006: *Federal-Provincial Diplomacy: The Making of Recent Policy in Canada.* Toronto: University of Toronto Press.

Solomon, Ty, 2014: The affective underpinnings of soft power. In: *European Journal of International Relations* 20(3), 720–741.

Stephenson, Paul, 2013: Twenty years of multilevel governance: "Where Does It Come From? What Is It? Where Is It Going?" In: *Journal of European Public Policy* 20(6), 817–837.

Wilson, Graham K./Wyn Grant, 2012: Conclusion. In: Wyn Grant/Graham K. Wilson (eds.), *The Consequences of the Global Financial Crisis: The Rhetoric of Reform and Regulation.* Oxford: Oxford University Press, 247–260.

Young, Kevin, 2013: Financial industry groups' adaptation to the post-crisis regulatory environment: Changing approaches to the policy cycle. In: *Regulation & Governance* 7, 460–480.

Zürn, Michael, 2014: The politicization of world politics and its effects: Eight propositions. In: *European Political Science Review* 6(1), 47–71.

Abbreviations

ABS	asset-backed securities
AIFM	Alternative Investment Fund Management
AIFMD	Alternative Investment Fund Managers' Directive
BaFin	Federal Financial Supervisory Authority (Germany)
BCBS	Basel Committee on Banking Supervision
BIS	Bank of International Settlements
BMF	Bundesministerium für Finanzen
BRRD	Bank Recovery and Resolution Directive
CCAR	Comprehensive Capital Analysis and Review
CCP	central counterparty/central clearing party
CDO	collateralized debt obligations
CDS	credit default swaps
CGFS	Committee on the Global Financial System
CFTC	Commodity Futures Trading Commission
CPSS	Committee on Payments and Settlement Systems
CRD	Capital Requirements Directive
CRR	Capital Requirements Regulation
DGSD	Deposit Guarantee Scheme Directive
EBA	European Banking Authority
EBF	European Banking Federation
ECB	European Central Bank
ECOFIN	Economic and Financial Affairs Council
ECOSOC	Economic and Social Council
EIOPA	European Insurance and Occupational Pensions Authority
EMIR	European Market Infrastructure Regulation
ESM	European Stability Mechanism
ESMA	European Securities Market Authority
FATF	Financial Action Task Force
FDIC	Federal Deposit Insurance Corporation
FINMA	Financial Market Supervisory Authority (Switzerland)

FNR	Fonds Nationale de la Recherche (Luxembourg)
FSA	Financial Services Authority (UK)
FSAP	Financial Sector Assessment Program
FSB	Financial Stability Board
FSF	Financial Stability Forum
GHOS	Governors and Heads of Supervision
G-SIB	global systemically important bank
G-SIFI	global systemically important financial institution
IAIS	International Association of Insurance Supervisors
IASB	International Accounting Standards Board
ICB	Independent Commission on Banking
IGO	intergovernmental organizations
IIB	Institute of International Bankers
IIF	Institute of International Finance
ILO	International Labour Organization
IMF	International Monetary Fund
IOSCO	International Organization of Securities Commissions
ISDA	International Swaps and Derivatives Association
LCR	Liquidity Coverage Ratio
MOU	memorandum of understanding
OCC	Office of the Comptroller of the Currency
OTC	over-the-counter
PFMI	Principles for Financial Market Infrastructures
SCSI	Standing Committee on Standards Implementation
SEC	Securities and Exchange Commission
SIFIs	systemically important financial institutions
SIFMA	Securities Industry and Financial Markets Association
SME	small and medium-sized enterprises
SPOE	single point of entry
SRM	Single Resolution Mechanism
SSB	Standard-Setting Body
SSM	Single Supervisory Mechanism
TLAC	total loss-absorbing capacity
UNDP	United Nations Development Programme
WTO	World Trade Organization

Contributors

Arthur Benz is Professor for Political Science at the Technische Universität Darmstadt.

Roman Goldbach is a political economist at Deutsche Bundesbank in the Department of Banking and Financial Supervision where he works on regulatory strategy and coordination in global banking regulation.

Scott James is Senior Lecturer in Political Economy, Department of Political Economy, King's College London.

Renate Mayntz is Emeritus Director of the Max Planck Institute for the Study of Societies in Cologne.

Lucia Quaglia is Professor of Political Science at the University of York.

Peter Ryan is Vice President, Federal Regulatory Affairs for Credit Suisse – Public Policy Americas. During the writing of this chapter he served as Senior Policy Analyst for the Financial Regulatory Reform Initiative of the Bipartisan Policy Center (BPC).

Lora Anne Viola is Assistant Professor in the Politics Department of the John F. Kennedy Institute at the Freie Universität Berlin (FUB).

J. Nicholas Ziegler is Associate Professor in the Travers Department of Political Science, University of California.

Hubert Zimmermann is Professor for International Relations, Philipps-University Marburg.